Family and the Politics
of Moderation

Family and the Politics of Moderation

Private Life, Public Goods, and the Rebirth of Social Individualism

Lauren K. Hall

BAYLOR UNIVERSITY PRESS

Jacket Design by Faceout Studio/Kara Davison

Library of Congress Cataloging-in-Publication Data

Hall, Lauren K., 1980–
 Family and the politics of moderation : private life, public goods, and the rebirth of social individualism / Lauren K. Hall.
 198 pages cm
 Includes bibliographical references and index.
 ISBN 978-1-60258-801-1 (hardback : alk. paper)
 1. Families. 2. Individualism. 3. Collectivism. I. Title.
 HQ734.H2545 2014
 306.85—dc23
                                            2013020151

Printed in the United States of America on acid-free paper with a minimum of 30% post-consumer waste recycled content.

To my family, including those I have lost,
those with whom I share today, and those I have not yet met.
But especially to Piper, whose presence in the world makes
the subject of this book infinitely more meaningful.

CONTENTS

Acknowledgments

I have been very fortunate during the writing of this book to have had wonderful advisors, mentors, and intellectual accomplices. Each devoted valuable time and intellectual energy to challenge my ideas and to sharpen my writing. There have been many colleagues, advisors, and friends who have supported me throughout the years, and the following is but a partial acknowledgment of debt.

Professors Gary Glenn and Larry Arnhart sparked my interest in the works of Burke and Montesquieu, and their careful and attentive mentoring helped guide my research and writing from that of a fledgling graduate student to what it is today (whatever that might be). They also, even after retiring, read through drafts at various stages of this work. Their thoughtful comments and criticism were crucial to helping me clarify my arguments. Larry's generosity as an advisor has known no bounds, and his willingness to respond to frantic e-mails with calm guidance will always be remembered with gratitude.

Steve Horwitz and Sarah Mackenzie Burns looked over early drafts of the chapter on family forms and helped me rein in what was becoming an unwieldy beast. Panelists at the Midwest Political Science Association and American Political Science Association meetings helped improve early formulations of the argument made in the book, and conversations at Liberty Fund conferences helped me locate sources and provide theoretical rigor. The support of a Jack Miller Center Summer Fellowship in the summer of 2010 allowed me to meet with editors including Steve Wrinn from University of Kentucky Press and John Tryneski from University of Chicago Press, both of whom provided generous follow-up advice.

Closer to home, I have had the unflagging support of the Department of Political Science and the College of Liberal Arts at the Rochester Institute of Technology for the three years it took to write the book and secure a contract. The Paul and Francena Miller Research Fellowship from the College of Liberal Arts in 2011 provided time off from teaching to finish the first draft of the book and the prospectus to send out to publishers. A Grant Writing Boot Camp Award from the Office of Sponsored Research Services at RIT provided me with course release time and funds for initial copyediting of chapters to be sent out for review. The Department of Political Science and my indefatigable chair, Sean Sutton, provided both intellectual guidance and flexibility with course releases and scheduling.

Carey Newman of Baylor University Press improved the content and the writing of the book immeasurably with attentive commentary and advice. Meanwhile, the support of the staff at Baylor ushered the manuscript through the publishing process with expertise and surprising speed.

Apart from academic support, in a very real sense this book starts and ends with the family. The timing of this book put the strength of my familial support network to the test as I finished the rough draft and secured a contract two weeks before my husband and I welcomed our first child. I spent our daughter's first six months of life rewriting and editing the final manuscript in between diaper changes and nursing sessions. This book could not have been finished without the help of an intergenerational platoon, to use Burke's words. My wonderful in-laws, Bill and Marilyn Lilly, watched our infant daughter on many a cold winter morning so I could stew over word choice and organizational structure. Their loving care helped me concentrate on writing, knowing that my daughter was in the best of hands. My own parents, Robert and Deborah Hall, in addition to babysitting, also provided detailed and thoughtful commentaries on early drafts of the major chapters. They have been my most consistent supporters and my most exacting critics.

Finally, my husband Brian Lilly's patience supported me throughout. He endured long workdays, writer's block, and occasional whining, with his usual unruffled cheer. In the early days of our daughter's life, his attentive care of both of us allowed me to strike a balance, albeit an imperfect one, between mothering and writing. For that and for his love I am grateful.

A Familial Fulcrum

The political project is a curious thing—always imperfect and never complete—because it is predicated on the continuous task of balancing the claims of individuals and the claims of the communities in which they live. The success or failure of this political project, creating harmony out of a multitude of voices, is dependent in part on the ideological foundations that help decide how the needs and interests of individuals are balanced and brought into harmony with the needs and interests of groups.[1] The wars of the twentieth century that claimed the lives of hundreds of millions of people were in part a failure of that political project—a failure to create cohesive communities out of discrete and diverse individuals.[2] That failure can be traced in part to the extreme ideological positions that flourished in the twentieth century, which prioritized individuals over communities and vice versa.[3] That these extreme ideological positions flourished, despite their horrific effects on human lives and happiness, can be traced to the loss of institutions that balanced, fulcrum-like, in the middle.[4]

The ideological clashes between extreme individualism and extreme collectivism can be seen in practical form in the clashes between fascism and capitalism and, later, capitalism and communism.[5] The fascist insistence on group cohesion and purity led to the mass murder of individuals whose ethnic heritage or intellectual beliefs differed from those of the group. The communist movement's adherence to collective egalitarianism resulted in a class-based purging of individuals, including those belonging to the traditional aristocracies of propertied landowners and the church.[6] Meanwhile, extreme laissez-faire capitalism supported social Darwinism in both Western Europe and the United States, where the poor were held absolutely responsible for their own poverty.

The incompatibility of both views—that the individual is all or the group is all—bred increasingly polarized political and economic positions in the twentieth century that made no concessions to the complexities of human life. The refusal to recognize that modern capitalism might have alienated humans from their social roots was pitted against the refusal to recognize limits on how much human nature could be stretched or molded to meet idealistic communitarian goals.[7] These intractable ideological positions persisted even after the end of outright warfare.[8]

Part of what made the ideological wars of the twentieth century so damaging was that ideological extremism coincided with social, cultural, economic, and technological changes that eliminated the strength of traditional buffers between individual and community claims. These so-called intermediate institutions—local governments, churches and religious organizations, political and social associations, and the family—were weakened by political centralization and imperialism, economic industrialization that led to urbanization, and the breakdown in traditional family structures caused by increased mobility away from small towns and extended family.[9] More than being simply weakened, many of these intermediate institutions were manipulated into serving the totalitarian goals of either radical communitarianism or radical individualism.[10] Church activities were closely controlled (or eradicated altogether), civil associations were limited or banned, and families were separated and replaced by ideological "brothers" and "sisters." Close friendships and family ties were purposely destroyed.[11] This "atomization" of society, the isolation of individuals from natural social groups like family and friends that formed the backbone of human social life and protected the individual against collective aggression, completed the totalitarian project, reducing the individual to a mere cog in the collective machine.[12]

Both radical individualists and radical collectivists found supposedly scientific support for their theories in the spread of evolutionary thinking ushered in by Darwin's work. The application of Darwin's work to human social life—known as social Darwinism—was unusual in that it was used to bolster theories of both individualists and statists. In Britain and the United States, laissez-faire capitalists who prioritized individual responsibility over community assistance pointed to the supposed "fitness" of the upper classes as the result of individual-level social and economic competition that would eventually eradicate weakness from the population. Meanwhile, progressives argued for state control over human evolution in the name of eliminating the weak for the benefit of the species. The result was mass sterilization programs that resulted in the forcible sterilization of as many as sixty thousand individuals in the United States alone.[13] The extremes of individualism and collectivism worked together in this instance to violate the rights and destroy the lives of tens of thousands of individuals.[14] Later totalitarian leaders viewed the forcible sterilization programs in the United States with approval; Hitler eventually used US state laws as templates for his own mass extermination program.[15] Social Darwinism, like fascism and communism, ignored the importance of intermediate institutions—like family, church, and civil and political associations—for understanding the success or failure of individuals. Instead of appreciating the complex causes of poverty rooted in social, cultural, and economic sources, success or failure became the function of atomized individuals pitted against each other in a winner-take-all competition.[16]

The failure or destruction of intermediate institutions in both Europe and the United States created a devastating cycle; as the institutions that mediate individual and community claims weakened, extreme political views like fascism and communism became even more polarized because no other institution was able to counter their effects. These intermediate institutions, hovering between individual and collective, served as a fulcrum between the two warring sides. When the fulcrum failed, the result was totalitarianism, the belief that the political life can and should engulf all other human goods.[17] The political world became the totality of human social life, structuring and controlling individuals from birth to death. Intermediate institutions like the church and the family became mere tools of the political—means to political ends.

While radical individualists like laissez-faire capitalists, due in part to their suspicion of collective activity, did not contribute as much as collectivists to the unprecedented death toll of the twentieth century, the radical character of twentieth-century liberalism, unlike its more moderate classical liberal precursor, inadvertently encouraged the collectivist streak that it denounced. From laissez-faire capitalism's insistence that each individual stand alone to Ayn Rand's later suspicion of social groups including the family, each contributed to the alienation that many felt in the modern industrial capitalist world.[18] This alienation served to fuel humanity's need to pursue a higher purpose. And, ironically, the individualistic emphasis on private concerns may have hastened the collectivization of society by eliminating legitimate public concerns.[19] Snapping kinship ties eradicated the final thread tying man to man, thus clearing the way for a movement that demanded total loyalty to the collective.[20]

Fascism, communism, and social Darwinism all shared in common an extreme view of the relationship between the group and the individual.[21] Collectivists' willingness to sacrifice individual rights and lives to idealistic collective goals was countered by radical individualists' unwillingness to moderate individual freedoms for the sake of any kind of collective action to assist the poor or those displaced or made vulnerable by modern industrialization. In both cases, individual lives and well-being were sacrificed for an extreme ideological position that accepted no compromise and recognized no moderation.

The world needed something in the twentieth century to remind individualists that humans were enmeshed in a social universe and that social relationships form the heart of the human experience. It also, however, needed something to remind collectivists that human individuals matter—that the meaning of human life comes from the unique individuals who contribute their talents and perspectives to the community. Both human sociality and human individuality require protection. The political project—how to ensure that these potentially conflicting claims are harmonized rather than allowed to destroy each other—failed in the twentieth century.

A Familial Fulcrum

While many intermediate institutions were effectively destroyed during this time, one alone had the ability to regenerate even in the direst circumstances, in part because of its universality and in part because of the strength of associations it creates.[22] The family emerges as a common element in the dialectic between individual and community. Its naturalness means that it regenerates, albeit in somewhat different forms, from generation to generation. Its foundational position at the center of human social life means that it affects each subsequent level of organization. It supports the importance of individuals because it teaches love of one's own. It supports sociality because it enmeshes us in a cooperative universe from birth. And perhaps most importantly, the bonds it creates are rooted deep in our nature and are difficult to eradicate. The family is therefore the root of the social individualism that resists political extremism from either side.

Well before the real-life clashes between individualistic liberal capitalism and collectivistic Marxism or fascism drew the eyes of the world, the
conflict between individual and community was playing out in political
thought over millennia. And for millennia, the family has loomed large
in the imaginations of individualists and collectivists alike. Plato famously
(and perhaps ironically) argued for the collectivization of the family to
ensure a just society.[23] Aristotle tried to moderate the Platonic position
by seeking a harmony between individual and collective claims, one that
included a strong domestic sphere.[24] The liberalism of Locke and Hobbes
rejected the moderate position of Aristotle, reducing the family to a mere
voluntary collection of individuals, characterized by consent and self-
interest, rather than affection.[25] In reaction to this overemphasis on the
individual, moderate philosophers like Montesquieu, Smith, and Burke
all sought to reassert the importance of the family for flourishing social
orders.[26] Each advocated a kind of "social individualism" that sought, like
Aristotle before them, to harmonize individual and collective claims.

The growing revolutionary movements of the eighteenth century
turned eyes from internal political issues to the grand politics of imperialism. The family was largely ignored during the revolutionary period,
though thinkers like Tocqueville briefly discussed the importance of the
family for moderating the individualism of American life.[27] The family
reemerged in importance in the nineteenth century as early Marxists ear-
marked the family, much as Plato did two millennia earlier, for extinction.[28] Individualists, in response to the communist threat, became more
entrenched behind extreme positions, and thinkers like Ayn Rand began
to view the family with suspicion due to the collectivist impulses it supposedly harbored.[29] Contemporary theorists like Rawls and Walzer, concerned
with distributive justice, struggled with the unequal impacts family life
creates.[30] Individualist theorists like Rothbard wrestled from the other side
with the nonconsensual bonds family life places on individuals.[31]

While political theorists of all stripes grappled with how the family
challenges political idealism, what has been only hinted at in political
thought is how the family is peculiarly situated between individual self-
interest and collective well-being. The history of political thought, viewed
through the lens of the family, resembles a precariously balanced seesaw,
swinging between the extremes of collectivism and individualism. The family serves as a balancing fulcrum that can, when strong and supported by
other intermediate institutions, balance these opposing ideological forces.

Viewing the family as a fulcrum is more than mere metaphor. The
strength of family life has very real implications for the political life of a

community and how that community balances individual and community claims, in both grand ideological debates and in mundane local resource allocation decisions. The weakness of the modern family exacerbates the polarization of our modern political rhetoric, forcing us to vacillate between individual selfishness and communal conformity, which in turn weakens civil discourse and makes real solutions to political problems even more elusive.[32] Modern debates about education; health care; care of the elderly, mentally ill, and disabled; reproductive rights; marriage laws; and welfare reform are all made more polarized, more vicious, and less likely to find compromise when the institution at the center of those debates, the family, is weakened or broken.[33]

While strong families will not, of course, prevent wars like those of the twentieth century on their own, they can help moderate ideological extremism by balancing human needs and reminding us of both our sociality and our individual worth. And while strong families may not entirely cure our current political rhetoric of its polarizing and extreme tendencies, they provide a bridge between the individual and the community by moving the care of individuals from a collective concern to a familial one. Strong families defang the collective's interest in the costs of individual decisions while placing individuals within a supportive social matrix. The family supports moderation by taking the burden of both individual lives and collective goals upon itself. It is one of the few institutions capable of doing so.

The family really is a fulcrum—the central point in the balance between our individualist and collectivist impulses. This fulcrum challenges radical individualism and radical collectivism, moderating political discourse. It preserves both our individual importance and our social nature. It supports political life at the same time that it challenges political goals. Precisely how the family acts as a fulcrum, what happens when it weakens or fails, and how political theories of all stripes have tried to manipulate it, weaken it, support it, or destroy it to fit their peculiar political ends is the subject of the rest of this book.

Chapter 1

Contemporary Liberalism, Human Nature, and the Family

The argument that the family serves as a permanent fulcrum that balances individuals and communities must first respond to a potentially serious criticism. Thinkers on the left argue that the family is a social construct or a mere contract between individuals and that it is therefore radically flexible. The family, according to these thinkers, is a relationship just like any other, whose functions can be replicated or replaced as needed. It is neither natural nor necessary for human happiness, at least in its traditional forms. As proof of this radical flexibility, those on the left point to the fact that the contemporary American family is dramatically different from that of even fifty years ago. Currently, 43 percent of children are born to unmarried mothers, and the divorce rate has reached 50 percent.[1] The media has responded with catastrophic-sounding headlines like "The Death of Marriage," while policy analysts and pundits respond with suggestions for ways in which government policies can alleviate the wide array of social ills the demise of the traditional family has caused.[2] The collapse of the family is not only the result of changing lifestyles and mores, but also the result of the contemporary liberal attitudes toward the family and how those attitudes structured and changed the debate over what families are for.

The belief in radical flexibility of family forms and functions stems from a liberal suspicion that a belief in universal forms and functions tends to support a patriarchal and inegalitarian family that stifles women and children and sustains inequality across generations.[3] Contemporary liberals attack this traditional patriarchal family in two ways. The first involves the denial that the family serves any particular societal functions other than those directly connected to the affectionate bond between individuals.[4] This initial attack allows liberals to move traditional functions of family life such as child care, education, and preservation of wealth out of the family and onto the broader community.

The second attack on the traditional family involves denying that family forms are connected to the functions family serves in the first place. Because the family serves no peculiar functions, there can be no justification for patriarchy, for example, other than tradition. The liberal alternative, following Locke, is to treat the family as whatever particular individuals believe it to be. The family becomes, instead of a link of blood relatives across generations with a consistent structure and function, a contract between individuals in the present, easily created and easily disbanded.[5]

In prioritizing individual consent and contract, contemporary liberals believe themselves to be protecting individual autonomy and privacy. At the same time, by moving traditional functions of the family like child care, education, and wealth preservation to the community, liberals believe themselves to be protecting the community from inegalitarian practices and outcomes. The liberal project eliminates altogether the family's unique position as an intermediary between the individual and the community. Liberals reduce the family to a mere contract between individuals while at the same time parceling out all but the most intimate of family functions to the broader community. Unfortunately for liberals, eradicating the family's intermediary position actually threatens individual liberty and communal equality in ways that are only now becoming obvious.

Liberalism and Ascendant Egalitarianism

Perhaps the most powerful and thoughtful example of this liberal critique of the family is given by Susan Moller Okin.[6] Her work on justice and the family attempted to decimate the previously conceived Rawlsian and Walzerian liberal understandings of public and private lives by arguing that what happens in the private sphere of the family has significant implications for the justness or unjustness of the broader society.[7] Because of this, the traditional liberal distinction between public and private must be radically rethought if not completely rejected. The family is both hierarchical and patriarchal, according to Okin, which creates unjust inequalities between the sexes. The education one receives in the family (particularly the gendered lessons of traditional families) shapes the way individuals see their place in the world and limits the kinds of choices they may make. The unequal affections created by family life perpetuate inequality through inheritance and perpetuate privilege over generations. Most important for Okin, however, is that the traditional liberal approach to treating the family as part of a purely private sphere—and ignoring the contributions to production and reproduction made by women in their reproductive and caretaking capacities—leads to a world in which the inequality of the sexes is reinforced by the family and replicated across generations. One ironic legacy of the patriarchal family is that as it breaks down, women who would have lived their lives at least economically cared for find themselves, after divorce, economically and politically disenfranchised, with the burden of child rearing on their shoulders, lacking the education and work experience to pull themselves and their children out of poverty.[8]

The traditional family (and its breakdown) creates an unjust political and social sphere. This connection makes it impossible to view the two spheres of public and private as separate. Okin argues that insofar as the family creates these unjust outcomes, the community is justified in molding the family in ways that protect the equal opportunities of women and children. One important facet of this project is to move women's role in the production of human beings from the purely private to a kind of recognized public role. Even more central to liberating women from the bonds of family life is providing child care and a specific kind of liberal education to children to take the burden of child rearing off families.[9]

Other liberal theorists go even further than Okin, attempting to break down the public/private divide altogether, calling for a "transformation of the domestic sphere to make it consistent with the requirements of free and equal citizenship."[10] This transformation is generally accomplished through education rather than through coercive law, but it also includes some elements of legal requirements, such as changes to divorce laws and even, it is hinted, compulsory state education.[11] The transformation of the domestic challenges closely held liberal beliefs, as recognized by liberal theorists themselves. In the move to eliminate sources of inequality, liberals have "destroyed the very space liberals attempt to protect."[12] The contemporary liberal adherence to fairness and egalitarianism conflicts with the traditional liberal respect for pluralism and privacy in nonpolitical areas of life. One stated solution to the problem is that citizens are entitled to privacy when it is "justified."[13] This solution implies that the private exists because the public allows it to, an upending of traditional liberal theory.[14] Communal egalitarianism replaces protecting the private lives and freedom of individuals as the central liberal principle.

The stated policy goals of contemporary liberals follow this new focus on egalitarianism. They advocate moving education as much as possible out of the home so that children are taught the principles of justice from a young age. Subsidized day care for all families would allow women to work outside the home and would further separate the family from its traditional educative function. Divorce laws would be rewritten to make women less vulnerable after divorce, including suggestions that wages be made out to both the wage earner and the caretaker at home as a way of publically recognizing the private contributions of the caretaker. All of these proposals shift responsibility for private decisions to the public sphere.[15]

Liberal scholars occasionally recognize that their adherence to the cause of egalitarianism fundamentally changes the way liberalism approaches the traditional split between public and private lives. Instead of being a primarily political viewpoint, contemporary liberalism moves closer to becoming a comprehensive theory, whose principles reach almost "all the way down" into every facet of human life. The blurring of public and private spheres places contemporary liberals in an uncomfortable position. Having argued that the values of contemporary liberalism do not always justify intervention in the family by the state, liberal scholars nevertheless assert that "these values should inform decision making within the family."[16] But taking the right to privacy seriously requires that parents be allowed to educate their children as they see fit. Education and day care, for example, are seen as legitimate alternatives to the family, but there is no discussion of those who voluntarily and purposely eschew such institutions, such as the home-schooling movement.

Liberals are therefore placed in the difficult position of advocating that a certain set of principles apply to the private sphere but lacking any clear way to enforce them or even encourage their use. The unspoken assumption is that the only way to actually achieve the liberal commitment to equality is to reject the (traditionally at least) equally important principles of privacy and diversity, in the name of egalitarianism. The privacy of the home and the values and education passed on within are rejected in favor of collective egalitarian goals, even if such goals are not shared by the families in question. Without an adequate grounding for how to rank contemporary liberal principles—why, for example, privacy is less important than equality—liberals are left condoning a shallow tolerance where private lives that adhere to the collectivist goal of egalitarianism are respected, but private lives that do not are challenged or restricted.

Liberal Policy Proposals and the Breakdown of the Family

Not surprisingly, this tension between privacy and tolerance on the one hand and egalitarianism and distributive justice on the other leads liberals into advocating some paradoxical public policies. Liberals advocate decreased state involvement in private decision making in situations like gay rights or abortion but advocate increased state involvement in private decision making when it comes to public health issues like obesity or contraceptive use or education. When it comes to the family in particular, liberals have allowed their respect for pluralism and diversity to devolve into a kind of unequally applied relativism—all family forms are equal except those that violate certain principles of distributive justice.[17] Liberals tend to support new family forms like gay marriage and single-parent families while treating traditional heterosexual marriage as either a patriarchal holdout or a dying tradition. Principled arguments for family forms like gay marriage are rarely made because principled arguments about the functions families are supposed to fulfill (such as preserving the well-being of children or providing financial stability) might be applied to other family forms like single motherhood, with less positive results. Fear of such judgments leads to a relativistic tolerance of family forms that effectively denies that the family serves any functions at all for individuals or communities other than being the foundation for purely private affectionate relationships.

Occasionally, the absurdity of this relativism is exposed, as in the case of the liberal defense of single motherhood.[18] Liberal public intellectuals have come forward defending single motherhood as a valid choice made by liberated women and a signal that women's dependence on men is fading. This defense demonstrates its own peculiarly liberal class blindness; some family forms, and not only traditional patriarchal forms, result in inegalitarian outcomes for women and children, and single motherhood in particular has devastating impacts on women's economic and educational outcomes.[19] The left's assertion that single motherhood has no negative impacts on either mothers or children not only fails to reflect reality but also demonstrates an unusual lack of concern for social and cultural contexts that lead to female vulnerability.[20] The implicit conclusion, that traditional marriage is a useless and dying tradition while single motherhood is a liberation from traditional patriarchy, is simply unsupported by any facts or theoretical foundations.

Contemporary liberals support single motherhood, not because it leads to better outcomes for women and children, but because it is not patriarchal and because to not support it would somehow shame women who do have children out of wedlock.[21] The irony of this liberal relativism is that the groups that marriage would help economically are precisely the groups that do not get married and, when they do, divorce at higher rates. Divorce, despite the 50 percent failure rate of marriages nationally, is actually relatively uncommon in middle- to upper-middle-class white families, who thus reap the financial boon of having one household to support with two incomes.[22] That liberals are able to decry female inequality and vulnerability on the one hand, while unequivocally supporting family forms that make women more unequal and more vulnerable on the other, demonstrates a very real theoretical conflict between toleration and distributive justice that liberalism has not effectively dealt with.

The practical way liberals deal with this fundamental conflict is to reject the idea that the family serves any form that cannot be fulfilled just as well by the community. Thus, the economic, political, and even caretaking functions of the family are passed off to the community in the forms of child care, nursing homes, and public schools. The liberal argument seems to be that the fault lies not with a particular family form but with our society's disinclination to take on the burden of parenthood. France, for example, provides "single mothers preferential access to excellent day care" instead of blaming mothers and fathers.[23] The question, of course, is whether even excellent day care can replace the love of two parents. If the family is a mere social construct, then perhaps it can. If it is not, then the liberal argument for radical toleration of family forms falls apart.

HUMAN NATURE AND LOVE OF KIN

The project to replace the family with community functions, leaving only the affections as the foundation of the family, rests on a particular view of human nature that suggests that humans are capable of universal benevolence, caring for one another regardless of kinship status, but that our particular social context (capitalism, for example) makes such benevolence difficult or impossible. This view goes back to Rousseau, and authors from Friedrich Hayek (Friedrich A. von Hayek) to Thomas Sowell to Steven Pinker have described the belief in a perfectible human nature as the fundamental theoretical splitting point between traditional liberalism and contemporary liberalism.[24] Contemporary liberals believe that human nature is no nature at all but is instead a reaction to particular social contexts. Change the context, and you change what it means to be human. In the case of the family, if patriarchal and capitalistic society could be eliminated, we could learn to care for each other without reference to kinship or other discriminatory judgments.[25] Thus, the relativistic liberal attitude toward the family rests on a particular understanding of human nature, one that is capable of universal benevolence or at least of caring similarly for kin and non-kin.

Unfortunately, the evidence from the human behavioral sciences suggests that, far from our being capable of universal benevolence, nepotism is written into our genes. Three important facets of human nature undermine the liberal argument for universal benevolence and the practical policy proposals that rest upon it. First is the human preference for kin, a preference shared by species as complex as primates and as (seemingly) simple as insects.[26] Humans are born with the disposition to discriminate between individuals, and it is precisely this discrimination that liberals seek to eliminate. The second problem for liberal theorists is that human infants have evolved to solicit the care of particular caregivers, not simply generic caregiving. Much of human psychological and emotional development is supported by having one or two stable attachment figures from an early age. This requirement loosens as children get older, but for infants the evidence is clear that secure attachment to a caregiver, not merely being cared for, is crucial for normal development.[27] Finally, humans are uniquely adapted to be members of families. A host of adaptations, including complex and subtle hormonal changes, prime humans to recognize and care for kin. Mothers, fathers, siblings, and even newborn infants are wired to love and be loved by kin.

All these various adaptations do not, of course, prove that family life is absolutely necessary for any one individual's survival. But they do indicate that family life, for most humans throughout human evolution, has been absolutely necessary for the survival and success of humans in the aggregate. And evidence from the experiences of orphans and those who have lost family indicates that family, while not necessary for survival, is indeed necessary for flourishing. The family is, in a very real way, prior to both the individual and the community, in that it is fundamentally necessary for both to exist and flourish.

Kin Selection

Universal benevolence is, unfortunately for idealists, made impossible by the very laws of natural selection. Reproducing one's genes is the foundation of natural selection, and behaviors that increase the percentage of one's genes that make it into the next generation will tend to be more common in the next generation, which will increase their probability of being passed on, and so on. The result of this selective pressure is that organisms that support other organisms that share a large percentage of their genes will pass on more of their genes, both directly and indirectly, into the next generation than those that do not privilege relatives. Behaviors have evolved in many species whereby genetic relatives assist each other in survival and reproduction, thus passing along those helpful genes.[28] Assisting those with shared genes is known as kin selection, and it is found in most complex animals that are able to recognize kin (either chemically as in insects or through social and behavioral cues as in primates).[29] Some researchers believe that kin selection is one of the most, if not the most, important mechanisms supporting humanity's high level of social cooperation.[30]

The high levels of sociality and cooperation found in human history are a legacy of the interconnected relationship between human family life and human intelligence. Humans have an unusually intense and enduring family life, even among our highly social primate relatives. Due to the social nature of primate life and the intelligence of primate species, care for offspring extends well past the usual age of independence in other mammals. Humans, the most social and intelligent of primates, have intensified family relationships to overcome certain biological hurdles. The conflicting pressures of high intelligence with limited hip size in human females mean that big-brained babies are born essentially premature, requiring the care of not just mothers, but fathers and the extended family, to survive.[31] The complex social structures facilitated by language require an extended period of adolescence for human children to learn the customs and traditions of their social group. This intense learning period, lasting for at least a decade and a half in most cultures, requires an intensity of familial relations unheard of in any other animal species. Family thus helps build our intelligence and sociality, which, in turn, requires long-lasting family relationships to help young humans navigate this complexity.[32]

Kin selection has resulted in a host of individual-level adaptations that support family life by avoiding role confusion and by creating emotional bonds between relatives. Incest avoidance is universal, for example, since incest leads to the proliferation of potentially lethal alleles (or genes) in the genome, at the same time that it confuses family roles and weakens family structure. Research suggests that extended contact before the age of three triggers incest avoidance, or what is known as the Westermarck Effect, the tendency for even nonrelated individuals to avoid mating with each other if they are raised together from a young age.[33] Women also seem to choose mates with different immunological traits from themselves.[34]

The most obvious adaptations, however, involve hormonal intermediaries that facilitate bonding behaviors. Significant research has been done on the hormones prolactin and oxytocin with newer research focusing on estrogen and testosterone. Both prolactin and oxytocin seem to be central to the creation of family bonds. Prolactin, a hormone that assists in lactation, is linked to protective and caretaking behavior in mothers and allomothers (those who care for children in place of mothers, either temporarily or permanently).[35] Males caring for offspring have been found to have higher levels of prolactin than males not caring for offspring in marmosets and the California mouse. Both are monogamous species where paternal investment is high.[36]

Similarly, oxytocin is a hormone that may act as a "mild sedative" shared between mother and infant during nursing.[37] It also assists in the birthing process, in bonding between mothers and infants, and between mates, and is present in increased levels during orgasm, perhaps to assist in pair bonding.[38] Oxytocin may be instrumental in supporting monogamy.[39] Cuddling, hugging, and holding hands have all been found to increase oxytocin levels in long-term mates. Both oxytocin and prolactin are found in males and females, and both are associated with caregiving behaviors in both sexes.[40]

The bond between mother and child, while often taken for granted, is more complex than initially thought and is by no means deterministic. Mothers, due to their ability to lactate, are the primary caretakers of young infants.[41] As a result of this close long-term relationship (in many traditional societies, infants nurse up to age four), infants and mothers have coevolved, exhibiting a series of adaptations meant (from the infant's perspective) to ensure investment by a mother and (from the mother's perspective) to help ensure her genes are transmitted into the next generation. Mothers and infants do not, as has often been assumed, have precisely the same interests. Mothers—due to environmental stressors, preexisting offspring, low paternal investment, and other resource allocation problems—often have to make difficult decisions about how much to invest in which children. At the same time, mothers are uniquely equipped to bond with infants.

Mothers are prepped for caretaking by endocrinological changes that occur during pregnancy, most importantly the increase of estrogen and progesterone. Levels of these two hormones fall quickly after birth and are replaced by prolactin and oxytocin. In the absence of oxytocin, primate mothers fail to bond strongly with offspring. Without oxytocin "monkey mothers tolerate offspring, but it's left to the infant to cling for dear life."[42] Primates, of course, require social learning as well. Motherhood needs to be practiced, and primate mothers that lack socialization often fail the first time they give birth.[43] This socialization starts early in most primate species. Babies are almost irresistible to primate females, particularly juvenile females. Primate species differ on the willingness of mothers to hand babies over to other females, but allomothering, or the tendency of other females to help overburdened mothers with offspring, is an important element in the socialization of young primate females and an important resource for mothers who need a hand.[44] The sensitivity of mothering success to social learning suggests that the lessons learned from our parents are very likely to be repeated with our own children.

While less research has been done on the bonding between fathers and young offspring, there is ample evidence that fathers can be "primed" in much the same way as mothers (though to a lesser degree) to invest in and care for their offspring. Recent research demonstrates that men "nest" just as women do, preparing for the birth of offspring, and men experience postpartum depression in uncertain environments just as women do.[45] Both of these behaviors indicate that fatherhood has important psychological and physiological effects on the male brain.

Physiologically, changes occur in the brains of new fathers that help create paternal bonds. Some fathers can recognize their offspring by smell, and this ability is positively associated with "paternal investment, affection, and attachment."[46] Men can identify their child's cry and experience heightened brain activity when they hear their own child cry.[47] Male hormones, like female hormones, shift after birth to turn men into fathers. Males exhibit changes in vasopressin levels that seem to facilitate bonding. Transgenic research has shown that a single gene change controlling the vasopressin system can lead polygynous mice to become monogamous. Vasopressin assists in bonding to a particular individual, and some studies suggest that the younger a child is, the higher the father's vasopressin levels are.[48]

Family life also affects male testosterone levels. Testosterone, the male sex hormone, is associated with competitiveness, aggressiveness, and sexual interest. Married men with children have lower testosterone levels than unmarried, divorced, or unfaithful men. These effects are strongest in the West, and some variation in other cultures may be due to the confounding variables of polygyny, less time spent with children, and cultural attitudes toward infidelity.[49] Testosterone levels are lower in males who sleep in the same room as their infants than in men who sleep in separate rooms.[50] Fatherhood characterized by high investment in children causes a reduction in testosterone, which causes a corresponding reduction in competitive, aggressive, and mate-seeking behaviors.[51] Some researchers argue that high competition (and the resulting violence of such competition) between men within groups results in a quantity over quality approach to child rearing, which would be reinforced by these hormonal changes.[52] Thus, the social environment plays an important role in determining the level of paternal investment to expect. The more competitive or aggressive the environment, the less likely it is for fathers to invest heavily in their children.

Fathers are also crucial to their children's development. A father's relationship to a child's mother provides signals to the child about the structure of mating relationships and the likelihood of male investment in children. Absence of committed males in a child's life increases the likelihood of early pregnancy and out-of-wedlock birth for girls and may increase the likelihood of antisocial behavior in boys.[53] In general terms, lack of paternal involvement leads to poorer educational, social, health, and psychological outcomes, though the effect ranges from large to relatively small depending on the study.[54] These effects are likely underreported, since many studies look merely at the presence of a male figure, rather than the presence of a biological (or adopted) father. Fathers are more likely than stepfathers to invest time and resources in a particular child; therefore studies that fail to distinguish between fathers and stepfathers probably underestimate the impact of father presence.

Infants in turn are not mere passive vehicles for maternal or paternal attachment. Infants demonstrate a host of adaptations, both physical and behavioral, meant to secure parental investment.[55] Babies seek out familiar faces and voices from birth and within a few days after birth have learned their mother's smell and prefer it to others.[56] Infants develop a fear of strangers right around the time they become mobile at six to eight months of age. Strange adult males are particularly frightening for infants, indicating that infanticide probably played an important role in human evolution.[57] Infants imitate facial expressions and by six weeks or so have developed "social smiles," perhaps as a way to bond with caretakers.

Humans have also been biologically primed to bond with siblings, though here the relationship is somewhat more complex. Sibling rivalry is a common theme in human life, and anyone who has had a sibling knows that such rivalry can reach violent levels.[58] Yet in contexts external to the family, sibling relationships are strong and often elicit the desire to protect and care for siblings. This dichotomy of behavior is evolutionarily logical since within the family siblings compete for attention and resources with each other. Outside the family, however, siblings are more related to each other than to any other member of the group. Thus, one would expect precisely this pattern: competition between siblings within the family and cooperation outside it.[59]

Generally, female children provide more direct care of siblings than male children do, but across cultures and across both sexes, siblings "cooperate with one another, form alliances, and provide each other social and economic support."[60] Such a pattern is both socially and biologically encouraged. In polygamous families where siblings and half siblings are encouraged to treat each other equally, individuals still make distinctions between half and whole siblings, and such distinctions have important consequences for the amount of resources individuals are willing to invest, either in terms of time or money.[61] Our preference for closely related individuals does not seem to be a mere cultural construct.[62]

Infants and "The Eyes of Love"

In addition to the propensity to care for kin more than for non-kin facilitated by hormonally mediated bonding, humans have evolved behaviors and needs that make it difficult for the community to wholly take on the burden of child rearing. In order to develop proper social relationships, infants need to be securely emotionally attached to a central figure or figures in their lives, usually a mother. This attachment to a primary caregiver acts as a kind of anchor in the storm of social development, allowing the child to learn social cues and navigate the difficulties of a new environment while returning to the safety and security of a loving caregiver.[63] Infants' need for a primary caregiver and the corresponding desire of many, if not most, new mothers to provide that kind of care make it difficult for policy makers to secure support for universal care for infants. The burden of child rearing, at least while children are in infancy, appears to be almost as biologically delegated to women as the burden of pregnancy and childbirth are.[64]

Attachment theory, or the importance of a committed caregiver for psychosocial development, was developed in the middle of the twentieth century after researchers noticed the abnormal development of war orphans, and has since been supported and refined by evidence from the biological sciences. In essence, infants are ready to attach to a (usually maternal) figure the moment they are born. This attachment is absolutely necessary for normal emotional and psychological development. Infants who fail to attach securely—usually a result of abandonment, neglect, or abuse by a central caregiver—exhibit patterns of behavior that move from "protest" to "despair" to "detachment."[65] Experiments with monkeys separated from their mothers demonstrate that even after short separations, the effects on the infant psyche are long lasting.[66] Human infants who fail to attach grow up to have trouble navigating the social world, including chaotic home lives and criminal or antisocial behavior. An infant's relationship with its primary caretaker (again, usually a mother) structures its attitude and approach to the world, and through smiles and imitation of facial expressions, among other behaviors, infants do what they can to elicit maternal and paternal investment.[67]

While infants can be raised successfully by fathers, the preference of babies for feminine faces and voices suggests that such a system was uncommon in human history. The universal desire of infants to suck almost continuously suggests a need to keep mothers near, partially to ward off hunger, but more importantly because mothers mean security and safety from the dangers of abandonment, predators, and strangers.[68] The benefits of breast milk for brain development are paired with the emotional and psychological benefits of having a loving mother close, thus making the nursing relationship particularly powerful for mothers and infants alike.[69] Infants' preferences for mothers (and the need for someone *like* a mother) create very real inequalities for the sexes. As one noted female biologist concedes, the debates over women's place in the world often ignore "the infant's often noisy two cents' worth."[70] Infants need someone to bond with, someone who is committed to their well-being and development, and that someone will likely have to make great sacrifices in order to fulfill these infantile needs.

The sum of the biological evidence is that the family is natural; people will prefer kin to non-kin, and these preferences will shape social structures. The available evidence also refutes the claim that families are whatever anyone wants them to be. Family forms exhibit patterned variability; while there is significant flexibility in the forms families take, some forms will better fulfill the needs and desires of the individuals in those families than others. And some family forms such as polyandry will be very rare indeed.[71] While the forms families take are somewhat variable, the consistent facts remain the same. Infants need primary caretakers who are committed to their care. Consistent caretaking limits the fluidity of the family, requiring stability over time. The coevolution of mothers and infants suggests that many mothers will be unwilling to leave young infants in the hands of strangers, and infants themselves will do better with mothers or closely related and committed caretakers. Fathers matter as well, providing resources and stability for the family as well as a model for how relations between the sexes should operate.[72] The presence or absence of fathers helps male and female children determine how they should approach reproductive decisions, thus perpetuating these reproductive patterns in future generations.[73] Particularly for children in high-risk environments, parents are absolutely necessary for successfully navigating complex social environments.[74] While evolution has built considerable flexibility into family forms, the rough ideal of the nuclear family with two stable partners raising related children, ideally assisted by extended family members, may well be the evolutionary standard for emotional and social development.[75]

From a policy perspective, the biological evidence for the family challenges liberal goals like social equality between the sexes and egalitarian economic structures, and it also challenges the policy means meant to get them there, like universal day care. Universal day care, at least for infants, will likely result in poorer outcomes for children than our current inegalitarian system of maternal care precisely because parents care about their own children more than those of strangers.[76] Committed and high-quality caregivers will be more accessible to those who can pay such individuals, while the poor will be left with less qualified and less consistent care for their children. Apart from forcing everyone in society to use the same day care system, government-subsidized day care perpetuates inequalities because it cannot get around the natural preferences of humans for their own kin. This same biological barrier rises up in reaction to other liberal alternatives to the family, such as death taxes and public education.[77] More than merely affecting liberal policies on child care, our evolutionary legacy challenges the assumption that the family is a cultural construct likely to disappear. Until technology or social change can short circuit the needs of humans to love and be loved by relatives, humans will be bound by these familial needs to a less than perfect world, at least from an egalitarian perspective.

The blindness of contemporary liberalism to the facets of human nature that make universal benevolence difficult is caused in part by contemporary liberalism's rejection of the more nuanced and complex traditional liberalism, and its difficult balancing act between various human goods. Traditional liberals like Locke and Hobbes believed humans were fundamentally flawed, and they constructed their theories around that flawed but stable human nature. Contemporary liberals moved away from Locke and Hobbes to the liberalism of Rousseau, convinced that negative facets of human nature are caused not by biology but by a particular social context that can be shifted and changed. Thus, instead of adapting human social contexts to human nature, liberals try to change our social contexts to change human nature. The family will disappear once women move into the workforce, children are raised by day care workers, and men are doing something (no one can agree on precisely what). What will be left in its place is a sort of universally benevolent welfare state with high levels of happiness and equality.[78]

Contemporary liberals are right that the traditional split between public and private is difficult to uphold because private decisions have profound public effects and public policies affect the shape and functions of private institutions. But part of why this split is so difficult to maintain—and what ultimately stymies the liberal attempt to unite the public and the private into one—is that the family is neither a wholly private nor wholly public institution. It falls somewhere in between the privacy of individual inner lives and the public sphere of political wheeling and dealing. It is natural, but affected by changes in customs, manners, mores, laws, and public policy. It has been home to inequality and slavery at the same time that it has housed the love and affectionate relationships that make human life worth living. This kind of complexity cannot be adequately captured by a simple theory of distributive justice that ostensibly bridges the public/private gap by fusing the two spheres. Contemporary liberals are right that the family must be scrutinized more closely by political theorists—but the analysis should include not simply the ways in which the family challenges our desires for egalitarian outcomes, but also the ways in which the family fulfills human desires, alleviates our incompleteness, and gives meaning to our public discourse. Without appreciating the family's perch in the middle—between generations, between individuals and communities, between the past and the present, and between justice and other human goods—policies intended to improve the human condition may very well end up doing great harm.

CHAPTER 2

MARXISM, COLLECTIVISM, AND THE FAMILY

Collectivist ideologies have been adversarial to the family since Plato's *Republic* first observed the fracturing effect of family ties on collective commitments. The family creates multigenerational ties that bind people to the habits, customs, and property of the past. Egalitarian collectives rely on the democratic decisions of the present members to allocate resources and make social and political decisions for the group, while the family carries the customs and habits of past generations, limiting the sovereignty of the present generation.[1] Families constitute private and disparate groupings within a larger social structure. These groupings have private interests and goals that can prevent collective action and compete with community goals. Moreover, the family is hierarchically structured. Even in the most egalitarian of families, the natural authority of parents makes egalitarian decision making and resource sharing difficult. Sex roles in the family lead to division of labor between men and women in the public sphere, which challenges egalitarian collectivism. Finally, and perhaps most importantly, the family's roots in our most fundamental desires as humans slow and impede radical social change. Because of its permanence and its position at the core of human life and human reproduction, the family erodes and moderates radical egalitarian collectivism and facilitates a more moderate balance between the individual and the community, between equality and autonomy, and between private attachments and public goods.

The Family, Simplicity, and Contradiction

The writings of Marx and Engels lay out most clearly the theoretical foundations for the collectivist rejection of the family.[2] Marxists single the family out for extinction because the traditional monogamous family supports both capitalism and the oppression of the proletariat. The family is a microcosm of bourgeois society, based, not on love or affection as the bourgeois claim, but on capital, labor, and private gain.[3] According to Marx and Engels, the relationship between man and woman contains within it the seeds of all other groupings.[4] From the relationship between man and woman "one can therefore judge man's whole level of development,"[5] and this early form of slavery, as Marx calls the dependence of women on men for survival, fuels the creation of property.[6] The dependence of women on men for economic survival results in women becoming "objects of commerce,"[7] as mothers and wives but also as prostitutes.[8]

Engels' historical analysis of property and the family argues that peculiar family forms emerge from particular economic conditions.[9] By linking family forms with economic modes of production, the battle against capitalism becomes a battle against all social institutions that support private relationships or facilitate the passing on of private property. The family, on this account, has no natural form but is radically variable. The family's traditional position as a natural and permanent facet of human life is reduced to a mere byproduct of class conflict. Each type of family contains within it certain central contradictions, linked to the contradictions of a particular economic form, which eventually lead to its destruction. Families are only transitional states that eventually succumb to the pressures of contradiction, rather than natural social groupings or covenants with God.

While polygamy, polyandry, and polyamory all create inequalities according to Engels, the family form most linked to capitalism and therefore to class oppression is monogamy.[10] Monogamy is peculiarly dangerous because it is "the first form of the family to be based not on natural but on economic conditions—on the victory of private property over primitive, natural communal property."[11] Family and property intertwine during the shift from communal agrarian families toward more mobile monogamous nuclear families of the industrial age. Privatization of property leads to privatization of the family as wealth accumulates in the hands of elites and securing property rights and inheritances becomes a central function of family life.

As a "cellular form" of society, monogamy highlights the "oppositions and contradictions" of capitalist society.[12] It is not the family per se that contains contradictions, but that peculiar form of the family: the nuclear family with division of labor based on sex, preservation of capital through inheritance, and a hierarchical structure, linked inextricably to capitalistic society.[13] Monogamous marriage is both a microcosm of the larger capitalist system and a direct result of that system.[14] The relationship between man and women created by monogamous relations represents the first "class opposition," and the first "class oppression" is the resulting unequal relationship between man and woman.[15] Women's confinement to the private sphere also robs the public sphere of the labor of half the population.[16]

Engels' "proof" of the transitory nature of the family relies largely on his contention that modern bourgeois monogamy contains within it certain "contradictions" that eventually destabilize it. These contradictions form the material dialectic. Monogamy coexists with prostitution.[17] The bourgeois support for family life coexists with their abuse of proletariat child labor.[18] The exploitation of members of the family by those within the family and the exploitation of proletariat families by the bourgeois constitute inherent contradictions that stem from the links between the family, the means of production, and private property.[19] The contradictions inherent in the modern family will eventually, Marx and Engels believe, cause it to wither away like the rest of capitalist society.

The specific Marxist criticisms of the family as the building block of capitalist oppression are part of a larger theoretical goal of the Marxist project, one that relies on creating a simple and ultimately monotone theory of human action. The "contradictions" Marx and Engels find in the family emerge from competing affections, interests, and desires. The conflicts arising from these competing goods may not be soluble by a dialectical history. Inherent in Marx and Engels' analysis is the belief that permanent contradictions are impossible in human life, that through the process of dialectic, one value or another will ultimately triumph.[20] Instead of grappling seriously with conflicts of human goods, early Marxists created an artificial coherence of thought by structuring their ideologies around the problem of class oppression. By inspecting all human life through that particular lens, other kinds of complicating factors—such as emotional attachment, need, and desire—become merely peripheral effects of that primary conflict, rather than real and complex moral dilemmas with a weight of their own. The problem with this myopic view of human life is not merely that it is wrong, but that it is fundamentally incomplete. Human life involves oppression, of course, but it also involves many other things. The reduction of human social relationships to the means of production limits our ability to evaluate the different values that different social relationships might support.

Many of the apparent contradictions Marx cites as proof of the family's corruption actually stem from delicate compensation and balancing between various human goods and conflicting human desires. The link between monogamy and prostitution, for example, is less a contradiction than it is the result of attempting to secure the benefits of monogamy to women and children while controlling male sex drives. This "contradiction," rather than supporting the rejection of monogamy, instead supports the recognition that different people with different interests, drives, and talents will create imperfect communities. Prostitution may represent the exploitation of vulnerable women by male sexual appetite, but the vulnerability of women and the existence of strong male sexual appetites are not transitory characteristics of a capitalist society but permanent facets of human life. Pretending that such characteristics are linked to a particular historical and economic epoch, and that such characteristics will change or fade away, distracts the community from real and difficult conversations about channeling appetites and protecting the vulnerable.

Permanent conflicts exist between men and women, between parents and children, and between families and the communities that house those families, and while these conflicts can be mediated, moderated, or channeled into other outlets, they are ultimately ineradicable because the variation in human life and the myriad ways in which humans interact are ineradicable. Marxists, by reducing human interactions to class conflict, destroy the diversity of moral goods at the same time.[21] While the vision of a society without conflicts of interests may be attractive, it distracts us from the difficult debates that politics requires about what kinds of moral goods to prefer in which situations and how to best balance individual desires with collective needs.

The Marxist project strives to create a society where everyone sings on the same note, where private interests are subsumed by public goods, and where diversity is unrecognized because such diversity leads to tragic conflicts between the individual and the community. The alternative to such a monotone society is to view society as a musical work in progress, with each divergent note contributing in some way to an overall harmony. Harmony requires working with diversity and recognizing that the outcome will be sometimes messy and sometimes tragic, but that such disorder is required for the balancing of individual and collective needs. There will be dissonance, of course, since the composition is being composed at the same time it is being played. But learning and adjustment is still possible, and lower-level disorder may be necessary to create a higher-level order.[22]

The family itself represents a harmony of values and desires because it brings together different voices informed by age, gender, occupation, education, and class into a group that acts collectively while moderating and balancing the differing desires of the individuals in the group. The interests of children for independence and control are balanced by their parents' desires for their children's safety and well-being, and the interests of grandparents may be weighed against those of parents and children. Spouses balance their love for their children, their relationship with their spouse, and external interests and desires that threaten the cohesion of the family.[23]

The conflicts that Marxists hope will disappear through the dialectical process are permanent facets of the human experience, unlinked to any particular economic or historical epoch. These conflicts can be exacerbated in situations where the needs of diverse individuals are not carefully balanced. Women's long (and ongoing) fight for equal political and economic rights demonstrates that some societies better balance the diverse needs of individuals in families and communities than others. But *balancing* will always be necessary, because no social condition will eradicate these fundamental conflicts between diverse individuals at different stages of life with different talents, interests, and needs. Progress can be made even within a complex and imperfect system, without relying on wholesale destruction of social structures like the family that are so closely linked to human flourishing. That women have successfully fought for equal rights worldwide while still retaining family ties is evidence that the balancing of human values is not a zero-sum game. Recognizing that balance, compromise, and moderation are necessary is a safer and more effective way to achieve change than waiting for (or instigating) a revolution.

Self-Interest and the Collective Good

The Marxist concern with simplicity and ideological coherence heightens their suspicion of the family's role in creating competing affections rooted in a particular time, place, and lineage. Familial attachments and affections create divergent interests within the community (often called "selfish" or "egoistic" desires by early Marxists) that pull members away from egalitarianism into private goods and differentiated desires at the same time that they fracture the attachment of individuals to the community. The family pulls the individual away from the community at the same time it pulls the individual out of himself. This middling position between individual and group confuses the relationship between the individual and the broader collective, creating complex and often contradictory sets of interests and desires.

Engels attempts to simplify the theoretical chaos the family creates by treating the family as a mere extension of the individual and of self-interest, rather than as a group partaking of both individual and community oriented values. The modern family is an "individualistic unit," according to Engels, and is thus dangerous to collective cohesion.[24] The early family, prior to the advent of capitalism, is free from self-interest, jealousy, and egoistic limitations on attachments.[25] Once capitalism takes hold, the character of the family becomes internally focused and love of kin becomes "egotistic and anti-social."[26] Instead of being the foundation for group loyalty, early Marxists view kin attachments as fundamentally opposed to the interests of the group.[27]

Kin attachments threaten collective egalitarianism because equality of conditions depends on equality of interests and affections. As soon as individuals' interests diverge from those of the group, the desire for equality diminishes, or rather, desires for different goods eventually erode the desire for equality. Unequal interests breed unequal conditions as individuals with differing interests, talents, and desires diverge further over time. Parents pass their talents to their children through education and the fruits of their talents to their children through inheritance.[28] Not only does the family create unequal interests, but it creates unequal affections as well. Family members care more for each other than for other members of the collective, and with that affection come resources and other material goods. Unequal affections lead very quickly to unequal material outcomes, which lead, in turn, to class conflict.

In order to keep both interests and affections homogeneous and channeled toward the collective, individual interests must be "subordinated" to those of the collective, and the primary source of these individual interests, the family, must be weakened.[29] Weakening the family begins with the careful education of children outside of the home and is assisted by the collectivization of property to eliminate familial loyalties based on inheritance. Kollontai believes that gradually loosening the ties between individuals and their families will lead over time to the strengthening of the collective and the eradication of selfish and individualistic desires.[30]

It is characteristic of the communist project that the first step toward phasing out the family is to change the meaning of the word. Engels' purpose in *The Origin of the Family: Private Property and the State* is to redefine the family by placing it within a transitory historical context. The family is not, according to Engels, a natural grouping but is instead a radically variable historical artifact that changes as the mode of production changes. Because its shape is not predetermined, the family can be merged into the collective until no distinction between the two is possible and no separation between private loyalties and public loyalties exists. This malleability is necessary to undermining the private loyalties at the heart of familial affection. If the family is a natural entity, it will recur and continue to challenge collective allegiance. Engels therefore rejects any natural foundation for the family. Everything from whom we consider kin (radically variable by culture and historical era) to incest avoidance (a useful invention to support sexual shame and further separate the family from other members of society) becomes linked to the means of production.[31] Redefining family is the first step toward the replacement of private interests with public ones.[32]

Private and Public Spheres

The divisive character of private interests and affections leads collectivists to collapse the functions of the private sphere into the public sphere, eliminating the main functions of the family in the process. The communist project is finalized when private interests are abolished (particularly private property and the family) and the public sphere becomes the sole center of human activity. The collapse of the private into the public is justified on the grounds that the distinction between public and private is false. What is called private is never truly private because the private sphere provides structure and support for inegalitarian social institutions like private property and sex-based division of labor.

The two central facets of the private sphere to be incorporated by the public, therefore, are private property and private affections, and the collectivization of both private property and private attachments starts with child rearing. Collective rearing of children separates parents and children before they create enduring private bonds. Women in particular ostensibly benefit from collective child rearing because moving children out of the home frees women from the most time-consuming of private duties, allowing them to participate fully in public life. As the primary victims and proponents of the domestic sphere, women's acquiescence would be needed to fully abolish the "monogamous family as the economic unit of society."[33]

Collectivizing the private sphere requires redefining reproductive activities in public terms. Motherhood is characterized as a "social obligation" and a "social task" rather than a private desire.[34] The collective must "assume all the cares of motherhood."[35] The collective also controls education, traditionally the purview of the family.[36] Apart from limiting private attachments, removing the education of children from the home breaks the cycle of poverty, allowing every child equal opportunity for education and self-fulfillment.[37] The collectivized family undermines the disparities in both affections and material conditions that are at the root of class conflict.

Elimination of private interests and affections homogenizes interests, not simply by reducing familial affections, but by eroding the weight of custom and tradition. Radically restructuring social conditions requires forgetting the customs and traditions of the past because such traditions limit progress. Unlike conservative thinkers who see traditions and customs as palliative and reassuring, Marx describes tradition weighing as "a nightmare on the brain of the living."[38] Traditions and customs not only limit progress, but they are also unnecessary; once the material dialectic has moved beyond an epoch of history, there is no need to learn from the past. Progress is inevitable and irreversible. The family threatens a progressive view of history because it embodies a nature that at once limits utopian progress while tying us to the past.[39] From family traditions to ancestors to homelands, the very idea of family is weighted with links to the past.

One way Marxists limit the weight of past generations is to segregate society on generational grounds, starting with the education of children by age group outside of the family. Rather than a historically rooted education passed down from generations of relatives, education is collective and uniform within each age group.[40] Generational segregation not only breaks the bonds of the traditional family, which is generally hierarchically arranged by generation, but also allows each cohort to be educated according to the peculiar needs of each generation in the present.[41] The education of the young is not the education in the past traditions of a people. For both children and adults, the transition to a new communist society is largely a question of learning new rules of organization and new emotional attachments, learning to reject the distinction between "yours and mine."[42] For many of the older population, such education may not be possible, and force may be necessary to restrain the most strident of the "individualists."[43] Once a generation has been raised outside the home, the disintegration of the family is largely complete as generational memory of the private sphere disappears.[44] Once the social question is "settled," collective education can turn its attention to the subjugation of nature.[45]

Generational knowledge is only relevant if one acknowledges that it is possible to learn from the past, which is unnecessary if social knowledge is relative to a particular economic mode of production. The communist collapse of the private into the public and the public into the demands of the present generation stems from the Marxist reduction of the private/ public distinction to economic considerations in general and to labor considerations in particular. Public interference in individual sexual relations, for example, is justified on the grounds that the state needs enough (but not too many) healthy workers. The education and care of children outside the home is justified as a way to bring women's labor into the recognized public sphere. In effect, Marxists reduce the private to the public and the public to current labor relations. Communism's radical reductionism facilitates marginalizing the family because human values such as freedom or love of kin are neither natural nor compelling compared to the ideological loyalty to class equality. Reducing human life to the means of production produces a theoretically cohesive doctrine that ultimately fails to reflect the complexity of human life.

Reducing human goods and values to material considerations causes Marxists to overlook the importance of the family for collectives and to underestimate its permanence in human life. The simplicity of the Marxist framework also mischaracterizes the split between public and private, failing to recognize that the family falls squarely in between the two and will be resistant to complete incorporation by one sphere or another. Familial decisions moderate selfish short-term interest by forcing individuals to balance or compromise their desires with the desires and wishes of the family. At the same time, the family moderates the collectivist impulse by forcing the community to recognize certain private (but not necessarily individualistic) desires that may challenge collective ends. The family forces the compromise between public and private because of its primarily private character and its public location.[46]

Proposed Marxist policies for the transition phase hint at how difficult the eradication of the family is likely to be. Instead of family ties merely withering away, undermining the family requires active collective interference and even coercion. Legal restrictions on traditional families may be necessary to loosen the bonds between parents and children, ultimately replacing the bonds of family to bonds to the collective.[47] As sex and reproduction become social activities, collective interference in the reproductive decisions of individuals on the dual grounds of public health and population growth becomes necessary.[48] Some Marxists have even championed government-run reproductive programs that would prevent feeble or diseased individuals from having children and would (presumably) encourage fit individuals to have children at rates consistent with collective needs.[49] For example, transition-stage policies would control the number of partners and the psychological state of the individuals involved in the relationship, as well as provide an end to economically based relations including prostitution.[50] Despite assurances that coercive force would not be used to disband the family, the collective will prevent some marriages, and in some cases, prevent reproduction of "unfit" individuals.[51] The main characteristics of the new Marxist family are its "freedom"—presumably meaning its lack of permanent bonds and equality of the sexes—and its sociality or public nature—as opposed to the "compulsively isolated" traditional private family.[52] Yet the coercive interference of the collective in sexual and reproductive decisions is anything but "free," and individuals, separated from kin, are stripped of the foundations of human sociality.

Another hint of the family's enduring power is that collectivists must co-opt kinship language to describe the individual's new relationship to the collective. Women and children "will be taken care of by society, which is like one large, friendly family."[53] This "society-family" replaces kinship attachments with affection for and attachment to the group. The early communist use of family phraseology to encourage attachment to the community unwittingly proves the strength of traditional kin ties. The use of familial language feeds off the strong emotional ties kinship creates. The collective can, to a certain extent, use these emotions to shift loyalties away from private kin bonds by redefining kinship as an ideological relationship rather than as a biological one. But the use of kin language in the first place implies that Marxists recognized the strength and enduring nature of kinship, even as they proclaimed its weakness and impermanence.

Nature and History

The collapse of the private into the public, supported as it is by the sovereignty of the present generation over the customs and traditions of the past, is directly related to the Marxist suspicion of nature and corresponding emphasis on a progressive dialectical view of history.[54] The dialectic that characterizes human progress also characterizes the natural world. Engels argues that nature is dialectical, not cyclical, and that the movement of nature follows a predetermined course based on material interactions.[55] Darwinian theory, Marx believed, supported the idea that nature itself was not a stable standard for values, because nature itself is characterized by a material dialectic.[56] The progress of man toward a true communist society involves rejecting the nature of Aristotelian philosophy, with its teleology and stable standards of right, and replacing it with a radical (and simplistic) Darwinian theory of nature whose leading characteristic is the progressive dialectic involving the gradual removal of contradictions over time.[57] Marx's insistence that knowledge comes from the world of sense leads to the conclusion that by simply changing the world of sense, one can change knowledge and thus human existence.[58]

The dialectical characteristic of nature assumes a lack of stability and permanence in natural human laws. The Marxist labor theory of value is merely one example of the relativistic nature of human values. Labor creates value, not nature. The standards for moral and social improvement stem not from who we are as evolved creatures, but instead from the kind of labor in which we engage (which, of course, changes over time).[59] Marx's labor theory of value assumes (much like Locke before him) that it is not nature but human effort that brings value. That this is a radical rejection of the ancient understanding that nature is a source of values is not an original argument.[60]

The relativism that characterizes natural laws extends into the political sphere.[61] Marx emphasizes not human nature, permanent and stable across generations, but material man, who only exists bound up with a particular time, place, and class. He criticizes the French revolutionaries, who erred by supposing that man has a nature outside the economic milieu in which he lives. The idea that man might have natural and permanent needs flies in the face of the Marxist belief that needs are dictated largely by the means of production and that humans can be liberated from these needs through the liberation from capital. The French revolutionaries founded their revolution on nature and thus failed. Marxists would move beyond nature, and only then succeed. Nature for Marx consists of power relations, just as the natural laws of physics are about power relations. Appeals to nature are nothing more than the ruling class attempting to justify their oppression at a particular point in economic time.[62]

The collectivist rejection of nature extends, finally, to the family, that most natural of human social groups. Family ties are particularly dangerous because they provide the foundations of humanity's possessiveness or the desire to *own*. The family supports this possessiveness because it links us to people who we claim as our own and because that preferential sense of *belonging* to a family supports our desires to acquire and pass on material possessions in the form of private property.[63] This possessiveness, so counter to collective attachment and collective goals, must be proven to be an artifact of history, not innate to human nature, if it is to be overcome.

The flexibility of the family in the progressive view of history is made possible by the communist rejection of the belief in the naturalness of human kinship bonds. A family that is natural, either because it fulfills certain stable human needs or because it represents a permanent natural order in the world, is fundamentally destructive of the revolutionary desire to change the social order. The family, as the fundamental building block of social organizations, must be malleable in order for the rest of society to change as well. The root of the communist project is the flexibility and relativity of the family: "Family and marriage are historical categories," because family "is part of the superstructure."[64] As historical systems change, the family fluctuates, becoming less and less central to human life until it withers away.[65] Marxists reject the importance of the family for the psychological, emotional, or sociopolitical well-being of humans because there is no permanent human nature or permanent well-being in the first place. Whether these early Marxists fully appreciated the fact, the success of the entire communist project depended on the answer to the question of whether the family is or is not a natural and therefore permanent facet of human life.

This characteristic Marxist rejection of nature is necessitated by the dramatic social change they hoped to foment. Humans must be able to create their own reality, and thus a nature that resists change is incompatible with this kind of radical freedom.[66] The fundamental difference between man and beast is not a unique human nature but is instead the ability to move beyond the given and to become creators, conquering the natural world in the process. For Marxists, nature provides no standard that man himself cannot change through the power of his labor, the ultimate creator of value. The only kind of legitimate social form is one carefully constructed, rid of contradictions, that replaces all private interests with public ones. The family—as the fundamental individualistic social form and as the form from which all other contradictions stem—is thus the central piece of the superstructure that requires destruction. The family is not merely dangerous for the practical consequences it has for egalitarianism; it is dangerous primarily as the theoretical bastion of the "natural" or of "human nature," which is the enemy of radical social change.[67]

The rejection of nature has profound consequences for Marx's theory of human sociality. Marx views the political and economic (or what he calls "society" broadly) as the only relevant social arenas.[68] By rejecting the family as a relevant social grouping, Marx effectively eliminates any need for private concerns or desires to be balanced or even acknowledged in the public sphere. Marx is correct of course that "if man is by nature social, he will develop his true nature only in society," but he mistakes the relevant kind of society because he refuses to recognize the existence of naturally existing social forms. Humanity's sociality is initially structured around family relationships, not around "society" as a whole. Humans are incapable of loving everyone equally; they must love those they know intimately, those who comprise the private social world.[69] Because Marx does not recognize the existence of innate characteristics, he also refuses to recognize that there might be social forms that limit and constrict the institutions on which he bases his social revolution. Effectively, Marx equates the social with the public, rejecting private or "intermediate" social groups that might limit or moderate the progressive goals of the collective.

While Marx is right that the family has profoundly inegalitarian tendencies, he undervalues the central role the family plays in social progress, albeit a particular kind of progress. Humans have, no doubt, progressed over time: morally, socially, and politically. But there is no indication that such progress is irreversible or that it is inevitable. Human progress occurs not because the historical dialectic dictates it, but because humans are capable of learning from their mistakes. This learning process, like so much else in human life, is imperfect and complex, and as a result human progress is imperfect and punctuated by setbacks and reversals. Nevertheless, learning still occurs. The family's role as the home of intergenerational contact and education is indispensable for this learning process. The family houses the knowledge of particular times and places not written down by historians, and it is this knowledge of particulars that allows humans to learn from the past and improve, however slowly. This kind of social change, the slow adaptation of individuals and families to their environments—geographic, economic, and political—is antithetical to the broad-based change collectivist reformers desire. It is slow and tends to preserve social order rather than overturning it.[70]

If history is not in fact inevitably progressive, if our nature continues to limit and hamper us with its imperfection and contradictory desires, the family serves a vital educative and stabilizing function. It preserves the memory of the past, and with that memory it supports generational learning. The family protects human choice by making it possible to remember the alternatives offered by the past and to choose between them in the present. Without these alternatives, the individual may be engulfed by the wheels of history, doing nothing more than providing the cogs on which History grinds forward. The refusal to recognize true human freedom—the freedom to choose well or poorly—is the obvious outcome of an ideology that believes the past has nothing to offer and that our link to that past, our family, is nothing but an artifact of economics.

The Moderation of Marx and the
Reemergence of the Family

It is perhaps not surprising that shortly after Marxism was implemented in real-world societies, the family swiftly reemerged and brought with it the complexity and diversity of human goods, conflicts of interests, and traditional sex roles that early Marxists sought to eliminate. The family reemerges in both large-scale Marxist experiments and in small-scale societies, and the experiences of the early Soviet regime and the later Israeli kibbutzim illustrate the durability of family relationships even in the face of hostile public policies.

Prior to the 1930s, the Soviets focused on literacy and job training programs for women, seeing them as an untapped labor force.[71] By the 1930s, however, the Communist Party in Russia had moved away from the communist ideal of liberating women from division of labor based on sex and had moved toward a traditional, patriarchal view of women's role in the economy. Part of this shift has been attributed to communism molding its ideals to the practical norms and values of the women they were recruiting, most of whom still saw themselves as mothers first, and workers second. Another reason may have been the economic benefits of the family in reducing the overhead of the new government by placing the cost of child rearing back under maternal control.[72] The regime had been so far unable to provide for women, and the problems of unemployment and prostitution were formidable. Traditional marriage with economic protections for women in case of divorce became necessary to ensure the economic well-being of women and children.

Despite clear policy prescriptions advocating the waning of the family in the so-called transition phase, society never moved beyond that phase.[73] As the Soviet regime increasingly rejected early Marxist attitudes toward the family and reoriented itself toward familism and away from collectivism, ideologically pure Marxists became more and more marginalized.[74] Those who criticized the movement away from the Marxist ideal of sex and gender equality were quickly silenced and their works carefully edited to exclude such criticism.[75] The legal framework followed the party line, with stringent abortion and divorce laws. Quiet resistance to these laws made them weak, but nevertheless the official position was that the nuclear family was "the basis for an orderly, productive society."[76] The endorsement of the nuclear family had the interesting effect of further weakening the extended family structure that had long been a mainstay of Russian life, further isolating the nuclear family and making control over families and individuals easier.[77] The return to familism thus occurred swiftly and early on in the Soviet regime, largely because Soviet leadership realized the importance of the family for economic and social stability, particularly in the transitional phase.[78] The Marxist revolution had not succeeded in destroying the family, but it had succeeded in isolating the family and reducing it to its nuclear form.

As true believers were gradually pushed out, their criticism of the regime became more subtle. Alexandra Kollontai, for example, congratulates the Soviet regime for allowing woman to "fulfill her natural duty . . . to be a mother, the educator of her children, and the mistress of her home."[79] While ostensibly placing her in line with the Soviet regime, her comment is actually subversive, given the traditional Marxist view of nature and women's position in it. An appeal to nature is a rejection of the ability of Soviet Marxism to radically restructure and ultimately conquer that nature. A regime that has made it possible for a woman to "fulfill her natural duty" is a regime that has fundamentally failed in its quest to bring about a new state of social affairs. The reemergence of the family demonstrates the failure of the communist project broadly.

It is not merely in large-scale and ultimately corrupt regimes like Stalinist Russia that the family reemerges in importance. The experience of the Israeli kibbutzim, considered one of the most successful long-term collectivist societies, suggests that the early Soviet experience with the family (theoretically hostile and practically friendly) is not an anomaly of that peculiar system.[80] Like Soviet Russia, the kibbutzim began with a clear ideological purpose: to create an egalitarian collective based on "each according to his need." Due in part to practical concerns (the lack of women in the early kibbutzim) but mostly to the ideological focus on equality, the family was practically nonexistent in the early kibbutzim.[81] The anthropological and sociological literature that followed these communities over the first twenty years or so catalogues a dramatic shift in the importance and centrality of the family in kibbutzim life.

The kibbutzim were originally touted by some anthropologists as being the first known social structure to do entirely without the family.[82] Children were raised communally, and contact with parents was limited by parental work schedules and separate living spaces. Husbands and wives were treated as separate and individual members of the group, and their economic contributions to the kibbutz were placed into the collective fund, thus eliminating the traditional economic role of the family.[83] Sociologists and anthropologists rushed in to study an unprecedented natural social experiment. What they found was that the death of the family had, in fact, been greatly exaggerated.[84]

More compelling than the fact that the kibbutzim did in fact host a vibrant family life was the evidence collected over generations that "familism," or the centrality of the family in the day-to-day affairs of the kibbutzim, had actually grown over time with each generation of kibbutzniks. Not only were anthropologists confronted with the need to explain the continued existence of the family in a community whose ideology clearly rejected such a structure, but they also had to explain why the kibbutzim, instead of becoming more collective over time as their ideological loyalties would suggest, actually became more familistic.[85]

Two of the largest qualitative and quantitative studies on the kibbutzim both found separately that the family began to play a more important role with the second-generation kibbutzniks, and the importance continued to grow with each successive generation.[86] Perhaps more important than attitudinal differences, the kibbutzim's policies themselves changed over time to allow for more individual family time, more parent-child contact, and even a shift toward family-oriented residences.[87] Such policies are noteworthy not merely because they are clearly averse to the expressed egalitarian and collective goals of the group, but also because they were opposed by many in the kibbutzim, particularly men.

Some have argued that the main catalyst for the shift away from communal child rearing was the desires of women for increased contact with their children. This is significant because it is women's freedom and equality that are threatened by the reintroduction of housework and traditional child rearing tasks. While men pointed out the dangers to female autonomy and equality posed by familism, the women by and large responded that they were willing to make sacrifices to have more time with their children.[88] The creation of an "hour of love," where women could meet and bond with their children during the day, and the eventual privatization of housing, demonstrated that collectivist ideology was slowly being moderated by the desires of families, particularly by the desires of mothers and children.[89]

The rationales behind the kibbutzim's original rejection of the family and its eventual reemergence mirror those given by early Marxists. The kibbutzim's initial suspicion of the family follows the Marxist concern with intergenerational ties and the "continuity of transmitted tradition."[90] Theoretically, the kibbutzim, as an avowedly revolutionary movement, could not sanction a social structure like the family that relies so heavily on tradition for its continuance. Practically too, most of the early kibbutzniks were young and single and had broken off ties with family in order to embark on this revolutionary path. Thus, for the early settlers at least, the family was both practically and theoretically averse to kibbutz life. As with the early Marxists, the kibbutzniks felt that private loyalties, seen particularly strongly in parental attachment to children, must be overcome in order to secure the success of the communal endeavor.[91]

At the beginning of a revolutionary movement like the kibbutzim, to succeed in a hostile environment, to become economically self-sufficient, and to protect oneself against the attacks of outsiders (a very real problem in Israel), one's loyalties to the group and to the group mission need to be absolute. The family was practically eliminated in this early generation. This early elimination of the family was short lived, however.

In the first generation, the question of the family initially was largely theoretical, but when the settlers began having children of their own, the landscape shifted. Families presented a source of "centrifugal tendencies," resulting in tensions between public and private loyalties that threaten cohesion.[92] The second generation was more family oriented than the first, and researchers cite spirited public debates over the appropriateness of family meals versus collective meals in the dining hall as evidence that the centrifugal forces of family life and collective attachment were causing obvious tension.[93] The outcome of this tension between family and collective was the eventual moderating of collective and public loyalties to make room for private familial bonds. Crucially, researchers of the kibbutzim found animosity toward the family in the extremes of collectivism and individualism. Pro-family arguments were, instead, rooted in a "moderate collectivism."[94] This moderation of collective goals resulted in a shift away from the segregation of individuals by generation to an intergenerational organization that reflected natural human groupings, by kin and across generations.[95] Even more crucial, the kibbutzim's commitment to equality was balanced over time against other human goods like autonomy, private attachments, and parental care.

The current kibbutzim are largely family oriented, with children living with their parents and meals eaten as families, not as a collective. The privatization of the family has been followed by economic privatization in many of the kibbutzim.[96] The same trend is seen in formerly collectivist communities outside the kibbutzim. Modern communes and "intentional communities" all demonstrate a move to make family life a central part of their mission, though the tension between family and community is still in evidence.[97] These movements all demonstrate the need to integrate the family with collective goals, even in the most radical and consensus-based groups.

Overall, the experience of collectivists in first abolishing and then reengaging with the family reveals a broad movement toward the moderation of ideological goals and ideals in the face of an ever-present family life. Attempts to abolish the family lead instead to a moderation of ideology itself by bringing values other than equality—such as attachment to kin, the desire for intimate human relationships, freedom, and a private sphere of action—into balance with the desire for equality. Such moderation of ideological principles allows the movement to better fulfill natural human social needs. These changes occurred despite the fact that the family creates emotional divisions, differentiates members of the community from one another, and shifts resources from the public to the private sphere. The compromise that collectivists have made with the family has been not merely a compromise in practice, but an erosion and moderation of some of egalitarian collectivism's most dearly held beliefs. That the family moderates these beliefs within an ideological community, without external assistance, and in the course of two generations, demonstrates its profound strength and endurance in human life.

It was a central goal of the early kibbutzim "to develop a new kind of human being, motivated by communal commitment and uncontaminated by private greed."[98] What the kibbutzim actually accomplished was *rediscovering* the human, in all its imperfect and complex glory. Human nature is permanent and stable, and social structures can no more change our innate desires in the short term than they can change our physical structure. Human needs for intimacy and familial relationships will challenge collective desires for equality and conformity.[99] While social structures are capable of controlling and channeling human nature, the strongest human desires, those for kinship and close family ties, must be integrated into any successful community lest they weaken that community's very foundations. The failure of radical collectivism as a whole, then, is not simply the economic problem as is often claimed but is instead the problem of human nature, beginning with the close bonds of kin.[100]

The Marxist rejection of human nature leads to a misunderstanding of the human goods required to support that nature. Radical collectivism fails because it fails to recognize the diversity of human goods that vary across the human lifespan and that extend beyond egalitarian concerns. Humans require a variety of human goods for true flourishing, and that variety begins in the family.[101] The family is natural and yet bound by custom and tradition, is private but with a strong public face, and is the home of affections that simultaneously pull us away from the community while creating deep roots. The family supports our complex human desires, provides room for human improvement, and nourishes our social nature and our private lives.[102] In this way it balances our individual and our social selves and provides a path toward a balanced community and an appreciation for equality, rightly understood.

Chapter 3

Ayn Rand, Individualism, and the Family

Individualist ideologies have no easier a time incorporating the existence of natural groups like the family than do collectivist ideologies. In recent years, Locke's contractual treatment of the family, for example, has been criticized as leading to an isolating individualism, and numerous critiques of the individualist neglect (at best) or rejection (at worst) of the family have been published.[1] The challenges posed by the family to individualistic ideologies are different from those faced by collective ideologies, though in both cases, ideological simplicity and consistency are threatened by the family's complexity and intermediate position. For individualists in particular, the family threatens the assumptions about human rationality and independence that form the core of individualist and libertarian theories.

The individualist emphasis on rationality and human choice is defied by the family's foundation on bonds that tie people together not through choice or consent, but through emotion and accident. Further, the family is inherently a collective enterprise, a natural social grouping where the continuity of the family unit itself often rises in importance above the well-being of any one individual. Finally, the family is founded on and perpetuates a system of human need and dependence, which conflicts with individualists' belief in personal responsibility and self-sufficiency. The individualist values of rationality, freedom, and responsibility are all moderated by the family as a social, emotional, and bonding entity, one that restricts human autonomy genetically, through habituation and education, and finally through emotional ties to the family itself. The family erodes and moderates radical individualism and opens individualistic libertarian societies to a more moderate balance between the individual and the community.[2]

Probably the most famous and most extreme adherent of individualism is Ayn Rand, and her work is useful to this analysis because her beliefs about the family are both consistent and largely negative.[3] Rand focuses on the family's role in limiting individual freedom, tying us to past generations, binding us in social groups that we did not choose, and creating cycles of need and dependence. Like Marx and Engels for the collectivists, Rand marks the most extreme version of individualism. Like Engels and Marx, Rand does not speak for many or even most libertarians or individualists, but precisely because her philosophy is so extreme, an analysis of her attitude toward the family can provide insight into how the family challenges even more moderate individualistic theories. Perhaps surprisingly, Rand's arguments against the family share many of the themes found in Marx and Engels' rejection of the family, including concerns about the stifling effect of history, the relationship between the public and private spheres, and the role of nature in familial desires. These similarities suggest that the family challenges extreme political views in similar ways.

The best starting place is Rand's work *Atlas Shrugged*, though evidence from her essays and interviews is also instructive. *Atlas Shrugged* is important not only because Rand herself saw it as the culmination of her fiction and the clearest articulation of her philosophy of Objectivism, but also because, unlike her other works, it is teeming with families, and Rand's treatment of the family is perhaps clearer in this work than it is anywhere else. *Atlas Shrugged* is ultimately a book about the worth of individuals and a rejection of collectivist philosophies. Rand was an escapee of Soviet Russia, and her rejection of the ideal of "from each according to his ability and to each according to his need" is complete and consistent. Rand's individualism rejects the ideas that "society" is anything other than a collection of individuals or that society has a "right" to demand that one individual help another. Unlike the simplistic interpretations of her work, Rand does not believe in selfishness as a good, but she does predicate all human relationships on voluntary cooperation. Coercion must be limited to protecting basic rights to life and property; no man can require the help or assistance of another.[4] Sociality is central to Rand's philosophy, though only if such sociality consists of a society made up of rational individuals.[5]

The story of *Atlas Shrugged* is the story of the replacement of reciprocal altruism (the morality of the trader) with pure altruism (the morality of the looter) and how a small group of men and women fought back. The protagonist is Dagny Taggart, a railroad executive whose philosophy of individual independence links her with a band of (mostly) men who rise up to challenge the increasing socialization of industry. Dagny's childhood relationship with Francisco d'Anconia, her later love affair with Hank Rearden, and her final passionate relationship with John Galt all embody Rand's belief that even love stems from rational assessments of another human's worth. These men challenge encroaching socialism by removing themselves and their talents from the world, escaping to an idyllic valley where they live by the code of trade. The gradual loss of talent and expertise creates a devastating loss of technology and industry that grinds the entire country to a halt. The antagonists in the book are a band of petty collectivist "looters," who use the language of brotherly love to enrich themselves and create dependency in others. They include Dagny's brother Jim Taggart and most of the political establishment, whose arguments in favor of taking from the rich to feed the (undeserving) poor end up impoverishing everyone.

Atlas Shrugged is, surprisingly for some, a highly moralistic book, though Rand redefines morality on rigidly individualist lines. For Rand, the highest and perhaps only moral relationship between individuals is that of trade.[6] The trader is neither entirely self-sufficient, nor is he selfish in the simplistic sense. The trader does not take what is not his due and does not give more than is deserved. The trader is the embodiment of the moral code of reciprocal altruism, and such altruism is the root of sociality properly understood.[7] The mistake of the looters (or collectivists) in *Atlas Shrugged* is to think that man's sociality relies on unreciprocated altruism or altruism without reference to desert. Real sociality, and the only kind of sociality upon which civilization can function, is the sociality of voluntary individuals "held together by nothing but every man's self-interest."[8] The other kind of sociality, that of requiring men to give their talents for their "brothers" without reference to work, talent, or relationship, breaks down into corruption and destroys the very foundation of the market.

The metaphor of the trader is the centerpiece of Rand's moral universalism. All relationships, not merely political or economic relationships, are or should be based on the morality of the trader.[9] Dagny's relationships with men are all based on the reciprocal giving and taking of trade, and these relationships, more than a little unbelievably, end with the amicable closure of a completed contract.[10] For Rand, any relationship based on anything other than self-interest and reciprocal trade is a relationship rooted in the morality of exploitation. This censure of relationships based on dependence or unequal contribution applies, of course, most forcefully to the family.

While Rand's work is often simplified to represent merely selfish gain, the characters in *Atlas Shrugged* actually represent a complex and compelling form of sociality. The men (and some women) who leave behind their industries and move to the valley cooperate voluntarily, and the three main male characters demonstrate deep affection for each other. Their affection is rooted in their shared values, and the monetary sacrifices they make are not actually sacrifices but trades that they make for their objective values. The accusations of emotional emptiness and hardened rationality leveled at the heroes and heroines of Rand's world represent the collectivist's demand that we must live for other people if we are to be moral, and part of that morality is the emotional, rather than rational, justification of human interaction.[11] Rand rejects such an emotional foundation for human bonding, arguing instead that love can only be based on rational values held by rational individuals.

Love is possible in a Randian world, but it is love that reflects the worth of the individual being loved and the values held by that person. Love reflects a value that one has in another person and thus is, for Rand, a kind of trade.[12] Rand's heroes will sacrifice their time, money, and perhaps even their lives for their own ideals and for no one else's. The sincere love of an ideal allows one to love those who share that ideal as well. And thus the book ends with two of the three main heroes, all of whom love Dagny as the ideal of the rational individual, giving her up without jealousy or rancor to John Galt, the most complete Randian hero. While the book's romances slip into the melodramatic, Rand's motive is clear: to envision rational individuals who are nevertheless capable of passion and love and who are characterized not by a hardened icy rationalism, but instead by the "capacity to feel too deeply."[13]

Rand's attempt to bring together rational self-interest and love of another person is part of an important and often-overlooked aspect of her project, the elimination of apparent contradictions between perceived opposites. As her philosopher Akston is famous for saying, "If you think you discover a contradiction, check your premises. One of them is wrong."[14] The apparent contradictions between reason and emotion, and between individual and society, could be overcome if one was objective and recognized the epistemological truth that the only things we know to exist are individuals, and thus individuals must be our starting point for moral worth. True emotion flows from reason, and the true society, the society of voluntary cooperating humans, flows only from individuals pursuing their rational happiness. There is a passing similarity between Marx's dialectical materialism and Rand's theory of noncontradiction, but Rand rejects the idea that history plays a foundational role in creating or eliminating contradictions. Her rejection of contradiction is ultimately a rejection of the Marxist premise in that for Rand, the material conditions are to be shaped and created by individuals and not the other way around.[15] Rand's philosophy is thus a rejection of dialectical materialism and the existence of any inherent contradictions in human life. What both Marx and Rand share, however, is a belief that human values are (or can be made) consistent and free from conflict. The family, as will be discussed, challenges this belief.

Rand solves the problem of contradiction by formulating an individualism that serves as a dogmatic alternative to a simplistic and radical collectivism. For Rand, the importance of the individual is being lost to the specter of "society," which takes credit for individual achievements and insists that individuals live and work for the benefit of others (or society as a whole) rather than for their own good.[16] In *Atlas Shrugged* the collectivist impulse is seen most clearly in the first stage of the government's plan to take over private business, the Equalization of Opportunity Bill, which used coercive force to reallocate resources and eliminate free trade in the name of equality.[17] The use of coercive force to create equal conditions is the first sign that the perceived well-being of the community is being placed above individual striving and success.

The Equalization of Opportunity Bill is prefaced by the philosophy of contradiction that Rand sees as so damaging to rational thought. Words change their meanings because meaning itself is entirely subjective. Pritchett's support of the bill is grounded in the philosophy of contradiction, which ultimately teaches men that they are of no objective use at all.[18] Rand, on the other hand, rejects subjectivity and lack of meaning in favor of concrete, objective meaning found only in individual rationality. For Rand, the radical subjectivity argued for by Marxists and postmodern philosophers ultimately leads to a rejection of the individual as important and the replacement of that individual with "society" as the final arbiter of worth. Rand's insistence on objectivity is that individuals, before they are taught to sacrifice themselves for the values of others, would and should objectively recognize their own worth because the worth of the individual to himself or herself is the only objective truth we have.

While the collectivist impulse, Rand believes, is based on the subjectivity of emotions, it hypocritically relies on cannibalizing natural human emotions to create a system in which the victim himself sanctions his own torture and destruction. An integral part of the collective enterprise, according to Rand, consists of using the language of the family to manipulate individuals into sacrificing their own values for the values of the "family" of society. The reoccurring appeals to "brother-love" or the good of the "family" is first seen in Rearden's own struggle with collectivist ideals, both in his parasitic family and his experiences with the "looter" government.[19] This simultaneous appeal of collectivists to both subjectivity and objective emotional attachments to family is part of Rand's more subtle critique of the ultimately incoherent and contradictory nature of collectivist ideology.

Rand uses the collectivist analogy of the society as a family, seen commonly in the Marxist literature, throughout *Atlas Shrugged* to demonstrate the parasitic nature of collectivist enterprises. In the initial instance, Rand's philosophy seems to reject only those who exhort us to treat strangers like family, as when the factory at Starnesville collectivizes.[20] The myth of fellow brotherhood used to coerce overtime and redistribution of salaries is soon exposed for what it truly is, as the requirement to work for no benefit soon reduces the factory's production and forces overtime of able workers and shirking among the rest.[21] Rand's commentary might then support the interpretation that she only objects to the misuse of familial affections on the grounds that such misuse in the name of the broader collective ultimately corrupts familial affections themselves. However, she frequently goes beyond disapproving of the co-opting of familial affections by the collective to counseling the rejection of the family completely, as when Dagny throws off her family entirely for their failure to share her values.

Rand's concern with the use of familial language goes beyond the immorality of manipulating strangers to care for each other as family. Her concern is that such manipulative analogies have the potential to become people's realities, creating devastating cycles of dependence. Rearden, for example, initially defends his decision to work for the sake of others, arguing that the looters are "a bunch of miserable children who struggle to remain alive, desperately and very badly, while I—I don't even notice the burden."[22] Individuals who rely on the state and others for support and survival are turned from rational individuals into desperate children, taking advantage of the strong, but ultimately controlled by the men or "fathers" at the center. Treating adult individuals like children is poisonous to the ideals of individual autonomy, personal responsibility, and rationality that Rand believes can be the only foundation for society.

True to Rand's rejection of contradiction, however, she seems to believe (at least in places) that there is no contradiction between taking care of one's own and contributing beneficially to society through trade. The engineer who is forced by government directive to send a train into a tunnel to meet with certain death ponders the changes that a society based on dictate rather than law, and emotion rather than reason, has wrought.[23] Before, there had been no conflict between caring for his family through honest work and the well-being of the wider community. Now, however, the politics of dictates and control leave him with no freedom, no autonomy to make the right decision—the individual in a dictatorship is left with no judgment or rationality to call his own and is forced to do whatever is demanded of him, regardless of the consequences. However, Rand's simplistic assurances that self-interest, love of family, and the well-being of the community are never in fundamental conflict is never adequately supported by the story of *Atlas Shrugged* itself, mostly because we never actually see real families in real, difficult circumstances.

Ultimately, Rand's attitude toward the family is somewhat contradictory, at least insofar as in places she supports the ideas of individuals caring for those closest to them, and in others she rejects the bonds of family as a limitation on the power of the individual to create his or her own way in the world and his or her own identity. The foundations of Rand's primary suspicion of the family are that the family is a barrier to free choice, a source of control, and a symbol of our need and dependence on others. All of these threaten the rational freedom of individuals to make their own life without the encumbrances of duties to other individuals.

Family, Chance, and Choice

The family is an obvious target of suspicion for Rand because the family counters and moderates the radical individual freedom that is at the root of Objectivism and Rand's vision of the trader. Instead of voluntary relationships purely based on trade, the existence of families creates or supports relationships based on chance, coercion, and accident. We do not choose our families, our children are born with personalities over which we have little control, and, crucially for Rand, values do not necessarily run in families. Families represent generation after generation of chance, accident, and sometimes coercion, and the end result is individuals who are bound to individuals in the past and present against their will. The family is the quintessential accidental relationship, and it binds us through custom, habit, affections, and genetics. These customary, emotional, and genetic bonds make it difficult for the truly entrepreneurial to remake the world in their own image.

Some writers have pointed out the lack of families and children in Rand's work. What is perhaps more surprising is that at least in *Atlas Shrugged* families are everywhere. The ancestry of many characters is laid out in detail, and in the main characters of Dagny, Francisco, Rearden, and John Galt, their family relationships (or lack thereof in the case of Galt) are absolutely central to the people they become and the decisions they make. That the decisions they make almost universally result in their throwing off family ties demonstrates how seriously Rand takes familial attachments and how dangerous she believes they are to the free will of rational individuals.

Rand's ambivalence toward the family is seen primarily in the characters of Dagny Taggart and Francisco d'Anconia. Both are the scions of wealthy industrial families, the descendants of completely self-made men, Nat Taggart and Sebastián d'Anconia. Clearly, both Dagny and Francisco share much of their ancestors' reliance on individual free will and independence, but Rand attempts (unsuccessfully) to make the resemblance over time as much a result of individual choice as of blind genetics. Dagny, for example, regrets that she is related to Nat Taggart: "What she felt for him did not belong in the category of unchosen family affections. . . . She was incapable of love for any object not of her own choice and she resented anyone's demand for it. But had it been possible to choose an ancestor, she would have chosen Nat Taggart, in voluntary homage and with all of her gratitude."[24] Of course, Dagny *cannot* choose her ancestors, and her attempt to distance herself from the contingent nature of their relationship simply underscores how much they have in common and how much she (may) owe to another person, generations before.

Dagny's case exemplifies Rand's suspicion of obligation and duty. Dagny does not want to *owe* Nat Taggart anything. Unearned duties are antithetical to the trader spirit. Dagny wants to feel love for him because he is worthy of love, not because she owes him love as a family member. Dagny rejects her familial duty to Taggart because it is a duty born of chance and not of choice. Rand explicitly describes the family as part of the "world of chance," and Dagny's rejection of Nat Taggart as an ancestor by chance, and her acceptance of him as an ancestor by choice, is characteristic of Rand's treatment of family ties.[25] Duties that are unchosen and unrelated to the actions of the individual are rejected, which of course means that the traditional family must be rejected as well.

Francisco shares the problem of unchosen ancestors, though in his case it is his own family who tries to control the lineage, linking familial membership to the freely chosen actions of Sebastián's descendants. When Dagny's brother Jim refers to him as a d'Anconia, Francisco replies, "Not yet. The reason my family has lasted for such a long time is that none of us has ever been permitted to think he is born a d'Anconia. We are expected to become one."[26] Francisco and Dagny both belong to families who share their values, and in Francisco's case, sharing those values is necessary for inclusion in the family. In the traditional family, sharing values is neither necessary nor sufficient to make a family, as Rand occasionally admits. Francisco would still be a d'Anconia even if his values rejected those of his family, and Jim Taggart, Dagny's brother, is still a Taggart, despite the fact that he, more than anyone else in the book, violates his family's standards and destroys the railroad his ancestors built. Rand's family by choice is both an extension of her extreme individualism and a rejection of the structure of traditional families in human life.

Other characters reject their families as well, most often for failing to reflect their values. The Starnes children reject their father's capitalism with disastrous results, and Cherryl, Jim Taggart's doomed wife, rejects her family for being parasitic and small, only to find herself married to the quintessential parasite.[27] Dagny in turn rejects Cherryl as her sister-in-law until she realizes that Cherryl shares the same moral vision, though Dagny's offer of sisterhood "through our own choice" comes too late to save Cherryl from her recognition of moral evil.[28] Dagny's rejection of Cherryl as a mere family member and her later acceptance of her as a fellow traveler emphasize Dagny's refusal of any relationship not created of her own free choice.

Rand occasionally slips, acknowledging or at least hinting at the debt we may owe our families, whether in terms of genetics or values. Francisco's abilities are described as "if the centuries had sifted the family's qualities through a fine mesh, had discarded the irrelevant, the inconsequential, the weak, and had let nothing through except pure talent; as if chance, for once, had achieved an entity devoid of the accidental."[29] Rand's recognition that Francisco is in some sense the sum of generations of genetics and habituation is then countered by her assertion that Francisco's debt to his family still partakes of the chosen, and that Francisco's abilities, though the result of chance, are by no means accidental. That the accidental results, in Rand's eyes, in "the irrelevant, the inconsequential, the weak" stems from her opinion of the role of families in individual development, and the families of her main characters, by and large looters and parasites, support her assertion that family membership is entirely a matter of chance and can be rejected on rational grounds.

Rand's ambivalence toward familial attachments and traits in her trader characters is reversed somewhat in her looter characters. Familial continuity is alive and well in looter families; Wesley Mouch is described as coming from a mediocre family that always chafed that their college educations were not better rewarded, and Lee Hunsacker bitterly expects his family name to make up for his own lack of accomplishments.[30] Rand herself seems to acknowledge that there are traits that families pass on that individuals do not necessarily choose freely. Even Dagny's irritation that she is Nat Taggart's descendant by chance and not by choice demonstrates that however much Dagny may wish to be self-made, she is always tied to and bound by a path that she has not chosen. Yet in both cases, Rand refuses to recognize the middle ground: that families are both chosen and accidental, that individuals are the compilation and combination of choices they have made and choices others have made for them, often before they are even born. Rand's refusal to recognize the middle ground forces her into a rejection of family bonds that further radicalizes her message and makes it unlikely to appeal to any but the most ardent individualist.

Rand's replacement for the traditional family is a family constructed by choice, not by chance. Rand's heroic characters universally throw off family ties for the relationships forged through trade. Dagny's brother Jim; Rearden's mother, brother, and wife; and John Galt's complete parentlessness all suggest that to be a true trader, one must choose his or her family based not on mere birth or habit but on a shared moral vision. Akston the philosopher refers to his pupils Ragnar, Francisco, and Galt as his "sons," defending them and protecting them as a father would.[31] Instead of descendants-in-fact, Rand replaces the family with "descendants-in-spirit," those who are chosen to share one's life based on shared values.[32]

Rand is vague on how a "family-in-spirit" would work in the real world. A mother in the valley raising objective and rational children tells Dagny, "There can be no collective commitments in this valley," and "families or relatives are not allowed to come here, unless each person takes the strikers' oath by his own independent conviction."[33] Yet families themselves are collective commitments, and the bringing of children into the world creates collective commitments that are largely based on chance. Simply disallowing families to move together to the valley does nothing about the families that will spring up on their own. Rand fortunately never has to confront this reality because in her world individual and collective commitments are separated completely, and one can treat the family just as one would any other group—as a collection of rational individuals rather than a tightly bound collective with its own interests, needs, and desires.[34]

Despite the practical problems with the family-in-spirit, Rand's rejection of collective commitments demonstrates a more serious theoretical problem with her approach. The family is by definition a collective commitment, one born of a peculiar blend of chance and choice, where individuals are bound to each other by affection and duty, if not permanently, at least for a time. The family is the one place where "from each according to his ability, to each according to his need" is, in fact, the most just and efficient way of allocating resources.[35] This inherent collectivism is challenging for Rand's moral universalism, which argues that all human relationships must be relationships based on trade.[36] More dangerous for Rand is the slipperiness of these collective identities. If collectivist values are allowed in the family, then why not make all of society like one big family? The collectivists in Rand's work and elsewhere do precisely this, referring to men as brothers and society as a family. The family's support of collectivist impulses creates a gradual shift in moral thought over time—the movement from morality consisting of sacrificing one's self for one's family quickly slides into the sacrifice of the individual for the village, the nation, and the world.[37] Rand's suspicion of the family and her insistence on moral universalism may be less of a rejection of the moral rules that could work in family relationships and more of a concern over what happens when those familial moral rules seep into the broader society. To avoid this problem Rand roots family love in trade, and love of children in the love of one's own values and conscious choice. How successful such a family would be in the real world is a problem Rand fortunately did not have to confront.

In the end, Rand's own novel leads us, unintentionally, toward the middle ground that she explicitly eschews. The family moderates the individual's ability to self-create, but it also provides a grounding for the values that Rand herself supports. Our bondage to families by birth, education, and custom is incomplete since the individual can, of course, cast off truly parasitic family members as do Rearden and Dagny. But Rand is forced to make these family members completely parasitic because her philosophy cannot adequately deal with the possibility that our families will share many of our values, but not all, that we can choose or change some membership in our families, but not all, and that we can overcome as individuals some of and perhaps even much of our early family experiences, but not all of them. The family represents the middle ground between chance and choice that Rand herself rejects. The family operates in this middle ground, and because the contradictions between choice and chance can never be fully reconciled, Rand's families are all extremes—completely contingent (and thus rejected) or fully chosen. The real family represents the moderation between chance and choice and thus moderates political goals like Rand's founded on rational choice.

Need and Dependence

Rand's concern with the family extends beyond its roots in accident and chance. The family also represents a relationship founded almost entirely on need and dependence, both of which are antithetical to Rand's vision of independent individuals who are solely responsible for their own success or failure. Rather than seeing the family as a collective of dependent individuals bonded together by affection and dependence, Rand sees the family as exploitative, the weak living off the strong.[38] Her concern with creating independent individuals leads her to eschew or ignore legitimate human relationships that might nevertheless be founded on need, dependence, or disparity in abilities.

Of course, there are different kinds of dependence, and Rand is not too simplistic to ignore that even the best trader needs things from other people. She therefore separates dependence and need into that of the trader and that of the looter. The trader is not, of course, independent of other people. The trader requires goods that others have, but he does not demand them as a right, but trades for them through voluntary relationships based on mutual need.[39] While the valley inhabitants depend on each other in the sense that they are highly interdependent, they are free to come and go and, more importantly perhaps, free to trade with whom they please. Rand's primary concern is coerced relationships, those based not on voluntary cooperation or mutual need but instead on coercion and dependence. The followers of John Galt reject appeals based solely on need in favor of appeals based on rational self-interest.[40] The proper way to need is "like a trader—who pays for what he wants. [Looters] say it like beggars who use a tin cup as a claim check."[41]

Trader independence relies on "recognition of the fact that yours is the responsibility of judgment and nothing can help you escape it—that no substitute can do your thinking, as no pinch-hitter can live your life."[42] The trader is not independent of all other humans, at least not materially, but the trader is independent in the most central of ways for Rand, that of rationality. The trader does not substitute someone else's rationality for his or her own. The looter, on the other hand, relies on others for his or her thoughts, ideas, and ultimately his or her survival since the blessings of civilization are largely procured through the ideas of great individuals.

Independent thought is a primary theme for Rand, whose belief in human rationality is the foundation for Objectivism as a whole.

Even families should be categorized by the trader's code of independent rationality and reciprocal altruism in Rand's world. Rand provides us with numerous examples of the looter family in action, most obviously in Rearden's mother, brother, and wife. Lillian Rearden describes her understanding of her marriage to Rearden, arguing, "What would make me happy, Henry? That is what you ought to tell me. That is what you should have discovered for me. I don't know. You were to create it and offer it to me."[43] The looter family requires family members to live their lives for the other members, expecting nothing in return. Part of this complete sacrifice is that Lillian sees her place as one of complete subservience to Rearden's greatness; Rearden's abilities negate any need Lillian might have to think or act for herself, to the point where even her concept of happiness is defined by her husband. It is no surprise then that Rearden chooses to cheat on his wife with Dagny, the independent trader who thinks and acts for herself and who does not *need* Rearden but who wants him because his reason, his character, and his accomplishments reflect her own.

A related characteristic of the looter family is that members of such families use their family names as replacements for true individual worth. Lee Hunsacker's bitter assertion that "my family name was just as good as any of theirs" is the assertion of a person who has given up on individual self-worth and who must ride the coattails of others.[44] True self-worth is central to Rand's understanding of love. Throughout the book, those characters truly capable of love are the traders, whose love of others is rooted in a rational recognition of the values and character of their beloved. Dagny's brother rejects this kind of love, requiring his new wife to love him not for his values or his accomplishments or his character but "for himself." His wife, understandably, has no idea what it means to love someone without reference to values, abilities, or character.[45] Rand's caricature of "unconditional love" is indeed problematic when taken to such extremes, and the looters warp the unconditional love of the family into an unconditional duty to care for each person collectively.[46] Rand creates families rooted in thoughtless love, baseless duties, and self-worth and value unlinked to any personal achievements. The man whose self-worth stems only from his family name is the same man who wants to be loved for nothing at all.

The John Galt version of the family, predictably, is that of traders.[47] Presumably this trade is based in a kind of reciprocal exchange of love and assistance, but Rand is never clear on this point, which is itself instructive. That husbands, wives, parents, and children "trade" does not tell us what is being traded or how one knows when the trade has become exploitative. Rand's avoidance of the kinds of trade involved in family life means that she fails to distinguish adequately familial "trade" from the traditional emotional family attachments that she finds dangerous. To be loved only for what one provides or offers to another person reduces the complex depth of human attachments to the mathematics of exchange that Jim Taggart rejects.[48] Such "trade" also cannot adequately deal with the reality that for long periods of life, real dependence means that any "trade" will be very one-sided indeed. Moreover, the problem remains that if Rand is defining any kind of emotional benefit as part of a "trade," she reduces the family to a trade relationship but cannot explain why family life is different from other kinds of trades (if at all) or why Rearden's mother's or wife's appeals to his sense of duty might not also fall under a kind of trader relationship.

The family is not a trade relationship, however hard individualists like Rand may try to argue otherwise.[49] Children, the disabled, elderly relatives, and other dependent people cannot provide goods for "trade" unless those goods happen to be emotional fulfillment. But there are times in everyone's life where family life simply is not fulfilling. It is difficult, exhausting, frustrating, and tiring.[50] No reader would want to exist in a family where one received literally *nothing* from the relationship, but Rand does not provide us with a clear alternative or at least not a realistic one. Rand's "trader" families eradicate the need and dependence of traditional families, but only by ignoring the very ways in which families are constituted. Families are not friendships or coworkers. Families are created out of natural affection and natural need.

The real weakness in Rand's assessment of family life is that she bases her theories on extremes, while family life itself usually eschews such polarity. The average family is somewhat exploitative but also based somewhat on rational judgment and trade. People provide their children with indiscriminate praise when they are young and then gradually expect them to deserve such praise as they grow. Because dependence and need are not always predictable, grown children who are struggling are often welcomed back into the home, but most people eventually have a limit on the altruism they will hand out to family members without return. No outsider can tell a parent when it is time to push out a parasitic child; the decision has to be made by the individuals involved. The family is neither simply a straight trader relationship nor is it a purely exploitative one. The family—as a social group based partly on chance and partly on choice, comprising multiple generations representing the different stages of life commingled—is simply too complex to be reduced to the platitudes of reciprocal trade.

The family's foundation on human need and dependence is made possible by the fact that it is also the natural home of "collectivist" sentiments. The family can meet dependence and need with altruism because it is the place where love of one's brothers is *literally* true. Real altruism, at least for most of human history, was sheltered in the family because the family has an interest in the care of relatives. While the relationship between a disabled adult child and his caretaker mother, for example, can hardly be considered "trade," the mother receives some kind of benefit from such caretaking, even though such activity may often be taxing to the extreme. The family has long been the place where children, the elderly, the disabled, and the mentally ill were cared for precisely because it was the place where reciprocal altruism was not necessary, where one's self-interest coincided as nearly as was possible in the human world with the interest of another.

It is hardly accidental that there are no truly dependent characters in *Atlas Shrugged*. There are no widows, no disabled individuals, no mental illness, and no elderly people in need of care. There are hardly any children, and the children who do exist are carefully tended to in two-parent families like that of the Objectivist mother of the valley. Rand has created a world in which true dependence, the inability to survive alone through no fault of one's own, simply does not exist, just as she has created a world where the moral adage of brother love is always exploitative. Rand's dependent characters, like Rearden's family and Dagny's brother, are loathsome to the reader because they are actual parasites, and the reader recognizes them as such.[51] But it is this kind of extreme case that is precisely Rand's weakness. She does not, because she cannot, include any examples of family members who have claims on their relatives due to actual disability, age, or bad luck. She is forced to provide only the extremes of family parasitism precisely because she recognizes that such cases are not the norm and that family members may have many, more or less legitimate, claims on the success of a strong relative that cannot be so easily rejected. Thus, her families are without dependent relatives in the same way that her ideal community is without insane asylums and nursing homes.[52]

Intergenerational Dependence

The problem of dependence and need in *Atlas Shrugged* extends further than the existence of dependent family members. Even more fundamentally, the family is the source of intergenerational interaction that makes the individual dependent on the past, a dependence that Rand rarely acknowledges. Rand's emphasis on extreme individualism ignores the importance of intergenerational activity that is often, though not always, rooted in the family. Genetics, inheritance, and education are all mechanisms by which previous generations influence the generations of the present, and yet none of these limitations on or contributions to individual success are discussed at any length in *Atlas Shrugged*.

Like Rand's concerns with using familial language as a basis for unfounded obligations, her suspicion of intergenerational obligations stems from its use to encourage the sacrifice of individuals of one generation for the good of another.[53] While Rand's demand that individuals not be sacrificed for not-yet-existent future generations makes intuitive sense, her analysis ignores the very real ways in which individuals are dependent on those who came before. Generations are, in fact, intertwined, most obviously in the family. Rand is right that forcing people through the power of the collective to sacrifice themselves for future generations of unrelated individuals is problematic. What is not problematic is the voluntary sacrifice of one generation for another, a common occurrence in family life. The responsibilities and duties we have to our families require that we do, in fact, sacrifice ourselves in various ways and to various degrees to the needs of the elderly or the young. The struggles of early immigrants to provide a better life for their offspring, a life in which they may never be able to take part, is a natural outcome of the desire to sacrifice for one's own. Beyond self-sacrifice, humans live in a world where the present is, in large part, constrained by the past through the customs, habits, and traditions that are passed to the present by the past, usually in the family. The past limits individuals involuntarily, and individuals limit themselves voluntarily to assist the future. However, it is the family that links these two kinds of limitations, not the coercive force of the collective.

While Rand tends to purposely downplay the role of the family in passing on values over generations, she also downplays how this familial inheritance might be important to her own project. Rand replaces the traditional family with a family of choice, a family created by shared values and a shared vision of the ideal moral world, partly because that shared moral vision is not always found within families. But, as the cases of Francisco or of Dagny and Nat Taggart suggest, the family is an important tool for passing on values. We influence the kind of people our family members will become by our very existence. Family members shape each other's morals, teach each other valuable lessons, and, for better or for worse, change each other as individuals. Rand's own novel suggests that our familial relationships are neither completely accidental nor completely chosen.[54]

One might argue that Rand only objects to those who use their family name as a replacement for self-worth.[55] Yet the worthless individual is again a straw man that no rational person would disagree with; surely most people would object to someone whose only source of self-esteem was family lineage. The more moderate argument is, as usual, overlooked, that family membership and the legacy of ancestors can serve to influence and heighten self-efficacy and self-worth precisely because they tie the individual to something greater and more enduring than any one individual can be. Living up to the standards of our forefathers and working to preserve what those before us created are both ways in which who we are as people can be influenced, positively, by our parents, families, and ancestors. Dagny's refusal to leave the railroad and go to the valley is at least in part influenced by her refusal to let the bridge Nat Taggart created be destroyed. Family life can influence our self-efficacy and self-worth in positive ways, something Rand implicitly recognizes but explicitly rejects.

Ownership: Public and Private Spheres

The family challenges another important theme in Rand's work, the importance of property or ownership. Self-ownership of one's talents, ideas, and capacities is integral to Rand's philosophy of Objectivism and is a central plotline in *Atlas Shrugged*, as the abilities and talents of the heroes and heroines are slowly usurped for public gain. The battle over Rearden Metal is perhaps the most obvious example, though Francisco and Wyatt's destruction of their mines and oil fields to prevent them from falling into the hands of the looters are poignant reminders of the importance of personal property. For Rand, ownership goes well beyond mere economic property rights. Ownership has a metaphysical import, related as it is to the rational capacities of individuals. Rearden struggles to make the looting government understand why he will not sell Rearden Metal, arguing, "Because it's *mine*. Do you understand the word?"[56] Rand's characters often take ownership for granted, as something that only traders can understand, and indeed the slow eradication of property rights over time is the catalyst for the eventual collectivization and corollary destruction of the country.[57]

Ownership or possession for Rand must come about as a result of rational action, not chance. The pride of possession, for lack of a better word, in children, for example, is not rational unless those children prove themselves to be also rational actors. Rand takes the Aristotelian belief that philosophy starts with what is one's own (i.e., one's own family and community) and reduces it to one's labor. Rand's philosophy is asocial but also a-emotional. Though ownership might result in passionate attachment, such ownership cannot begin in such attachment but only in rational accomplishment. Because much of family life is rooted in irrational attachment largely unlinked to accomplishment, Rand rejects the accidental biological family and replaces it with a family of rational choice based on shared values. Yet most of what is owned or possessed is not owned exclusively but is shared across generations and across space. Children are really a shared possession (insofar as humans can be possessed) of our ancestors, our spouses, relatives, and to a lesser degree friends, community, and society, which provide us with the goods to raise them. Such partial possession requires an acknowledgment that the accomplishments of individuals are always rooted in a social context.

Rand's minor characters recognize the importance of emotional possession better than her major characters. The love of family members for each other is occasionally given heroic characteristics, though these instances are always found in minor characters who never rise to the level of actual heroes or heroines. The engineer who must choose between feeding his family and letting a train full of people die chooses his family, and Rand treats him sympathetically. In her narration of the eventual breakdown of civil society in the midst of collectivization, she describes a woman with a broken jaw who was slapped by a stranger for forcing her child to give away his toys.[58] The stranger recognizes the love of one's own, immanent in both the love for one's children and one's private property.

Rand's own individualist heroes rise above these minor characters by rejecting even the ownership created by biological family ties as illegitimate. Rearden separates his work from his family life, and when his mother entreats him to employ his brother Philip by making a claim of kinship, Rearden's response is "What has that got to do with it?"[59] Rearden refuses to admit that his brother's biological relationship to himself might create an accidental and irrational bond that nevertheless creates real duties and obligations. While not completely separated from character or accomplishment, such duties are still real and an important foundation for human social life.

Property rights are complicated by family life again because there are no pure private property rights in the family. Rand's suspicion of the family takes root in part because our family lays claim to our property simply by virtue of being our family. The inherent collectivism of family life—the treatment of each according to his or her need and not ability—is extended into the broader society by the looters. Children have a right by merely existing to part of the property of their parents, and most legal systems throughout human history have recognized the automatic duty of sharing resources created merely by the birth of a child. A clear system of ownership based solely on rational faculties is simply not possible in the family, since we own or claim ownership over things that are not the result of our rational activities, and others can claim ownership over our property merely by existing. The family requires a different property ethos, one that is legitimately collectivist, that recognizes the different claims of duties and rights imposed on the different members simply by existing and by the nature of the bond that ties family members together.[60] Rand's understanding of ownership, because it is universal across all social contexts, forces us to treat the family as a mere collection of individuals, bound together merely by voluntary association.

Rand's theory of ownership also ignores the overlap between public and private spheres. Rand contrasts her own theory that property is always private and always the outcome of one individual's rational capacities against the extreme looter theory that nothing belongs to anyone because everyone owes their lives, abilities, and success to the collective. This bright-line distinction between public and private is useful in the abstract, but it fails to reflect the ways in which public and private lives intersect. While even Rand recognizes that the public/private distinction is hardly clear-cut, she only recognizes the seepage of the public into the private and not the other way around. The benefits of John Galt's machine would have been dramatic for society had society allowed him to profit off it. Rearden Metal would have made most people's lives better, but the desire to take everything from the individual, to turn everything that is private gain into public good, eventually strains even Rearden's altruism, and the system collapses. Rand does not, however, pay sufficient attention to how the private actions of individuals affect the public in other ways, nor does she incorporate social groupings that are both public and private, like the family, into her scheme.

The relationship between the individual and society (or other individuals) should be a symbiotic one; both require each other to survive and flourish. In Rand's novels, the relationship is parasitic, with society as a whole (which really consists of the majority of lazy individuals) exploiting the strong. Rand's solution is a purely private system where all human interaction takes place through voluntary interactions between individuals and where all property is private and originates out of individual effort and ability. Rand and Marx both recognize the difficulty of balancing between the public and the private, and both reduce the public or the private to modes of production. Marx retreats to a materialism that reduces the private to the public, while Rand reduces the public to the private sphere of individual rationality.

Nature and Familial Desire

Like the Marxist one, Rand's revolutionary project must deal with the limitations of the natural world, and Rand's approach requires redefining the relationship between human nature and the natural world. Rand rejects the collectivist tendency to define true human nature as fulfilled in some kind of natural, preindustrial age. On the collectivist's logic, modern industrialism, far from being the culmination of human nature and rationality, pulls us away from our natures and from nature itself. The collectivist approach is to simplify, to move us back toward a more natural way of life, one that represents man's early, supposedly collectivist past. Dagny, the quintessential industrialist, is criticized by one of the intellectual elite as "a woman who runs a railroad, instead of practicing the beautiful craft of the handloom and bearing children."[61] The speaker's contrast between the evils of industrialism and the utopian simplicity of preindustrial crafts ignores the gains in human health and welfare made by industrialization and new technology. Dagny's self-reliance and devotion to production are used as examples of modern industrial greed by collectivists and are indicators of our movement away from the natural state.

The collectivist movement to reverse industrialism in favor of some more "natural" life is actually a way to control the masses. Dagny realizes this when the government leaders destroy the Minnesota rail line, and thus her railroad: "Men who live by pulling levers at an electronic switchboard, are not easily ruled, but men who live by digging the soil with their naked fingers are."[62] The rejection of civilization by the looting government leaders indicates their complete abandonment of individual worth and the blessings of civilization for individuals. Instead, the politics of control and coercion replace self-worth and individual responsibility for the simple reason that precivilized humanity is easier to rule than civilized humanity The criticism of Dagny for her rejection of traditional feminine tasks like hand weaving and child rearing is merely one example of the promotion of primitive economies because such economies are easier to manipulate.

Rand rejects the exaggerated collectivist view of primitive human nature, instead embracing the other end of the spectrum, reducing nature to the rational abilities of individuals. These rational abilities culminate in the industrial triumph over the natural world.[63] Rand believes our natural desires, including those for family and children, are holdovers from a nature that is best conquered by human ingenuity. Dagny herself, the quintessential Randian heroine, never shows an interest in family life, and even her sexual activity is described as being part of her rational fulfillment, rather than fulfilling a passionate biological need.

Yet by ignoring the fundamental biological desires to reproduce and raise children, Rand must contort human life into ever more unrecognizable forms. It is precisely because family life is a profound natural desire for most people that Rand is forced to paint biological family life in unrealistic extremes. Dagny's brother and Rearden's mother, brother, and wife are the antithesis of everything Dagny and Rearden stand for. Both families try to destroy the individual, and both individuals are forced ultimately to reject their families in order to preserve their freedom. In reality, of course, the choice is rarely this stark. We resemble our families whether we like it or not, and the act of being raised together, of sharing the same environment, the same genes, the same values, may lead to different personalities, but rarely does it lead to wholly different value structures. Our natural instincts for family in turn support the processes that tend to make families alike. Because she rejects these limits on human self-invention, Rand rejects natural familial bonds and any natural desires other than that for rational self-fulfillment.

Modern Libertarianism and the Moderation of Rand

While Rand's work was popular at the time she wrote, she has never been taken seriously as a philosopher, even among those most likely to share her views on the importance of individual freedom. If Rand's passionate defense of individualism continues to be read and enjoyed, why is she still something of a marginal figure in the libertarian community? Few people consider themselves Objectivists, and even fewer consider themselves Randians. Part of the answer seems to rely on an acceptance by most individualists of the dependence and contingency of human life, a contingency that Rand herself refuses to acknowledge. Most libertarians reject the metaphysical freedom of Rand in favor of more moderate kinds of freedom like political and economic freedom.[64] The individualism inherent in Rand's philosophy needs to be moderated by the recognition that there exist natural social groupings that might restrict the freedom of the individual but that are nevertheless important for individual development and flourishing.

Most individualists and libertarians, like Rand, do not pay much attention to the family. Libertarian discussions of family typically revolve around force or fraud in family matters, including abuse or neglect of children and when the state can lawfully intervene. When the family is mentioned, libertarians and individualists disagree on the proper relationship between the family and liberty.[65] Some argue that the family itself needs to be run on libertarian principles, with the rights and desires of children being given equal weight with those of the parents.[66] Others fail to deal with the family at all, focusing instead on the coercion of the government rather than coercion by related individuals. Others focus on the epistemological foundation of the individual, arguing that "only individuals exist, think, freely choose, or act."[67] But families also exist, and while they may not think on their own, they often act collectively, and some individualists fear that recognizing one legitimate source of natural collective action could potentially legitimize other kinds of collective action, putting one foot on the slippery slope toward despotism.[68]

Forging a Middle Ground

The family moderates extreme individualism because it forces us to recognize a social grouping that is natural, not completely chosen, governed by both emotion and reason, and founded in part on dependence and need. Rand would presumably accept a family that is an extension of one's rational self but not a family that is merely an extension of one's biological and passionate self. In reality, the family is both. And this balance between our rational and passionate selves, between our rational desires and our passionate bonds to other people, is the middle ground into which Rand dare not step. Rand's moral absolutism rejects the middle ground on principle, and the characters who espouse compromise are vilified. Rand's moral absolutism stems in part from her belief that human life is characterized by one big slippery slope.[69] The truth of the matter, however, is that human life is characterized by balance and compromise. The family is a mix of goods, a balance between human flourishing and human tragedy, accident and choice, emotional attachment and rational judgment.

Rearden's mother's resentment that she is not more important than his work exemplifies the black-and-white nature of Rand's philosophy and how it fails to reflect human life as really lived.[70] The decision to choose between work and family is not an absolute decision as Rand might suggest. Real individuals are not forced into being terrible sons and husbands in order to be excellent workers. Human life is about compromise precisely because it encapsulates many desirable goods, all of which need to be balanced against one another and against the need for a complete life. This balancing act is difficult, and many people lead imbalanced lives. Humans live with that imbalance because it is a result of an imperfect human nature, and because it is precisely the attempt to balance many different goods that leads to a full and flourishing life. The demand to choose between work and family (or between freedom and equality or between accident and choice) is legitimate only if you recognize a strict hierarchy of human goods whose apex is the rational action of productive labor. Those who recognize a different hierarchy, a different ranking, are, according to Rand, weak, emotional, and ineffectual. Those who recognize goods that compete with productive labor are labeled collectivists.

Rand's passionate defense of the individual nevertheless reveals an important flaw in a collectivism that requires the subordination of individual desires to the will of some fictitious "collective." Whether one's focus is technological innovation or the benefits of close family and friends, individuals are indeed the source of good in society. That Rand is right about so much makes her books worth coming back to. But missing from her analysis is the importance social groups play for individual fulfillment and flourishing. Individuals matter only within a social context. Our families and friends matter because they are individuals, but also because they provide us with the social context in which to understand ourselves and our own worth. The family is the social grouping in which individuals, while not perhaps being most *objectively* valued, are the *most* valued because it is in the family where individuals are most known. Rand criticizes collectivism for turning everyone into a blank page, but individualism presents an equivalent problem, since radical individualism separates individuals from their social moorings and has the potential to turn individuals into nameless, faceless persons in a crowd of other people. Families are important precisely because they are the original (though not always the most unbiased) social group to recognize individual worth.

Rand's suspicion of the family's links with collectivism leads her to lump the family in with collective ideologies and forces her to create an individualistic morality that rejects the importance of context in moral decision making.[71] More moderate individualists and libertarians reject Rand's metaphysical freedom in favor of political and economic freedom because the former is constrained by all sorts of groupings, organizations, and affiliations that we find desirable in society, not the least of which is the family.[72] The family forces the moderation of Rand's principles because most people will not accept a philosophy where the freedom of the individual is pitted against the social grouping on which individual desires and capabilities are founded. The resulting focus of many moderate individualists on political and economic freedom rather than metaphysical freedom is one reason why many, if not most, libertarians and modern individualists do not pay more attention to the family. Unlike Rand, they take the family for granted as a natural part of human life, necessary, beneficial, and ultimately impossible to eradicate.[73] The most "moderate" libertarians recognize "the division of ethics into two languages: a language of liberty for dealing with issues in the political order and a language of virtue for dealing with issues in the nonpolitical order, that is, for choices concerning oneself, family, friends, and acquaintances."[74] Moderate libertarians preserve a distinction between private and public, rather than collapsing the two into each other.

It is Rand's proclivity for black and white, for moral absolutes, that ultimately undermines her philosophy. Radical Randian individualism fails to persuade because there are no such things as completely isolated individuals, and the choice she tries to force between individualism and collectivism is ultimately a false choice. Rand's families are all extremes as a way of forcing us to choose; the family must be either chance or choice, either looter or trader, either dependent or independent, either public or private, either standing alone or falling together. The real family is, of course, all of these things and none of these things. What makes family life so precious and so infuriating is that it is complex, neither freely chosen nor violently coerced, neither dependent nor independent, neither wholly public nor wholly private, neither based on the individual nor based on the community. Instead of eradicating the family or contorting it to fit into an extreme view of individualistic freedom, many libertarians have instead moderated their dedication to freedom and have become adept at living in "two worlds at once."

CHAPTER 4

MONTESQUIEU, BURKE, AND THE MODERATE FAMILY

While Marxists and Randians fear the family because of the way it challenges ideological purity, other thinkers have championed the family as one of the bastions of moderate political systems. The works of Montesquieu and Edmund Burke are emblematic of the eighteenth-century attempt to balance the increasingly polarized conflict between collective sovereignty and individual autonomy.[1] Central to this balance are intermediate institutions that perch, like fulcrums, between the claims of individuals and collectives. These intermediate positions bring together individual and collective claims by supporting humanity's natural sociality. Both Montesquieu and Burke believe that natural social groupings provide the best balance between our individualistic and social natures and that this balance between our individualistic and social natures supports a corollary balance between liberty and equality, a balance that became especially difficult in the twentieth century. The family's role as the natural home of a kind of "social individualism" makes it the most stable and most central of these intermediate institutions.

Both Montesquieu and Burke's works are located in the broad tradition of classical liberalism, a tradition in which community cohesion is balanced against individual freedom. These thinkers advocate the meshing of nature and custom through a spontaneous order that starts in the family and expands into the broader society. Unlike Marx and Rand, these moderate thinkers support the importance of intergenerational relationships as a balance between the need for change and the need for stability. They promote a balance between public and private lives that recognizes the interconnected nature of public and private spheres but nevertheless supports the creation of a private sphere of action that includes a generally autonomous family. Finally, by balancing the claims of the individual and the community through the medium of natural familial affections, their theories champion a reformulation of the conflict between individualistic liberty and collectivist equality, one that harmonizes the two by softening the claims of each. These softened claims promote the equality and liberty of the "civil social man," or what might be referred to as liberty and equality "well understood."[2] These classical liberals support individual liberty protected by a robust and pluralistic social order, and moral equality protecting the rights and privileges of everyone in the collective.

Though the family and familial analogies play central roles in the works of Montesquieu and Burke, little scholarly attention has been paid to these aspects of their works, even by thinkers working explicitly on the family.[3] Burke scholars often focus on the intergenerational compact, or Burke's rejection of Lockean contract theory, but they fail to address Burke's intentional analogy between the family and the state.[4] Scholarship on Montesquieu dissects *Persian Letters* and *The Spirit of the Laws* for lessons contra despotism but fails to address the importance of family forms, particularly polygamy, for his analysis.[5] Both thinkers address the importance of balancing nature and custom, public and private, and the needs of individuals and groups in order to create complex, pluralistic communities that support a range of human goods and values.

The Family and the Meshing of Nature and Custom

As the works of both Marx and Rand make clear, the interaction between nature and custom is pivotal in the balance between individual and collective needs. Collectivists like Marx reject nature because it is an uncompromising limitation on the power of human invention and social evolution. Individualists like Rand reject nature as a limitation on the power of individual reason and choice. Moderate political thinkers characterize nature as a limitation on radical change of both kinds, but they reconcile this limit on human ingenuity with nature's role in providing a standard for social and political systems that support human flourishing. Far from being entirely inflexible, natural desires can be molded and channeled within certain limits through gradual adaptation to particular circumstances. Human life is a complex combination and intertwining of nature, custom, and reason. Moreover, because humans are naturally social yet naturally self-interested, the natural desires of humans must be made compatible with the needs of other individuals and the stability and function of the group to which those individuals belong. Politics, then, is the balancing of these natural desires against the desires, needs, and interests of the group at a particular point in time. It is the harmonizing of our universal nature and our particular needs. Instead of rejecting nature as radical individualists and collectivists do, Montesquieu and Burke recognize nature as a limiting factor on human political skill, and recommend that social change occur slowly over time as a way of adapting such change to the nature of the people themselves.

The interplay of nature and custom is central to Montesquieu's discussion in *The Spirit of the Laws*. Montesquieu's gargantuan work is not devoted solely to positive laws, but instead looks at how different kinds of law, including natural law, interact.[6] While Montesquieu seems to reject nature as a standard in places, natural laws assert their power by limiting the customs and habits of the people.[7] Montesquieu criticizes local laws and customs when they threaten the purpose of a particular social group or when such laws and customs offend the general laws of nature that undergird all human laws and customs.[8] His account of the family straddles the complex claims of nature and nurture by focusing on the specific ways in which diverse family structures support the state and how regime principles can manipulate and potentially damage family relationships.

Montesquieu discusses two foundational natural laws, the natural law of defense and the natural law of modesty. While he never actually defines what he means by a "natural law of modesty," the meaning emerges from his examples of civil and political laws that violate underlying natural law. Forcing girls to declare their premarital sexual activity with their husbands prior to marriage, condemning to death a woman who does not declare her pregnancy and whose child dies, allowing young girls to choose their husbands, allowing divorce to be decided by a third party, forcing wives (or children) to be witnesses against their husbands, and involving children in the discovery and reporting of adultery are all civil laws that violate the natural law of modesty.[9] Two controlling variables seem to be at play in these examples. Either a given case represents a violation of the autonomy of the family to make decisions solely affecting the domestic sphere, or the example refers to a decision about sexuality or reproduction that should be kept private (i.e., within the family).

Montesquieu, characteristically, does not give a detailed analysis of where these natural laws come from or what the sphere of "modesty" is, but it is clear from his discussion that natural laws should take precedence over civil and political laws that might conflict with them. Natural laws form the basis for our mores, Montesquieu believes, and these violations of modesty, though created to "preserve the mores, overturned nature, in which the mores have their origin."[10] The family is crucial to the balance between nature and custom because, while its origins are in our natural desires for reproduction and intimacy, it provides the first education in the customs and mores of the community.[11] Thus, political rules that conflict directly with our natural desires, particularly with the autonomy of the family, should be avoided.[12] The resulting order is a nested system of laws, starting with the natural laws that are protected in the family.

Burke also focuses on the interplay between nature and custom, and he too sees family life as an important intermediary between these different facets of human life. Like Montesquieu, Burke rejects the state of nature of early liberal thinkers. Unlike Montesquieu, he eschews most talk of nature as a useful foundation for rights, focusing instead on the rights of a "civil social man."[13] Burke's incorporation of nature plays out in a complicated analogy between the family and the state that ends in a social contract rooting individuals to their particular society through familial affections. Burke uses the phrase "second nature" to differentiate the man rooted in family, time, and place from the abstract human nature (and attendant rights) of the early modern liberals.

Far from rejecting nature altogether, Burke seeks to illuminate the ways in which our customs arise from our nature. As Montesquieu believes the mores have their root in nature, Burke believes that our customs and habits are worth preserving because they reflect the gradual adaptation of our natures to our peculiar circumstances. Such growth resembles the gradual organic growth of plants, and Burke uses organic analogies throughout his work to underscore the danger of uprooting society from its natural and customary groundings in the name of an abstract metaphysical nature.[14]

Rather than relying on a simplistic conventionalism, Burke believes that nature is a central limiting factor on political change. He describes the inheritance of customary privileges as "the result of profound reflection; or rather the happy effect of following nature, which is wisdom without reflection, and above it."[15] The British, instead of using the Lockean and Rousseauian abstractions of nature as the grounding for their rights, have used the example of the family, a natural grouping that nevertheless partakes of and is shaped by custom, as the foundation for their political structure.[16] Inheritance is how we receive our rights, not as a God-given gift as individuals, but as individuals in a social context. We receive rights as individuals from our families. This method of rights transmission ties the individual inextricably to a community and ensures the continuity of custom while following nature.[17]

This familial analogy serves another purpose in Burke's theory, binding the individual through familial affections to the larger social group. Rather than a rational social contract as the binding mechanism between individual and community, the affections nurtured in the family become the material for social cohesion. Burke rejects the French metaphysical conception of nature, arguing that no rationally based philosophy has ever successfully replaced the naturally rooted reliance on familial affections and inheritance of rights.[18] Nature is found not in humanity's reason alone, as the rationalistic Locke (or Rand) would suggest, but instead in the natural affections for family, hearth, and home, which eventually extend to one's homeland.

This affectionately grounded nature allows for the gradual adaptation of a universal human nature to the peculiar circumstances of a people. When describing the wisdom of the ancient legislators, Burke argues that these men did not rely on "the metaphysics of an undergraduate" or on "the mathematics and arithmetic of an exciseman."[19] Instead, these early legislators recognized that man is social and that laws must be adapted to civil life as well as man's natural desires.[20] This combination of nature and custom requires that laws be created for the peculiar people to whom they will apply, and not to a generalized "human" who belongs nowhere and to no one. Burke echoes Montesquieu's assertion that governments must be made to suit their people. Far from promoting relativism as some have claimed, both Burke and Montesquieu root their understanding of politics in an organic intertwining of nature and the customs that grow out of natural and stable human desires.[21] The family, representing as it does the most natural of our desires and the most natural of social groupings, is the foundation for and the mode of transmission of this civil social nature.

A moderate meshing of nature and custom protects both the individual and the community from the dangers of a rejection or radical mischaracterization of nature as a standard. The collectivist rejection of nature leads to a belief that radical social change is desirable, and the individualist rejection of nature leads to a belief that the individual owes the community nothing for his success or failure. Because the family arises from natural desires but is shaped by customs and traditions, the family occupies an intermediate position between nature and custom that assists it in moderating the separate and sometimes conflicting claims of individuals and the communities to which they belong. The family slows social change by rooting such change in natural human desires and protects the permanent desires and interests of individuals against calls for radical collectivization. On the other hand, by educating individuals in social mores and values, the family creates social individuals who are ready (at least in theory) to enter and contribute to society. Finally, because the family and property are so closely linked (a fact that Engels found sufficient justification to support elimination of the family altogether), the process of inheritance not only operates in the passing down of manners and mores but also applies to material possessions and land. These possessions, linked as they are to the laws and customs of the country in which they are passed on, operate to further strengthen the link between the individual and the community in which he or she is born. The family is thus a protector of individual needs and desires, particularly those desires rooted in natural affections for privacy, family life, and property. At the same time, the family protects the community by passing on customs and traditions and creating a clear way of passing on property claims.

The balancing of differing goods and values in society is the goal of politics, and it is not fully possible without the connection between our first nature and our second, between the family and the state. This "conformity to nature in our artificial institutions" supports the bringing together of our "first nature" and our "second nature," the first being the natural human affections that arise spontaneously in the family, and the second the manners, mores, and other accoutrements of society that are acquired beginning in infancy.[22] It is this seamless meshing of the natural and the customary that creates a moderate constitution that supports the affections of the people as it secures their liberties.[23]

Burke on the Weight of History against the Sovereignty of the Present

The intergenerational nature of the family, rejected by both collectivists and individualists, is essential to the moderate political project.[24] Montesquieu and Burke believe intergenerational relationships support moderate governments because they provide a link between past, present, and future, because they moderate and slow political change, and because intergenerational thinking promotes the importance of individuals in social groupings at the same time that it underscores individual dependence on the group. The family, the primary and most natural intergenerational social group, helps balance the claims of individuals of multiple generations and their communities over time.

The importance of intergenerational relationships is the heart of Burke's criticism of the French Revolution. Burke begins his critique by rejecting the radical argument espoused by the French revolutionaries that each generation has the freedom to remake society according to its will. For Burke, each generation is dependent on the actions of the past, and the extension of that dependence is a duty to preserve those goods that past generations have given us.[25] The present generation is not wholly sovereign because its actions rely on the activities, plans, and sacrifices of the past. Moreover, the most important political goods—the constitution, the structure of government, and the manners and mores of a people—are not goods created by one generation, but instead are the inheritance of the past and should be preserved when possible for the future. As a result of this intergenerational dependency, politics is a partnership over many generations, "a partnership not only between those who are living, but between those who are living, those who are dead, and those who are to be born."[26] Burke's intergenerational contract is the foundation for his family-state symmetry, a symmetry that forms the foundation for all individual rights and duties.

This intergenerational contract is not merely symbolic; it is a very real contract passed down in large part through the mechanism of inheritance in the family. Burke replaces the individualistic social contract of Locke with an intergenerational social contract where individuals are born into a society through their families and they inherit their rights and privileges as members of that society, and not as individuals. This contract links our "lower" with our "higher" natures.[27] The linking of the lower with the higher natures can be understood as a reference to human dependence and need.[28] Each human during his or her life span will partake of both a lower and higher nature. Dependent when young, humans grow, reap the rights and privileges handed down to them by previous generations, and pass those benefits on to their children. The intergenerational contract does more than link the lower and the higher natures over time and within society; it also mixes these lower and higher natures, dependence and independence, rationality and need, in the same individuals over the course of their lives. The social contract for Burke, instead of a one-shot contract between individual and society, resembles much more the links in a chain that stretches backward and forward in time.

The links of this chain are supported by the affections we feel for society, and these affections are bred and nurtured in the family. Burke's contract language differs from Rand's in that he frequently uses emotional language to describe the link between individual and society, referring continually to the importance of the sentiments to cement our social relationships.[29] If these sentiments are the supporters of our duty to country, it is clear from whence they come. Our love of country starts in our "little platoons" of family, friends, and neighborhood, only later extending outward to the broader public world.[30] Familial love and its collectivist impulse tie us to the broader community, just as Rand feared they would.

These "inbred sentiments," by attaching us to our home and homeland, limit radical change by creating a stake in the present and an attachment to the past. The sentiments, unlike reason, promote conservatism (in the broadest sense of the word) because individuals desire to conserve that which they love, regardless of whether or not the beloved object is in fact rationally defensible. Burke does not go so far as to say that the loveable is entirely separable from the rationally defensible, but he believes that a purely rational justification for one's political regime and traditions may not be possible and that insisting on such a justification is almost always dangerous.[31] Burke's sentimental defense of the community is both more stable and less dangerous than rational appeals to the supremacy of the collective because it stems from the desires of individuals themselves to protect not what is the community's, but what is their own.[32]

The individual and the collective, instead of being opponents with conflicting values, are instead part of the same whole, a kind of harmony of values and ideals that remains rooted in the natural human desires made immanent in the family and supported over time by links of custom, tradition, and inherited rights and privileges.[33] This harmony secures the voluntary obedience of citizens to the laws of the land, promoting social stability and individual liberty at the same time. The connection between nature and custom "incorporated into politics the sentiments which beautify and soften private society" and which "cover the defects of our naked shivering nature."[34] This naked, shivering nature is at least partly an allusion to the threat of force lurking at the bottom of any government's claim to authority and obedience. Linking the family to the state, even if metaphorically, helps secure individual freedom and community stability at the same time, no small feat.

Burke, Montesquieu, and the Balance between Public and Private

The harmony between individuals and collectives supported by the family does not, however, provide a clear answer to the question of when public interference in the private sphere is legitimate or justified. Private decisions have enormous impacts on public decision making, and no strict dividing line between public and private spheres can accurately describe the complex interplay between the two spheres. Rather than insisting on a total separation between the two spheres or the collapse of one sphere into another, moderate thinkers attempt to find principled arguments for what kinds of private activities warrant public scrutiny. Both Montesquieu and Burke provide a partial solution to this problem of private/public interaction and, unsurprisingly, each of their solutions are grounded in a respect for a generally autonomous family that fulfills certain natural functions. How well the family fulfills these natural functions then becomes the basis for public judgment and debate. The partial solutions offered by Montesquieu and Burke provide the outline for a constitution that supports natural human desires for family life, individual autonomy, and group membership.

Montesquieu's first step in defining the legitimate scope of the public and private spheres involves his ranking of the different levels of laws and his belief that each area of law remains somewhat independent from the others. Montesquieu envisions a kind of nesting of different types of laws, and these different kinds of laws are ordered based on their origins (nature, custom, church, or government) and on the generality or specificity of their ends. Natural, political, civil, and domestic laws form the core of the categories of laws that deal with familial issues like divorce, inheritance, procreation, and sexual crimes.

The presentation of these laws moves from the most general and universal (natural laws) to the most specific (domestic laws). Natural laws, dealing as they do with all of humanity, are the most general since they apply to everyone regardless of time and place. Political laws, dealing as they do with the relationship between citizens and their rulers, are next because while they deal with a specific political order, they deal with the entirety of that political order. Civil laws, dealing as they do with relationships between citizens and other citizens, have a higher level of specificity because they deal with the gradual evolution of customary law and particular cases. Finally, domestic law, dealing as it does with particular families and the governance of those families, is the most specific of all categories of laws Montesquieu lays out. These different levels of law are related to one another in that each is linked and limited in some ways by the more general laws that come before. The natural laws of modesty and self-defense form the foundation for political, civil, and domestic laws. Each set of laws has its own sphere of action, and the things that relate to that sphere should be decided as far as possible by the laws (and lawgivers) of that sphere and by no other.

One consequence of this nested legal structure is that it carves out a significant private sphere for the family. Private activities like adultery and homosexuality are reserved for civil or domestic punishment. Excessive interference in sexual matters violates the natural law of modesty, which requires that such matters be settled as much as possible by the individuals directly involved. Interference by the community in domestic or sexual affairs is undesirable in part because such interference tends to negate the purposes of familial relationships, one of which is to fulfill the natural human desire for intimate human relationships.[35] While most decisions are best left to the family, Montesquieu recognizes that the family is not a purely autonomous sphere. Though largely protected by the indefinite character of the natural law of modesty, domestic right's place as the most specific of the different kinds of laws indicates that the size of the private familial sphere will be limited by previously existing civil and political laws (which, of course, will also be limited themselves by the universal claims of modesty).

Some examples may elucidate how this nested legal system operates in practice. Montesquieu examines several instances when the civil and political laws may justifiably intrude on what seem to be purely individual or familial decisions. In the cases of celibacy, marriage, homosexuality, and incest, society may have a compelling reason to intervene in what are properly domestic decisions. Usually, however, the intervention Montesquieu advocates is not civil or criminal penalties for particular kinds of domestic and procreative decisions but the more benign removal of legislation and social conditions that support or incentivize such activities. Celibacy, for example, Montesquieu dislikes because, as an extreme itself, it supports its opposite extreme, "libertinage." Celibacy encourages individuals to "flee a union that should make them better in order to live in one that makes them ever worse."[36] Montesquieu refuses to outwardly criticize religious celibacy, though he does maintain that its original use was to provide "distance from the cares and encumbrance of a family" in order to support the "speculative life."[37] Montesquieu suggests that most humans will be unhappy in celibate systems because celibacy prevents the fulfillment of our most natural desires, one of which is sexual intimacy and procreation. While celibacy should not to be punished, law should not encourage it lest it foster unnatural relationships by diverting men from the natural relationships of marriage and family.[38]

Similarly, Montesquieu recognizes the social and political importance of marriage, arguing, "Of all human acts marriage is the one that is of the most interest to society."[39] Its importance in the civil sphere suggests that it should be ruled then by civil laws.[40] Marriage's importance for procreation and the continuity of the community, its role in inheritance and the stability of property, and its influence on the mores of the people themselves suggest that marriage laws will span both private and public spheres.[41] As always, however, these civil laws regarding marriage are limited by the natural laws of self-defense and modesty. The natural law of modesty protects the individual from excessive intrusion into his private life and from excessive punishments for primarily private acts. Montesquieu attempts to forge a balance between private desires and public needs through the use of his nested legal structure. Domestic laws influence civil laws, which are in turn limited by the natural laws of modesty and self-defense. Montesquieu's framework allows some intrusion of the public into the private, but limits that intrusion to civil laws and their moderate punishments.

Homosexuality and incest provide the best examples of Montesquieu's prudential approach to law because they are, in some ways, the most extreme challenges to the preservation of a private sphere. In both cases, the public import of these activities is clear. But as in the case of celibacy, he suggests removing laws that might support or encourage such behavior, trusting to human nature to limit such behavior to a minority of situations.[42] Incest is to be avoided because it perverts the natural end of marriage.[43] But it is precisely because incest is unnatural and perverts the natural ends of marriage that Montesquieu believes that, given a moderate constitution and well-constructed civil laws, the temptation toward incestuous relationships will be minimal. Similarly, while he does not deny the belief of the time that homosexuality is a "crime against nature," nature itself is the best prosecutor of this particular crime. Where civil institutions are not set up to encourage such activity (such as among the Greeks), it is unlikely to make much headway.[44]

Such a moderate position toward activities that, in Montesquieu's time, would have had no vocal defenders indicates the strength of natural human sociality and its ability to protect the community from individual excess.[45] The balance between individual and community is best found by following nature. The best protector of that nature, not surprisingly, is the private and intimate attachments of the family. Regimes that support the natural affections of the family life and avoid excessive interference in familial affairs are more likely to have families characterized by affectionate bonds between husbands and wives and parents and children that will preclude incest and other potentially destructive private activities.

Montesquieu's approach to navigating public and private conflicts provides a principle approach to navigating the public/private split. He avoids a stark delineation between the two spheres, recognizing that private decisions have public impacts and vice versa. At the same time, he maintains a prudent restraint toward the domestic and sexual world. The community has an interest in the goings on in the private sphere, Montesquieu acknowledges, but interference in the private sphere may destroy that sphere's ability to police itself. It is better, Montesquieu suggests, to trust the natural feelings and inclinations of human nature. Our natural desires for intimacy and autonomy will create stable, affectionate families that preserve individual worth while supporting our natural sociality. This kind of balance is only possible, however, in a properly constructed constitution, one that builds off nature and whose laws are properly ordered. The proper ordering or nesting of different types of laws supports a complex and pluralistic balance between private and public in which natural, customary, and domestic laws support and refer back to one another in the process of balancing and promoting human needs.

Montesquieu's approach is firmly grounded in nature and the moral standard that nature provides while also respecting cultural and political variation. He is guided by the principles of natural human desires (procreation and intimate pairings being two of the most important) and their relationship to human communities, but he is also guided by a consequentialism that cares about the purposes of human groups and their importance to individual well-being. The purpose of the community is to protect individuals and provide for the common good. The purpose of marriage is procreation and the moderation of sexual desire. In both cases, laws (and individual actions) that violate or negate the purpose of those social groups should be eliminated or proscribed. Since part of the goal of any functioning group is to balance the interests and needs of the individuals making up that group, groups ought to preserve the balance of power between individuals in those groups, as well as between groups themselves. This is particularly important when it comes to balancing the claims of individuals, families, and the community. One way to preserve this balance is to preserve an autonomous sphere for familial and private decision making, particularly when dealing with sexual acts that are difficult to prosecute by the state.

Montesquieu's system of ordering private and public lives falls somewhere in between the radical individualism of Rand and the radical collectivism of Marx and Engels. Unlike radical individualists like Rand who refuse to recognize a legitimate role for the public in individual decision making, Montesquieu recognizes that private acts have public consequences, and that the family is not an entirely autonomous group, particularly when the family itself conflicts with the protection of individual rights. Unlike Marx and Engels, who refuse to recognize a sphere of individual action separate from that of the community, Montesquieu recognizes that the family is a central part of human life and therefore a central part of civil and political life. Political and civil decisions impact family life, though often in unforeseen ways. While the community cannot help but take part in domestic decisions like marriage and divorce, such intervention should be moderate and balanced against the natural right of modesty and the need to protect the purpose of family life and the intimacy and privacy that purpose is founded upon. Finally, this balance between public and private is part and parcel of the Montesquiean project to balance powers against each other to provide for moderate and humane rule. Such balancing requires that the family place itself as the primary (but not the only) intermediate institution between the interests of individuals and the power of the community.

Burke's Moderate Balancing of Individual and Community

Burke also supports a moderate position between public and private interests, though his balancing act has less to do with carving out a private sphere for the family and more to do with using the family as an intermediary between the individual and the community. Burke's interpretation of the social contract emphasizes that no man is an island and that the state of nature for man is a social state, not an individualistic one.[46] Yet Burke is not a collectivist. He is deeply concerned with the well-being and freedom of individuals, but he believes the best way to protect individual rights is through the social order itself, albeit a very particular kind of social order, one that has grown and evolved over generations. It is no accident that such growth occurs primarily within the system of inherited rights and privileges passed from ancestors to descendants. The entire Constitution of England can be understood as a buffer between the interests of the individuals of the present, the needs of the present community, and the values and gifts of past generations. The primary medium through which this great intergenerational compact operates is the affections, and these affections are rooted in strong family life.

That Burke sees the emotions as the primary social bond between individuals is evident throughout his political works, particularly in the prevalence of words like "heart," "breast," and "sentiments," which he frequently uses to exhort and remind those who he believes have forgotten their duties. The emotions play a primary role in the preservation of the state.[47] Rationality is necessary but not sufficient; what binds us to home and hearth is not rational speculation but emotional and sentimental bonds. Our attachment to place does not come from a rational argument about one place's superiority to any other, but is founded on a respect for the ancient that is emotional in nature.[48]

The passions support social bonding, but they also support the moral sense that is at the root of human social life. The emotions help us recognize the limits of reason while reason helps the emotions find consistent grounding. Each without the other creates a distorted morality.[49] The interplay between reason and emotion creates a harmony between the individual and his or her community because it allows for rights and duties to be reconciled, balancing our social and our individualistic selves. This meshing of rights and duties forms the foundation for the "civil social man," and it is no accident that familial affections form the basis for how rights and duties are brought together.

The emotions are not only a foundation for society or the prerequisite for agreement and political debate. Burke's emotions operate as a filter through which metaphysical principles can be safely applied to political life.[50] This filter facilitates the application of abstract rights to real-life social contexts. Burke does not deny the existence of natural rights. His major concern is to reject false or misapplied rights language in favor of a theory of natural rights that is compatible with human nature and human social life.[51] The use Burke makes of reason in the realm of theory and the heart in practice is critical. The "real rights" Burke speaks of here are not the abstract, rational, individualistic rights of the contractarians. Burke explicitly rejects the social contract of Locke and Hobbes.[52] Instead of accepting these rationally arrived at and individually focused rights, Burke looks for a rights language that is moderated by the claims of the heart. Burke's theory of rights is built on our "second nature," or the interaction between nature and custom, rather than the abstract state of nature of the social contract theorists.[53]

Burke believes that a properly constituted rights theory is more than merely theoretically important. He believes theories based on the abstract rights of men are actually dangerous to social life. They harden the heart and corrupt the moral sentiments that bond the members of society together. Because of their extreme individualistic nature, abstract rights undermine the social emotions.[54] The "rights of man" accustom individuals to think in terms of abstract individuals, instead of in terms of socially rooted creatures whose existence depends on the bonds to community and society that absolute natural rights break.[55] Burke rejects the dichotomy between reason and emotion, arguing that rational principles properly understood and the moral sentiments properly understood support each other and form a buffer that helps mediate the different claims of the individual and society.[56]

Far from rejecting the existence of rights altogether, Burke merely disagrees with the proponents of natural rights on the best way to preserve natural rights in the political sphere. Both individual rights and human social life need to be preserved, and thus some safe medium must be found that helps us balance their sometimes conflicting claims.[57] Reason alone cannot provide this safe medium because it lacks the necessary link to human social life. The sentiments, however, help balance abstract rights against the needs of the communities to which individuals belong. In this vein, while Burke tends to associate abstract reason with rights claims, he also explicitly connects the emotions to duty.[58] Because duties are a social phenomenon, they belong properly to the sphere of emotions, or at least they are protected by the emotions. Thus, both rights and reason can be moderated by the duties protected and grown from our emotional attachments to our particular time and place.

These attachments, according to Burke, are rooted not in custom alone, but in nature and in that most natural of social groups, the family.[59] A statesman must "preserv[e] the method of nature in the conduct of the state," and such a strategy is not merely "the superstition of antiquarians" but is based on the "spirit of philosophic analogy."[60] He defends himself against accusations of being a mere traditionalist by arguing that society is rooted in nature and that the attachments one feels for the state are naturally rooted, as our affections for our family are. The analogy between family and state is explicit: "We have given to the frame of our polity the image of a relation in blood; binding up the constitution of our country with our dearest domestic ties; adopting our fundamental laws into the bosom of our family affections; keeping inseparable, and cherishing with the warmth of all their combined and mutually reflected charities, our state, our hearths, our sepulchres, and our altars."[61] All rights are moderated and reflected off the social affections, which are in turn rooted in our families, that ground our duties to the community and the state as a whole. Religion, state, and family are all supported and protected by the affections rooted in the love of one's own, which counteract the individualism of traditional rights language.

A prime example of these moderate rights for Burke is private property. The right to private property, far from being a purely selfish right as Marxists would claim, is instead one of the primary balancing points between individual self-interest and community commitment. The inheritance of property takes the selfish impulse to acquire and makes it social by ensuring the passage of what is acquired to future generations. Inheritance of property through families conserves not just property but also the complex system of laws, habits, and mores that property creates, at the same time that it socializes the individual by making him or her beholden to those who came before and responsible to some degree to those who come after.[62] Private property creates a commitment to a community by giving individuals something worth preserving. It does this so effectively precisely because it relies on self-interest and the self-interested love of one's own, rather than on universal benevolence. By "graft[ing] benevolence even upon avarice," property rights elevate self-interested love of one's own to a community-building virtue that conserves and protects laws and social orders.

Burke's socialized and moderate rights are more closely connected to— or rather, encompass—duties because they are more closely connected to our social nature and because they stem from our natural familial affections. These rights are moderated by our attachments to time and place, reflected and moderated by prejudices, and a part of society rather than separate from it. These moderate and socialized rights provide hope that there might be a way of recognizing both duties and rights without making them identical or subjecting one to the other. Socialized rights rely on an intergenerational compact that links individual and community over time and goes beyond mere individualism toward a complex understanding of compact that links individuals, families, and communities. Part of this project is the balancing of individual interests against the legitimate needs of the community. Burke rejects the abstract rights of the French because he believes that they are incompatible with the meshing of our first and second natures. In some sense, this meshing is an artificial construct, but even though some facet of our allegiance to the state may be based on "pleasing illusions," it is precisely these pleasing illusions, the analogy between state and family, that provide for political moderation. The connection between nature and custom "incorporate[s] into politics the sentiments which beautify and soften private society" and which "cover the defects of our naked shivering nature."[63] The balancing of differing goods and values in society is the goal of politics, and it is not fully possible without the connection between our first nature and our second, between the family and the community.

Unlike collectivists, who see in the family unadulterated selfish individualism, or the individualists, who see the family as the foundation for a simplistic and dangerous collectivism, Burke recognizes that the family moderates the claims of both the individual and the community. The family is that which, while serving our individualistic love of our own, also links us to the broader community through familial affections. Habit, education, and affection within the family solidify connections to others at the same time as they teach love of one's own. The family provides the links between the individualistic rights on which Rand focuses and the collectivist duties of Marxists. In the process of linking our abstract rights to our social duties, the demands of both are moderated, softened, and made humane.

The Family and Political Complexity

The moderate position the family occupies between the spheres of public and private and between the individual and the community supports the complexity of human political and social life and a pluralism of human goods and values. Both Montesquieu and Burke, unlike Marx and Rand, recognize the existence of permanent conflicts of interest in human life, conflicts between individual interests and community interests, between liberty and equality, and between privacy and public well-being.[64] By balancing the claims of the individual and the community through the medium of natural familial affections, Burke and Montesquieu avoid a direct conflict between individualistic liberty and collectivist equality by filtering these values through the affectionate and social lens of family life. Montesquieu uses the language of balancing of powers, while Burke's interpretation relies on a harmony of interests. In both cases, complexity and moderation in the political realm are linked to the family's role in supporting both individualism and community goals.

Montesquieu rejects the simplistic political teachings of Marx and Rand because just as human nature is permanent, human political problems are permanent. Contradictions and conflicts are part of human political life. Instead of attempting to eliminate these contradictions, Montesquieu uses them as the foundation for his moderate political regime.

Moderate governments, unlike despotic regimes, are difficult to maintain because they require the careful balancing of different goods.[65] Moderate government requires that we acknowledge the existence of eternal conflicts, whether between the individual and the community or between various human goods, and use those conflicts to create a system where neither individuals nor their communities are sacrificed. It is only in this careful balancing of a variety of goods that liberty is possible.[66] The proper balance between nature, custom, and political rule and between private and public spheres requires a robust family structure to balance these complex claims because the family is rooted in nature and facilitates social habituation through the affections.[67]

The best constitution, according to Montesquieu, is a complex constitution that combines liberty in relation to the citizen—secured by mores, manners, and civil laws—and liberty in relation to the constitution, secured by fundamental laws and the balancing of the three main powers of government. Montesquieu's political theory is a rejection of the simplistic and mathematical theories of those who believe a universal political theory can be built upon abstract ideas like rights or class conflict. The family—because it occupies a unique position between the particular and the universal (no family is ever quite the same, and yet family life is itself universal)—provides the foundation for all other intermediate institutions in Montesquieu's analysis. The family facilitates the balance between the individual and the community, between public and private, and between nature and custom.

Like Montesquieu, Burke supports the preservation of difference in political life, and he, like Montesquieu, relies on the slow evolution of constitutions over time so that positive laws can be made compatible with the customs, habits, and mores of the people they are to rule. Instead of a balancing of powers, Burke uses the term "harmony" to describe the ideal political constitution, and his use of the word is not accidental.[68] Politics for Burke, much like for Aristotle, is the bringing together of different and diverse interests, needs, and goods to create a comprehensive whole that is characterized not by "an excellence in simplicity, but [by] one far superior, an excellence in composition."[69] The goal of politics is thus not to eradicate or eliminate contradictions, as it is in Marx and Rand, but to bring those contradictory elements into a harmonic whole.

Just as this harmony promotes a balance between individual and community interests, it also helps balance the claims of liberty and equality. Burke emphasizes both liberty and equality in his work, but his liberty is the liberty of the "civil social man" and his equality is a moral equality, unconnected to equality of property or social class.[70] In both cases, he uses the affections for one's own, stemming from the affections for kin, to create a social individualism or an individualistic communitarianism, where liberty and equality come together as compatible with the rights of individuals and the stability and health of the whole.

Burke's position is, like Montesquieu's, a rejection of the radically simplistic and pure ideologies of Rand and Marx, though with a slightly different emphasis. Burke rejects the Randian independence of the individual, arguing that each individual in society is dependent on those who came before and thus has a duty to protect and pass on that legacy to those who come after. At the same time, Burke turns Marx's criticism of private property as a primarily selfish institution on its head and instead grounds much of our social duties in the inheritance of property. Instead of fracturing our affections for the community as Marx argued, the family is the source of affection for the community and moderates our selfish individualism by rooting us to those around us. Burke's analysis of the relationship between individual and the community is fundamentally moderate, meant to preserve a harmony of interests, particularly the harmony between individual rights and communal duties. The family serves as facilitator of that harmony, bringing together our higher and lower natures and assisting both individuals and communities to modulate their tones.

Chapter 5

Family Forms and the
Social Individual

Not all family forms facilitate the social individualism that Burke and Montesquieu believe to be the foundation for political moderation. A family that supports moderation must itself be moderate, which means it must balance the needs of the individuals within the family against the needs of other family members and the stability of the family unit itself. The moderate family must also help to maintain a balance of interests with the broader collective. Moderate families may take a range of different forms, but they will share certain important characteristics, and these characteristics are more likely to be found in some family forms than others. The moderate family is capable of adjudicating domestic or private issues on its own, with the use of its own resources; it will, therefore, be self-sufficient. The moderate family will also be a balanced family, in that it harmonizes the interests of its members, avoiding oppressive coercion of one member by another. The moderate family will also be an intergenerational family, tying individuals to others across generations, preserving stability over time. Finally, the moderate family emphasizes social individualism, rather than collective identity or atomic individualism. It will help mold individuals to become citizens because they are bonded by affection and inheritance to their community. It will simultaneously assist individuals to maintain autonomy within the broader collective by preserving individual worth within these close bonds. The moderate family thus creates individuals who are capable of balancing private and public relationships and for whom the conflict between individual and collective is moderated by the affectionate attachments of individuals to the community to which they belong.

This self-sufficient, balanced, and intergenerational family is essential to individual and community interaction because it influences how much control the collective or public sphere may claim over individual- or private-level decision making. Collective control over private decisions is usually justified on the grounds that private decisions incur significant costs that must be borne by the public sphere. But centralization of decision making incurs costs of its own, and the more the public becomes involved in private decision making, the more volatile public discourse becomes. The more the public becomes involved in private lives, the more clashes occur between private individual decisions and public values. Debates over the kinds of marriages to recognize, whether abortion should be legalized, whether contraception should be paid for out of public coffers, and how to fund and assess the quality of public education, are all debates that, for better or for worse, would not polarize the public sphere had the family maintained its strength in supporting itself and fulfilling its role in taking primary responsibility for children.[1] Public solutions to the failure of the family are costly and may create adverse moral and economic effects.[2]

Despite the drawbacks of collectivization of family functions, more and more traditionally family-based activities—from education to nourishment to psychological health—are being moved from decentralized families into the public sphere.[3] There are many and complex reasons for this change, some of which are demographic, including more women working outside the home and the increasing mobility of individuals away from families, and others of which are cultural, such as the shrinking of the family itself as fewer people reproduce and the increasing rate of out-of-wedlock births that result in single-parent households. These trends create an asymmetry between individual and collective interests that, tragically, undermines the beneficial aspects of both individualism and collectivism.[4] Individuals separated from families and at the whim of the collective for entitlements become isolated, members of no group at all. Meanwhile, the increased power of the collective over traditionally intimate decisions strains community resources and pushes community members against each other as resentment grows toward noncontributing individuals. The damage done to both individuals and their communities further undermines the social individualism advocated by Montesquieu and Burke that supports both individual autonomy and community interests.[5]

Such social individualism relies heavily on the family to habituate and form individuals who are both autonomous and independent but who are also thoughtful and conscientious citizens. As family forms change, the ability of the family to maintain this precarious balance erodes. Three increasingly common family forms are particularly relevant to modern political discourse in that each fails to accomplish the ends of the ideal "social-individual" family. Single parenthood, polygamy, and nonreproduction all fail to achieve one or more of these primary goals, and this failure destabilizes the relationship between individual and community, leading to isolated individuals and weak communities. The family form that best preserves social individualism—monogamy in its various forms—encompasses the benefits of the family offered by Montesquieu and Burke in that it balances nature and custom through intergenerational relationships and preserves a balance between public and private by limiting the costs it imposes on the public sphere.

Single Parenthood and Familial Self-Sufficiency

Since the Moynihan report laid out the dangers of single parenthood to social stability in 1965, single parenthood rates have soared, with roughly 41 percent of children now born to single mothers.[6] In African American communities, the percentage rises to 72.5 percent.[7] The increasing isolation of parents into single-parent units restricts parents' ability to handle the economic, social, physical, and psychological needs of their children on their own. The loss of self-sustaining families forces individuals to rely on the collective for the economic, educational, psychological, and emotional resources traditionally provided by family life. This reliance on the collective, by blurring the lines between public and private, in turn increases collective interference in the private sphere as a way to ensure that community resources are being properly allocated. The result is a collapse of public and private spheres into one another.

The economic costs of single parenthood are perhaps the most obvious. Single parents typically rely on less than half the resources of married couples, which, among other things, makes them more economically vulnerable than married couples to changes in employment. Because most single parents are mothers, and because women are more likely to be negatively economically affected by pregnancy, birth, and infancy, single-mother households in particular are more economically vulnerable and more likely to require public assistance. Because many single mothers have children when they are young and before their educations are complete, they have difficulty finishing their educations and have a lower than average earning potential for the rest of their lives.[8] As a result, single mothers have much higher poverty rates than married couples in all developed countries.[9] The economic aftermath of these realities is that single-parent families struggle not only with half the normal economic investment predicted by the lack of a partner, but also with much less than half the resources of stable married couples due to lower education levels and more unstable employment. Census figures indicate that married couples have, on average, more than ten times the net worth of single-parent families.[10] These economic patterns are passed to the next generation, since single parenthood increases the likelihood that children will drop out of school and have children outside of stable marriages.[11]

Reduced economic independence, unsurprisingly, leads to increased economic dependence on the state. In the United States, the recipients of food stamps; Medicaid; welfare; Women, Infants, and Children (WIC) benefits; subsidized school lunch programs; subsidized or free day care; Head Start programs; and public housing are overwhelmingly single mothers and their children.[12] Legal enforcement mechanisms must be crafted to ensure that fathers provide some resources to their dependent children, and the family court system has grown in size and expense as single-motherhood rates have risen.[13] State expenditures for tracking down "deadbeat dads" have increased as the collective struggles to constrain costs for children's day care, health care, and education. The foster care system is increasingly strained as fractured families fail to provide adequate care for children.[14] Children from single-parent families have worse health outcomes and are more likely to be incarcerated over the course of their lives than children from married families, increasing costs for both the overburdened health care and criminal justice systems.[15] The overall expense to taxpayers of non-monogamous child rearing has been estimated to be perhaps as much as $100 billion each year, an amount that many argue justifies collective regulation and monitoring.[16]

The lack of economic self-sufficiency of the single-parent family has led to increasing calls for collective control over individual decision making. Proponents justify parental licensure, one of the more extreme policy options, on the dual grounds of the psychological damage done to children and the economic damage done to the state caused by fractured families.[17] With every policy assisting single parents comes additional calls for intervention and control over private reproductive decisions. Incentives such as providing child care for mothers to encourage them to enter the work-force and linking public assistance with "child immunization, child school attendance, paternity identification, and child support collection" encourage individuals to tailor their private and reproductive decisions to meet communal goals.[18] Such public programs often, however, have unintended side effects, one of which may be an actual increase in the incidence of out-of-wedlock child rearing.[19]

It is not just in access to economic resources that the single-parent family is at a disadvantage. The psychological and emotional costs of single parenthood on children are also significant. Where children are separated by divorce, even when fathers try to stay involved, the rate of paternal contact with children drops dramatically.[20] Perhaps due to this lack of paternal contact, girls raised by single mothers are more likely themselves to become single mothers at young ages.[21] Boys raised by single mothers are more likely to drop out of school and become involved in drugs and other criminal behavior.[22] Children of both sexes are more likely to have impulse control and learning problems, making them less likely to be as successful as their peers raised by both parents. Children of single parents require more remedial work in school and may be grade levels behind their peers.[23] It is unclear whether these psychological and behavioral differences are due primarily to the absence of fathers per se or to the simple fact that a single parent of any sex is simply more constrained for time, resources, and mental energy to provide adequate structure, discipline, and the stability necessary to raise successful and well-adjusted children.[24] What is clear, however, is that single parents have a more difficult time providing for the economic, social, and psychological needs of children than two-parent households.

The policies offered as solutions to the problem of single parenthood usually entail replacing the fractured single-parent family with state-provided care. State-sponsored day care, school lunch programs, and extended school days collectivize traditional functions of family life, replacing parental contact with paid teachers, counselors, and other specialists. These "solutions" by and large assume that the primary function of the family is one of economic resources, rather than emotional or psychological growth. The collective, while able to replace the family in some of its functions, cannot provide the same kinds of emotional investment in children that parents in traditional families can, meaning that while physical needs are provided for, emotional and psychological needs go unaddressed. Studies of institutionalized children consistently demonstrate that while basic physical and medical needs may be met, children raised in orphanages or other institutions show decreased emotional functioning, which impacts social relationships and the development of moral reasoning. These effects persist over the life span.[25] Neglect of emotional needs creates isolated individuals who are unconnected to the broader community and whose affectionate bonds to other individuals are undermined. The result resembles the liberal individual of Locke and Hobbes, bound only to the broader community by contract, rather than by affectionate bonds.[26]

The emotional and psychological neglect that follows from the collectivization of the family stems from a confusion between the roles family members play in each other's lives and the functions families fulfill.[27] Roles are irreplaceable relationships in a person's life that can only be filled by one particular person. An individual playing a role is important as an individual and cannot be interchanged with another person. A function, on the other hand, can be fulfilled by anyone, and individuals who fulfill functions are interchangeable, characterized not by their individuality but by the activities in which they engage.

The family is unique among social groups in that it is characterized more by roles than it is by functions. A mother fulfills a role for her children, one that another human being can never fill completely; she is not simply replaceable by another woman of the same age. A day-care provider, on the other hand, fulfills a function. Someone fulfilling a function may be able to turn that function into a role, as in the case of a day-care worker who, through compassion and patience, plays a central role in the life of a child. In general, however, roles and functions do not always or even typically coincide, and the difference between the two affects the importance of individuals as individuals and their worth in the broader collective. While the collective can replace some of the traditional functions of families, such as the economic function, it cannot replace the roles that family members play in each other's moral, emotional, and psychological development. Replacing these unique roles with functions takes irreplaceable individuals and turns them into replaceable employees. Individual worth is slowly eroded in place of interchangeable functions.

Individual worth—and the rights and duties that attend such worth— is made possible by kin relationships because such relationships are where individuals *matter* in the deepest sense. Families are our first experience as role-playing individuals, individuals who are important for our own sake, not for whatever function we fulfill, and the erosion of that individual importance affects the way in which the collective interprets and protects individual worth and the rights that extend from that worth. In a world of functions, the individual is no longer important in his own right but is instead important only in the capacities in which he serves the community or through the activities in which he engages. The assumption of the kibbutzim was that parenting was a function that could be fulfilled by anyone. The result of that experiment was children who wished to be cared for by real parents and parents who wished to be able to fulfill a unique and irreplaceable role within the family. Recognition for one's public work is only one facet of personal worth and not the most important.[28] Individual worth is not tied wholly to the public functions of individuals, as collectivists would have us believe, or to the market value of one's work, as individualists like Rand argue. Instead, such worth emerges from the roles individuals play in relation to other human beings.

Polygamy: Liberty and Equality

While single-parent families are the most obviously problematic family form in terms of prevalence, other, more marginal family forms may have important consequences for both individual worth and community cohesion. Polygamy, common in the developing world, is reemerging in the United States as a viable family form in light of recent television shows like *Big Love* and *Sister Wives*. While polygamous unions are often criticized for their exploitation of public assistance, the real issue is that polygamy creates an imbalance of power between men and women and weakens traditional kin ties.[29] This imbalance between male and female roles encourages collective involvement to prevent abuse. By failing to protect the interests of the individuals in the family unit (in this case, the interests and rights of women and children), the polygamous family distorts the family's position as an intermediary between private and public, necessitating public interference.

Polygamy is illegal in the United States in large part because of the clearly detrimental outcomes of polygamous unions, particularly for women.[30] Polygamy is associated with higher rates of spousal abuse, higher rates of maternal mortality, low rates of female education, and other negative social, political, and health outcomes.[31] Health outcomes for women and children are lower in polygamous than in monogamous households.[32] These negative outcomes can be traced to the fact that polygamy is almost always associated with imbalances between male and female interests, and the power that males wield over female decisions often leads to a cultural preference for male over female children. Such preferences for male children in turn reduce resources for female education and health care from infancy through adulthood.[33] Some kinds of polygamy, like that of fundamentalist Mormons in western states, are correlated with sex-ratio imbalances that result in the abuse of young men and young women by older elite males.[34] Polygamous marriages in the United States, for example, are often characterized by coercive force against girls and women and against young males who might challenge or interfere with the ruling patriarchal elite. While some of these problems may be linked to the secrecy required by legal prohibitions, the general pattern of coercion is one that can be found across most polygamous groups.[35] On an international level, the patriarchal nature of the family in traditional polygamous cultures becomes intertwined with the political and legal system, making protection of wives and children from abuse and neglect more difficult.

The coercion of women and the devaluation of female children create neglectful and abusive situations in which the interests of individuals are not protected by the family unit. The same is true of abusive or neglectful monogamous relationships, but the problem is exacerbated in polygamous unions because the imbalance between male and female power is so extreme and because the cumulative effects of polygamy over generations exacerbate the imbalance between male and female interests. As more men take multiple wives, the sex ratio of available mates decreases, leading to increased competition for females.[36] This competition for mates lowers the age of first marriage for females, leading in the extreme cases to child marriage.[37] Adolescent females are less capable than older women of protecting themselves against the psychological and physical coercion of older husbands. Combined with the strong pressure from a girl's own family to stay in the marriage, a young bride may be powerless against her husband's desires, lacking allies, resources, and psychological maturity to rebel against abuse.

The division of interests of the sexes is worsened by the imbalance in investment in children in polygamous unions. A male's interest in his children (as well as his economic resources) is spread out over the children of multiple mates, while a female focuses her resources on her biological children. Studies show a decrease in paternal investment in individual children in polygamous unions, and such a decrease can leave children vulnerable if their mother dies or if the marriage dissolves. Because of their lack of status and resources, mothers may not be able to protect their children in the case of remarriage. In some polygamous communities, adolescent boys are ejected from the family and the community upon a mother's remarriage since they are considered competitors for resources and mates.[38] The polygamous family, in large part because of the separation of male and female interests from one another, fractures the family's natural bonds. The result is a family form often held together solely on the basis of coercion.

The reliance of polygamous relationships on coercive male authority stems from another problem common to polygamous unions, namely the dilution of kin ties, particularly those between father and offspring.[39] Male investment in individual children is necessarily lower in polygamous unions than in monogamous unions because the numbers of children are so much greater. Moreover, some have argued that because male attention is directed at procuring new mates rather than at existing relationships and their offspring, the overall investment in children is even lower than one would find in a monogamous union with the same number of children.[40] This reduced investment dilutes family ties since children have little access to their father's material or emotional resources. Siblings from different mothers are also less bonded than siblings from the same family unit, even when such distinctions are carefully avoided.[41] The consequence of these diluted ties is that what seems to be an extensive family structure is actually reduced to a kind of single-parent family, where children are bonded primarily to their mothers and have little interaction with or investment from paternal figures. The dilution of kin bonds makes the polygamous family more fragile and courts external community involvement for the same reasons single-parent families do—a lack of self-sufficiency. Community involvement may be even more urgent, however, due to the increased incidence of abuse and neglect.

In addition to failing to protect individuals, polygamy also damages communities by introducing expansive kin ties that promote hierarchical, patriarchal, and nepotistic characteristics that challenge community cohesion and liberalization. The patriarchal nature of polygamous families encourages authoritarian male control, which, when extended into the broader society, challenges democratic decision making and emphasizes patriarchal family lines as legitimate claims to rule. Nepotistic and hierarchical cultures have lower levels of social capital, which reduces the efficacy of other intermediate institutions.[42] Nepotistic patriarchy, while not only found in polygamous societies, is strongly linked with polygamy and can be found in societies as culturally different as Arab polygamous tribes in the Middle East and fundamentalist Mormon polygamous communities in the American West.[43]

Even more than the problems of nepotistic hierarchy, the prevalence of spousal abuse and neglect of children in polygamous families strains communities by challenging liberal democracy's dual commitment to privacy and the protection of rights. Suspicion of abuse and neglect requires public interference in the private decisions of polygamous families at the same time that the community struggles to uphold its commitment to religious toleration. Liberal democracies have not been entirely successful in balancing these different interests, though a kind of consensus has emerged in attempting to control the effects of polygamy rather than its form. Pursuing polygamists on the basis of their family form alone has not proven successful, nor does public opinion seem to support state intervention solely to prosecute the crime of bigamy. The public supports controlling the effects of this family form, including prosecution for sexual abuse, statutory rape, and abuse and neglect of children.[44] The secrecy required by criminalization in many states may make it even harder for authorities to protect women and children.

With the effectiveness of criminalization in question, existing research is mixed on whether indirect policies can help eliminate polygamy by providing opportunities for women. There is some evidence that polygamy declines as female education increases, and as countries develop they often outlaw polygamy.[45] As women's options expand, both within and outside of the home, their desire to participate in polygamous unions decreases. A community that allows women equal political rights and protects those rights against male oppression and coercion is less likely to produce women who believe their long-term interests are served in unequal marriages with multiple partners. Other kinds of social structures may help make polygamy less common. Societies without dramatic wealth inequality may make it less likely that very wealthy men expend their wealth in attracting multiple wives. Legal protections for women's property and support for female education from a young age can be important protections against polygamous unions.

At the same time, female empowerment policies, while they have some effect on reducing the prevalence of polygamous unions, are not nearly as effective as enforcing monogamy with criminal penalties. Neither the carrot of economic opportunity nor the stick of criminal punishment seems entirely effective, perhaps because polygamy is rooted in biological sex differences. Polygamy remains resistant even to cultural change because it is a natural outcome of the differences between male and female reproductive potentials. Males who have the resources to control the reproductive potential of multiple mates will be inclined to do so, and women who lack access to resources may be inclined to share powerful men with other women. Controlling polygamy and limiting its more egregious effects when possible may be all that is possible given these reproductive realities.[46] Liberal democratic institutions alongside criminal penalties may be the most effective way to do both.

The Atomic Family and the Loss
of Intergenerationality

An increasingly common family form in the developed world is the tendency toward limited or nonreproduction—an "atomic family"—and though its effects are less immediately damaging than those of either single parenthood or polygamy, they may be even more pernicious in the long run.[47] The atomic family is the smallest possible family unit, consisting of one person or two partners with one or no children. Minimal or nonreproduction engenders increasing numbers of children born without siblings and increasing numbers of individuals with no family at all. The atomic family has become more common due to concerns about overpopulation, the increasing costs of raising children (including out-of-control educational costs), the decision to have children later in life, and the increasing focus on individual comfort and self-fulfillment, which makes sacrificing material comfort for a large family unattractive to young people. The decision to have only one child, if carried out on a large scale over two or more generations (as is the case in China, for example), creates a generation of individuals who have no siblings, aunts, uncles, or cousins. Their unchosen familial relationships (as opposed to chosen relationships like spouses) are confined to their relationships with their parents and perhaps their grandparents, should they still be living.

This reduced familial footprint has important consequences for both the individual and the broader society, both through a reduction in intergenerational relationships and an overall reduction in the number of high-value relationships in which an individual participates. Atomized families reduce intergenerationality by separating generations from each other, which contributes to a society oriented toward the present rather than balanced between the past, present, and future. The loss of familial relationships also reduces the number of high-value relationships an individual has, which threatens individual worth. The elimination of the family as the intermediate buffer between individuals and collectives isolates individuals from one another and requires more community intervention to care for increasingly vulnerable populations.

Intergenerationality benefits both individuals and the communities in which they live by moderating both the individualism and the collectivism that are in tension at the heart of liberal democratic theory. It does this not by denigrating the importance of the individual or the group, but by placing the individual in a social context, bounded by past and future. Individuals with grandparents, parents, and children of their own are more likely to be aware that their actions will influence the kind of world their children inherit and that decisions they make will preserve or destroy the decisions and actions of their own parents and grandparents. This longitudinal view balances the principles of liberty and equity over generations by moderating both and making them compatible with each other.[48]

Burke's discussion of social liberty and moral equality is merely one example of how the often starkly defined principles of individual liberty and collective equality can be moderated and softened when placed within a generational scheme because intergenerational contact reminds us of the principles of the past and the needs of the future. Individual liberty is softened in an intergenerational context because the individual's "self" is expanded to include other individuals at different stages of life with different needs. Collectivistic equality is softened as well because the demands of the collective must be moderated by the principles of the past and the needs of the future, and because the collective is forced to recognize a social grouping prior to and more permanent than the collective itself—the family.

On a practical level, families balance intergenerational claims because they consist of multiple generations of individuals bound by affection. It is in families, rather than in other kinds of social groups, that individuals are most motivated to sacrifice their short-term selfish interest for their long-term expansive self-interest, including the well-being of their children and the communities in which those children will live. Such self-sacrifice includes teaching children how to share finite resources, plan for the long term, respect individual needs, and recognize changing needs across the life span. The family teaches these skills in childhood when they are best learned and with individuals with whom the child is emotionally attached, both of which facilitate the internalizing of these lessons. These intergenerational relationships help balance potential conflicts between individuals and their communities because they place individuals in a social context while reinforcing the importance of individuals as individuals.

A second problem caused by atomic families is that they reduce the number of permanent high-value relationships in which individuals participate. The family is the home of high-value permanent relationships because family members are bonded together by both blood ties and by affection, which results in a permanency that few other human relationships create. Familial relationships are different from every other kind of human relationship because they defy dissolution, even over time and place.[49] This persistence means that individuals are, from birth, placed in a network of permanent social relationships that undergird the changing relationships of the broader society. Individuals fall back on these relationships in times of strife precisely because they do not decay the way friendships decay. Even when a dysfunctional familial relationship creates estrangement, the actual relationship does not disappear, and individuals may find themselves drawn again and again back to familial relationships even when such relationships are coercive or unhealthy. The permanency of family relationships make them both fulfilling and exasperating. This permanency, this sense of no escape, forces individuals to work hard to maintain familial relationships, even if the other party is someone with whom no one would willingly choose to associate.

Because of this permanence, familial relationships are more immune to political and social change than other kinds of relationships, which protects individual worth in times of uncertainty. While an individual might cast off friends with whom he or she disagrees politically, an uncle or aunt cannot be cut off so easily. While *contact* can be cut off, the aunt or uncle continues to be a relative, whether or not that is desirable. Family relationships, unlike other kinds of relationships, are not predicated on individual desires and are therefore not dissolvable on individual whim. The collective may even be moderated by these high-value relationships because the existence of permanent familial relationships requires compromising political values in the name of family harmony.[50] A kin relationship may survive serious political disagreement or long distances, while a friendship crumbles under the strain.

In a world of atomic families, relationships—instead of being rooted in private and permanent blood ties—are usually public and temporary. Individuals without kin ties are atomized within their social networks, with fewer permanent relationships on which to rely when economic or political instability arises. As individuals become more isolated, they become more susceptible to abuse and neglect at the hands of strangers. Even more troubling is that the individual has no one to counter the weight of collective abuses. Atomic individuals have fewer permanent private relationships, relationships that are peculiarly privileged and which the public, generally, acknowledges as separate from and largely immune to collective interference.[51]

The duties we owe our families, duties that arise out of the peculiarly permanent nature of familial attachment, are the foundation for a durable social support network that emphasizes individual importance while linking individuals across time and space. The loss of high-value permanent intergenerational relationships creates a crisis for individual worth.[52] Rhetoric about abstract rights to the contrary, individuals only matter to other individuals who care about their well-being. Abstract rights claims are only enforceable when someone cares enough to enforce them. Those with permanent relationships to other members of the community who are invested in their welfare and whose survival and well-being are linked are more likely to have such advocates in times of trouble. Work on social capital demonstrates that social networks, which include close ties with family, have significant consequences for the economy and the health and welfare of those living in those communities.[53] Individuals who are protected by close relationships to others are also more likely to value and protect the individual worth of others.

The tenuous position of the elderly in modern societies exemplifies the problem of individual importance. Elderly members of large anonymous societies are vulnerable because their individuality may be sacrificed to collective needs like efficiency or resource scarcity. Because the elderly contribute little directly to the economic well-being of the community and their care is particularly costly, their interests may be ignored in favor of younger and more productive members of the group. Some collectivist theorists ignore the elderly precisely because they are nonproductive. In some radical cases, they remove the elderly from the collective altogether.[54] The "nonproductive" elderly matter only when there exists a network of people who share a permanent relationship with them. While stories of mistreatment of the elderly by relatives are common, elderly people who lack any family network are much more vulnerable to abuse.[55] Traditional societies, where individuals live closely with kin, are more likely to respect the elderly, not for their material contribution to the group, but as individuals. The intergenerational nature of family life increases the probability that individuals will be valued throughout their lives. Even in the collectivist countries of Scandinavia, the elderly are protected primarily by kin relationships rather than by government-provided resources.[56]

It is not just individual worth that is harmed by a loss of intergenerational family relationships and the permanent bonds that result. The community is harmed by a loss of pluralism, because individuals who choose their associates are more likely to become entrenched in a particular worldview. A loss of diverse viewpoints, or at least the segregation of such viewpoints into like-minded groups by self-selection, can lead to a community that is incapable of reaching compromises when conflicts between values and interests of different groups arise. The family, by forcing us to associate with people with whom we may have little in common, encourages political moderation. It takes the individual out of himself or herself and expands the understanding of "self" at the same time that it forces the individual to confront, sometimes daily, individuals with beliefs, interests, and goals different from his or her own.

Despite the importance of the family for both the status of the individual and the long-term interests of the community, both individualists and collectivists have the tendency to support the increasing atomization of the family.[57] For egalitarian collectivists, a reduced birth rate allows women to become more equal in public roles, minimizing the amount of time spent in the private sphere. Reduced fertility puts less strain on community resources, at least in the short term, and reduces hierarchical relationships, resulting in more egalitarian systems. A reduced fertility rate may reduce strain on the environment, one of the primary concerns of modern collectivists. For individualists, childlessness allows individuals to freely choose with whom they associate, avoiding the tangle of dependence and accident that familial relationships entail. Childlessness liberates men and women from the bonds of family life and allows them to rationally choose how to live their lives without requiring sacrifices from other people. The atomized family reduces the immediate strains of need and dependence on individuals.

In practice, however, the growing trend of nonreproduction challenges both collectivist and individualist thinkers because it erodes the social individualism on which both theories rely. Collectivists need the emotional and psychological support for individuals that the family provides and that the community is ill equipped to provide. Individualists need the family because it supports the importance of the individual in the face of collective demands. Both theories need the long-term thinking that family life promotes via intergenerational relationships that provide stability to communities by rooting individuals in a complex web of affectionate and supportive relationships. A world without the family is one where both individuals and communities are worse off because it is a world ultimately rooted in nothing more than self-interest.

The Ideal Family and the Harmonizing of Individual and Collective Claims

Given the drawbacks of single parenthood, polygamy, and nonreproduction and the impacts these forms have on political systems, it is essential to outline the kind of family forms that promote political moderation. Theoretically, the ideal moderate family form will serve as a strong buffer between private and public lives, preserving both and harmonizing, as far as possible, the interests of individuals and their expansive self-interest with the interests of the communities to which they belong. Such balance requires a family with certain characteristics: self-sufficiency, permanency, internal balance between its members, affectionate bonds, and intergenerational strength. Single parenthood, polygamy, and nonreproduction all lack one or more of these characteristics and are therefore less able to preserve a moderate distinction between private and public spheres or to moderate between the claims of individuals and their communities.

A self-sufficient family will decrease community involvement in private decision making and help to preserve distinct spheres of public and private action. A family that preserves a balance between the interests of its members, particularly the interests of men and women, will decrease inequality at both the private and public levels and will decrease the need for community protection of individual rights against coercive or abusive relationships. An intergenerational family, where members maintain contact with each other throughout the life cycle, stabilizes community norms and values and places the individual in a social framework that helps turn selfish impulses of the moment into an expansive self-interest that encompasses the past, present, and future. Finally, the affectionate family preserves individual worth by uniting individuals within a network of caring and invested companions while preserving community cohesion by bonding individuals to the community in which that network exists. By encouraging voluntary obedience to community norms and values, both individual freedom and community strength are nurtured.

In practice, the family form that is most likely to display these characteristics is a family consisting of a monogamous couple and two or more children.[58] Monogamy is more likely to be self-sufficient than other family forms because two adults contribute to the care of the children resulting from the union, which affords twice the investment, resources, and time to children than single-parent families. Further, monogamous pairs do not split their investment among the children of multiple unions, the way polygamous fathers do. A monogamous family is thus more able to provide for itself both in terms of emotional investment and concrete resources than either single parenthood or polygamy.[59]

Monogamy provides a stronger intermediate buffer between the individual and the collective than either single parenthood or polygamy because it balances the interests of the sexes by tying both sexes, despite their different reproductive interests, to the same set of offspring, thus equalizing as far as possible the investment each sex makes in children.[60] In the traditional monogamous family, the female provides intensive care of young children while the male provides her with the resources to support that family. In the less traditional monogamous family, these duties may be split even more evenly, with fathers participating actively in the care of the young and mothers working outside the home to earn income to support the family. In either case, the investments of both sexes are equalized, which helps balance the different interests of males and females.[61] Polygamy and single motherhood, on the other hand, end with males lowering their investment in the offspring of a particular union, leaving females with the burden of both caring for offspring and earning income for the family.[62] Women and children are thus increasingly vulnerable and dependent on community assistance.

In addition to balancing the interests and investment of the sexes, the monogamous family preserves intergenerational relationships that balance the community's need for both change and stability. Intergenerational relationships protect both individuals and society against both radical social upheaval and social stagnation, and monogamy helps support these intergenerational relationships through robust emotional bonds that extend into the broader community. Close relationships with individuals of other generations provide individuals with insight into the challenges and values of the past and provide direct access to history from the people who lived through it. Intergenerational relationships limit the sovereignty of the present generation because they allow the weight of past tradition and values to press on the goals and projects of the present. This weight, however, protects the interests of different generations and individuals at different stages of life because it slows social change and allows the gradual incorporation of innovations into the existing social structure. Such slow change protects both individuals and the community against radical calls for revolutionary flux that might destabilize the community and encourage the violation of individual rights. Simultaneously, the family adapts to meet the changing needs of its members from different generations, but in a way that recognizes individual needs. Intergenerational relationships allow members to mold and shift their values gradually through intimate associations between kin belonging to different generations.[63]

At the same time that monogamy links individuals from multiple generations, it also bonds individuals tightly within the family itself. It does so by extending the emotional bonds of single parenthood to two parents while providing tighter emotional bonds between family members than polygamous families can create.[64] Both parents, linked equally to their offspring, are present in children's lives. Sibling ties are likely to be stronger in monogamous families than polygamous ones because siblings are equally related to each other.[65] The stronger the emotional bonds between kin, the more likely they are to protect each other's interests and needs across the life cycle and to apply those emotional attachments to the community at large. Burke's "little platoon" starts with strong bonds between children, parents, grandparents, aunts, uncles, and cousins that create intergenerational links that persist past maturity. These emotional bonds thus protect the individual by enmeshing each person in a supportive network of high-value relationships that extend backward and forward in time.

While they protect individuals, intergenerational emotional bonds also preserve the stability of the community by tempering purely individualistic desires. As Burke argued, individualistic claims of right are softened by emotional attachment to kin and community. These emotional bonds thus help prevent radical social change from either direction. An individual who views him or herself as a part of a larger whole and whose emotional well-being is inextricably linked with that larger grouping is less likely to support wholesale revolution than is an individual whose emotions are unfixed on any particular aspect of social life. In effect, the emotionally bonded family is the nursery for social altruism.

The affectionate and intergenerational bonds between family members in monogamous families promote a more stable balance between private and public spheres. The monogamous family's extensive generational structure solidifies its position as the foundation of community activity. At the same time, its self-supporting nature creates a private sphere of action that resists communal interference. A self-sufficient family fosters a sphere of individual autonomy in sexual and reproductive decisions largely protected from public interference. A self-reliant family also frees up the community to focus its efforts on truly communal goals. Strong private and public spheres that resist excessive overlap balance the claims of individuals and the broader community by harmonizing private decisions and public needs.

Moderate Monogamy and the Publicly Private

Obviously, not every family produces positive benefits for individuals or the community. Even the best families contribute to public outcomes, both positively and negatively, and these public effects cloud any sharp distinction between public and private activities. The private decisions of individuals to have children or not affects the economy and social and political stability.[66] Different family forms can create negative political and social outcomes, particularly for women.[67] Abusive or neglectful families can create unbalanced or needy individuals and put strain on social welfare programs and the criminal justice system. Families can pass on traditions that may be at odds with the values of the broader society.[68] Families may violate individual rights, requiring state or collective intervention.[69] Private decisions about child rearing and child care can lead to inequalities between the sexes in the public sphere.[70] The question is not whether the collective has an interest in the private decisions of individuals in families, but what kinds of outcomes and effects are important enough to justify public intervention.

While most people recognize that serious abuse or neglect is sufficient grounds for interference in private familial decisions, what constitutes abuse or neglect is highly variable. It is often defined on a case-by-case basis, and social welfare workers and family court judges are often given discretionary power to determine when intervention is necessary. Usually, where familial decisions have direct and negative impacts on the rights of individuals, some collective intervention is considered justified, just as collective intervention is justified to protect the rights of individuals in other contexts. The harder cases are those where family life has important indirect social consequences that may not affect individual well-being directly but may have important consequences for strongly held social and political values. These more difficult cases of balancing public and private lives include the debates over the role of women in the public sphere and the current contentious debate over same-sex marriage. It is not accidental that even in these more difficult cases, monogamy can provide a partial solution to the problem of balancing public and private lives.

One of the more difficult issues to challenge the autonomy of the private sphere is that women's equal participation in the public sphere is challenged by family life. Moderate sex differences in the desire and ability to bear and nurture children, caused by either socialization or innate biological differences, create an imbalance in who takes on private and public roles.[71] Such differences also affect which parent controls economic resources and political power. Monogamy, far from creating or requiring economic and political parity, may contribute to unequal outcomes for men and women, particularly when paired with traditional beliefs about male and female sex roles. Partly because of the burdens placed on women by pregnancy, lactation, and nurturing young children, women are underrepresented in the most challenging public fields of business, law, and politics.[72] Many progressive thinkers believe these unequal outcomes in the public sphere justify intervention in the private for the sake of the public. The policy prescriptions proposed by these thinkers, however, rely on the important and unproven assumption that women would, if they could, hand off child rearing to husbands or day care.[73] The experience of many women is that such a choice is an agonizing one, and it may be best left to those who are most familiar with the talents, desires, and interests of the individuals involved.

Where such desires about work and family arise from individual choice, an imbalance between men and women in the public sphere may be unavoidable. Coercing women not to care for their young children for their own good is not an effective strategy.[74] At the same time, that men and women differ on average in their desire to care for young children does not necessarily require stringent and inflexible sex roles within all families, as advocated by some on the conservative or religious right. Women are neither rigidly programmed to take care of children, nor are such maternal desires mere social constructs that can be manipulated by social change. Women, like men, have a complex set of desires that include both private and public roles. When children are young, many women will choose (aided by bonding hormones like oxytocin and prolactin) to emphasize their private duties to their children over their public duties as citizens and leaders. When children are more independent, many women will choose to move outside the home, engaging more with their communities. Because monogamy comes closest to balancing the differential desires of men and women, it can assist in balancing the claims of public and private lives by allowing individuals, along with their partners, to decide what kinds of roles they want to fulfill, both publically and privately. It also assists women by evening out the resources provided by both sexes and may allow men to take on more of the burden of home life at different stages of children's lives. While not perfect, the support monogamy provides for both women and men who choose to balance private and public lives is integral to protecting individual autonomy and community well-being.

A similar debate about public interference in families for the sake of community outcomes centers around same-sex marriage and traditional families, and this debate takes on a predictably polarized character. Liberals argue that we should "stand on the side of love," supporting any familial relationships in the fight to justify legal and social recognition of same-sex unions. Conservatives, on the other hand, argue that we need to protect "traditional" marriage, or the union of a man and woman, often with the assumption that those men and women will espouse traditional gender roles within marriage. Liberal relativism is pitted against conservative absolutism, with neither side willing or able to moderate their claims.

Unfortunately, neither relativism nor absolutism works well in practice.[75] Family forms are not neutral with regard to their outcomes. The liberal use of relativism to defend a moral good is actually problematic for gay marriage advocates themselves, partly because it undermines their arguments by creating a slippery slope toward other family forms, but also because the assertion that all family forms are equal is empirically untrue.[76] Relativism in this case is incoherent because it requires individuals, in their defense of what they believe to be a positive moral good, to argue instead that there are no such things as positive moral goods apart from individual desires. Ultimately, gay marriage is *not* defensible from a relativistic "stand on the side of love" position. Gay marriage is not defensible merely because it is based on the love two people feel for each other or because all personal desires lead to rights that must be legally protected. If the sole reason for supporting same-sex marriage is that it represents the private wishes of two people who love each other, and all such wishes must be respected by the community, then on what grounds would we restrict incestuous relationships and bestial relationships and polygamous marriages? These comparisons are precisely the kinds of comparisons that same-sex marriage advocates would like to avoid and yet cannot defend against because they have eliminated all arguments for same-sex marriage as a positively defensible family form.

Same-sex marriage is not defensible because any kind of union is justifiable. It is defensible because it creates a family that fulfills the functions that its advocates want families to fulfill and creates social individuals who are capable of balancing their self-interest with broader community needs. If same-sex marriage creates stable unions where children are loved and invested in by two people, regularizes sexual activity, and provides children with legal, social, and economic protections, it should be embraced by the community in the same way heterosexual monogamy is embraced.[77] Because such marriages bond members of the community who would probably not otherwise enter into heterosexual relationships, the impact on sex ratios is minimal, and the creation of an imbalance between the sexes in the marriage market is unlikely. Same-sex marriage, like heterosexual monogamous marriage and unlike heterosexual polygamy, balances the interests of the various members of the family in such a way as to protect the natural desires of these individuals. Same-sex marriage, like heterosexual monogamous marriage, represents a harmony of interests, rather than an autocratic arrangement like polygamy.

Changes in public opinion over the last ten years suggest that heterosexual individuals have noticed that same-sex monogamous couples behave much like heterosexual monogamous couples and pass the benefits of monogamy onto their children.[78] Opposition to gay marriage is dropping not because people believe that any kind of marriage is a good marriage but because experience with gay couples has demonstrated to many that families headed by gay couples fulfill the kinds of functions they want families to fulfill. Such a change in public opinion does not seem likely in the cases of incest or polygamy because those family forms do not fulfill the functions or roles families should serve. Even when liberals refuse in the abstract to acknowledge differences in family forms, most people are still able to distinguish in practice between beneficial family forms and those that are dangerous to the balance between individual autonomy and social stability.

Conservatives, on the other hand, undermine their own position just as surely when they reject same-sex marriage out of hand as a danger to traditional marriage. By taking an absolutist approach to monogamous marriage, conservatives are forced to reject family forms that may create precisely the kinds of values they would like to see in the public sphere. Committed same-sex partners are more likely than single-parent or polygamous families to create the kind of self-sufficient and responsible citizens that conservatives prefer. Two parents of either sex are more likely to be able to provide the economic, psychological, and moral stability that children need than single-parent families. At the same time, such unions avoid the kinds of imbalances between partners seen in polygamous households. Same-sex marriage avoids the dependence on state aid that conservatives dislike and provides children with strong intergenerational relationships that help moderate the pace of social change.

The conservative blind spot applies not merely to same-sex marriage, but also to concerns over women working outside the home. Conservative absolutism on the subject of marriage alienates women who reject the implicit argument that only a particular kind of monogamy, one ordered by traditional gender roles, is stable enough to preserve the kinds of values conservatives care about. In reality, most women now work outside the home by preference, economic necessity, or both. The economic realities that make a two-earner home necessary are changing the face of the family as the conservative movement holds to a style of family life that is disappearing. Conservative animosity toward both same-sex marriage and the two-earner monogamous family may in fact undermine the conservative message that families are the essential foundation for social and political life by creating a standard of which all families will fall far short. By implicitly criticizing all but the most traditional family forms, conservative absolutism alienates individuals who would otherwise support conservative arguments for the importance of the family.

Apart from liberal relativism or conservative absolutism, there are ways of structuring monogamous families that enable individuals to find a family form that fits the unique variables of their lives. These variables may include group-level variability such as social mores, political structures, and economic and legal variables. They may also include individual-level variation such as personality, talents, interests, and stage of life. Allowing for some variation within the broad category of monogamy allows family structures to fit the needs of the people families are meant to serve. Far from being either relativistic, as liberals would have us believe, or perfectly fixed, as conservatives argue, family forms exhibit a patterned variability.

We should not tolerate *all* family forms, because some family forms are better at others at harmonizing the different needs of the individuals who make them up and are therefore better at balancing between individual and community claims. At the same time, family forms are not absolutes. There is no one single way of structuring family life that will fit all societies, political systems, economic needs, or individual talents and personalities. The most one can say is that some family forms create more stability and better outcomes for the individuals within them and the societies of which they are part than other family forms. Within the broad category of "monogamy" one might find same-sex couples, traditional paternalistic relationships, and nontraditional egalitarian relationships. What they all share are the broad characteristics of monogamy that provide stability and a balance between individuals and groups: a general equality of investment between the partners in the union, the concentration of economic resources in one family and on one set of children, an intergenerational structure that supports a balance between the values of the past and the present, and a size and structure that facilitates the creation of deep and abiding affectionate attachments that spread outward to the community.

Political Moderation and the Familial Fulcrum

The ideological extremism that characterized the grand politics of the twentieth century has been moderated in some ways by the end of the world wars, the rejection of both communism and fascism by the developed world, and by the seeming ascendancy of liberal democracy throughout the developing world.[1] It might seem as if the conflict between the individual and the collective has been solved. Liberal ideals ostensibly satisfy the desire for individual freedom at the same time they support a devotion to equal rights that satisfies our collectivist tendency toward equality. As many commentators have pointed out, however, the ascendancy of liberal democracy is neither as universally beneficial nor as complete as some might have us believe. Liberal democracy, some argue, has led to a torpid emphasis on comfort and minor technical advances, eschewing thymic concerns with nobility, greatness, and human meaning.[2] The "last man" created by liberal democracy is no more complete than the radical individualist of Rand or the collectivist hive worker of Marx. Indeed, this "last man" partakes of the worst of both individualism and of collectivism in that he is isolated from others around him, concerned only with his individual comfort, but he is also a conformist, never rising above the average of man.[3] This liberal "last man" falls into a kind of mediocrity, concerned neither with individual nor collective greatness. Liberal mediocrity, some have argued, fuels the rise of radical religious sects like political Islam precisely because it fails to satisfy natural human desires for greatness.[4]

Perhaps as a result of the unintended consequences of liberal comfort, the victory of liberal democracy has been called into question, both at home and abroad. The twenty-first century, supposedly a time for peace and self-congratulation, was instead born into tragedy and uncertainty. The first decade of this century saw ideological clashes based again on conflicting ways of life, this time a clash between religious piety and liberal freedom.[5] The twenty-first century has also seen tragic events at home—school and workplace shootings, attacks on our military and representatives, and an increasingly polarized political climate that has failed to reach consensus on issues from social mores to economics.[6]

The family, too, has changed forms and weakened in part as a result of the liberal democratic ideals of equality and individual freedom. An increasingly mobile society fueled by capitalism has spread families farther and farther apart. As more women work outside the home, the balance between men and women and between parent and child has shifted. Two earners are necessary for most people to earn an adequate living in an increasingly competitive marketplace, which puts more pressure on day care and public schools to provide education in traditional subjects as well as manners and mores. In the working class, the separation of marriage and procreation caused in part by liberalism's gradual erosion of traditional mores and religious beliefs has led to children being born into increasingly fractured homes.[7]

The family's ability to counter either the stultifying comforts of liberal democracy or the ideological and religious extremism that opposes it might seem limited. Yet even in this weak form, the family still balances ideological extremism to some extent because, almost no matter what form it takes, it forces us to balance our individual and social selves. Its intermediate position between generations, between individuals and communities, between past and present, between equality and liberty, between principle and pragmatism, between complexity and simplicity, and between perfection and imperfection allows the family to naturally balance a diversity of human goods and values in a way no other institution can.

But this persistence does not mean we can ignore the family's weakness. Understanding what families should do and perhaps are no longer doing is crucial to identifying weaknesses in our social and political communities. Because the causal arrow between political moderation and familial form works in both directions, weakened family forms can lead to political immoderation, and political immoderation can weaken the family. In both cases, a greater understanding of what the family actually *does* can help us better understand what it is that we want *communities* to do. There are some lessons the family imparts regardless of whether it is weak or strong, precisely because these lessons have to do with the broader human condition and how individuals and communities intertwine.

Why We Need the Family

The first lesson the family teaches is a lesson of humility.[8] Perfection is not possible in human life, and family itself is one reason for this imperfection. No one ideological system will support entirely the broad range of human goods. No belief system is capable of simultaneously supporting our conflicting desires for comfort, for belonging, and for greatness. The family, precisely because it challenges equality, liberty, and a host of other human ideals, forces us to accept those ideals in a more modest, more realistic, more human form.[9] This imperfection arises from the fact that the family is the first social group in which compromises between individual autonomy and collective activity must be worked out, and the balancing of these different ideals is never perfect and never complete. Conflicts between spouses, between parents and children, between siblings, and between the nuclear family and its extended relations, all require the balancing of interests, values, and ideals over time. Human needs change across the life cycle, and groups themselves are always in flux as individuals are born, marry into and out of new families, and eventually pass away. This constant flux and the imperfect and incomplete balancing that results promotes an awareness that human goals and ideals must be approached, like marriage itself, reverently, discreetly, advisedly, and solemnly.

A humble approach to social and political change in turn promotes a reconsideration of the meaning of political moderation. Rather than mere compromise or a peace based on disinterest, the best families, like the best communities, seek a vibrant harmony. An emphasis on harmony, not conformity, can be instructive for an increasingly pluralistic society, one riven by competing cultural, ethnic, religious, and ideological identities. The family is not a conformist collective. It is hierarchical, made up of diverse individuals serving in different roles, with different strengths and weaknesses, who all nevertheless contribute to a flourishing community bound together by affection. Family members do not always agree on political ideals or even religious beliefs. What they should do is respect one another, be invested in each other's fortunes and misfortunes, accept the limitations of their own and others' abilities and ideals, and seek a way forward that preserves their different beliefs while creating a space in which others can do likewise. This space is not founded on blind toleration, but should be devoted to spirited and sometimes painful debates over the beautiful, the good, and the meaningful in human life. The difference between harmony and conformity seems little appreciated in the current political climate. Disagreement, instead of a starting point for debate, is now a wedge doused in vitriol. The family supports harmony because it starts with individuals who are inextricably connected with each other, whose happiness depends on each other, and who benefit from each other's differences even when those differences rankle.[10]

The successful creation of a harmony depends on the existence of individuals whose social selves are properly balanced against their individuality. Harmony is not merely compromise or centrism. It does not require the abandonment of deeply held beliefs in the name of agreement. It does, however, require individuals who are capable of shifting their own beliefs up or down a note in order to better fit with the chords being struck around them. That delicate balancing act is only possible with individuals who are secure in their individualism but who are also attached to the collectives to which they belong. Individuals who are confident in their own powers and self-worth but who are also affectionately attached to their communities will be able to critique these communities when they err, while loving them enough to desire their preservation. The confident individual, attached to his or her community, is the heart of social individualism and the harmony that results.

Supporting harmony also forces us to embrace complexity in our social lives and in our ideological commitments. Families require individuals to simultaneously harbor seemingly incompatible passions and interests. Independence is countered by need and love. Rivalry is attenuated by affectionate bonds. Individual choice is balanced by unchosen traits. Egalitarianism is countered by a diversity of needs. No family can be founded on a single value, mercilessly pursued. Equality, liberty, justice, and piety are all tempered by the complex emotions of trust, affection, and conflict. Ideological purity is incompatible with affection and love because human relationships require flexibility, patience, and forgiveness. Complexity is required in part because humans are fallible and imperfect—and thus groups of humans will be fallible and imperfect—but also because there are many human goods that must be balanced against each other.[11]

Recognition of fallibility and respect for the complexity of human goods lead to the last, and perhaps most important, lesson the family can teach us in our increasingly mechanistic and technological age. In a world of technical means and near constant information, the family anchors us to the ends of human life. The family is the home of affection and love; it teaches us how to bond with other human beings. It provides an end to counter and a context for the myriad technological and mechanical means that are sometimes mistaken for ends in themselves. The great leaps in technological innovation that have made human life so much better over the past century free us to spend time doing that which is most meaningful— become the most we can become as individuals and provide support for those we love and value.[12] While it is possible to periodically become lost in these means, convinced that a particular technology or public policy is an end itself, the family recalls us, as it were, with a twitch upon the thread. The daily growth of children, the aging of parents and grandparents, the loss of loved ones and the entrance into the world of new lives, all remind us, lest we forget, that there is more to life than the technological conveniences, pursuit of comfort, technical mastery, and barrage of information that liberal democracy has made possible.

These lessons—of humility, of complexity, of harmony, and of meaning—like all other lessons in life, cannot be learned unless we are paying attention. There exists no human institution capable of standing in the way of willful human ignorance or arrogance. But the family's strength lies in its persistence. As long as we reproduce, we will be bound to other humans in a way that goes beyond consent and beyond equality.[13] It is a bondage that both challenges and strengthens political ideals because it links us to others and reminds us of the fragility and imperfection of all human goals.

What the Family Needs

Crucial to its success as a fulcrum between individualistic selfishness and collectivist conformity is the recognition that the family cannot act alone. A fulcrum without something to rest on balances nothing. The family, like all important human institutions, requires helpmeets to keep it strong and balanced. The complexity of human sociality requires many other kinds of institutions—cultural, social, political, and legal—to support the family, just as family life supports the social and political worlds. While the family rests in the most fundamental sense on human nature, that nature may be subject to change in a way never before possible. New biotechnologies such as surrogacy, cloning, and genetic engineering may challenge our notions of families and will require careful debate and consideration as societies and individuals decide how far changing human behavior and capacities should go.[14]

Beyond our biology, the family requires social and cultural supports if it is to play its role effectively. The family needs strong and engaged communities, the traditional places where families have thrived. Neighborhoods where families come together, where children are shared, and where values and ideas, bobbing below the surface, are engulfed in the daily activities of productive work, raising children, and contributing to a shared space. Other intermediate institutions, still struggling to find their foothold in a changing economy and the changing social mores of the twentieth century, will help build a solid resting place as well. Churches, civic organizations, parent groups, sports clubs, and all the other ways we socialize outside of formal state power serve to strengthen family ties because they also strengthen our social individualism. These intermediate collectives, as they could be called, balance each other and prevent collective conformity because each has an end or goal peculiar to itself. Each of these intermediate institutions broaden and strengthen the base on which the family, and ultimately the delicate balancing act between individual and collective goals, rests.[15]

Finally, and perhaps most importantly, we need to resurrect the belief, now almost forgotten in modern political polemics, that the solution to most problems humans face cannot be found in either the state alone or in the isolated individual. Political solutions to problems, clumsy at best and dangerous at worst, have failed to provide true *human* solutions to the problems of violence, mental illness, poverty, and isolation. Complete solutions to these problems do not, of course, exist. What do exist are charity, succor, and comfort, and these supports to our human fragility are only found in the cracks between the state and the individual. They abide in private charities, loving families, benevolent churches, temples, and mosques, and in the private actions of neighbors caring for neighbors.

The family will succeed in resurrecting its central place in human life when we make more room for these intermediate institutions, when we accept that public policy is limited in its ability to reach human things, and when we open ourselves up to other people's needs—not through coercive power of the collective—but by recognizing the individualism of the other and by participating in a vibrant social life that includes collectives of various kinds with varied ends. This recognition requires that we view collectives as an essential part of what individuals need to flourish but also that we treat individual freedom and autonomy as central to the diversity that makes pluralistic communities successful. For now, the family occupies one of the most perseverant of intermediate positions, a fulcrum on a perhaps crumbling base, balancing—sometimes failing but often succeeding—the best parts of our social and our individualistic selves.

NOTES

Introduction

1   Aristotle criticized Plato's belief that the city should be a unity, arguing instead that "the city is in its nature a sort of multitude," made up "not only of a number of human beings, but also of human beings differing in kind." Aristotle, *The Politics*, trans. Carnes Lord (Chicago: University of Chicago Press, 1984), 56. Chantal Delsol, following Aristotle's thought, argues that "to constitute a world is not only to live together in a group, band, or collectivity, for the purpose of better satisfying basic needs; even more, it is to weave together coherent meanings that allow us to exist on earth as wayfarers capable of speaking about ourselves." Delsol, *The Unlearned Lessons of the Twentieth Century: An Essay on Late Modernity*, 1st ed. (Wilmington, Del.: ISI Books, 2006), 58. Each author believes that a central balancing act of politics is preserving both individuals and the communities to which they belong.

2   While there were many contributing factors to these wars—ethnic and religious conflict, changing economic circumstances, new technologies, and social and cultural shifts—the ideological roots of these wars are also clear. Francis Fukuyama argues, in part, that the wars of the twentieth

century were primarily ideological conflicts between Western liberalism and the various illiberal ideologies of imperialism, fascism, and Marxism. See *The End of History and the Last Man* (New York: Free Press, 1992).

3   Chantal Delsol argues that the failures of the twentieth century were caused by "the obscure weight that sinks utopias: a truth about man that limits the omnipotence of the will in the drive toward perfection." Delsol, *Unlearned Lessons*, 29. She further argues, "Totalitarianism made humanity barbarous by depriving humans of their cultural world" (58). That cultural world includes traditional laws and mores that help balance individual meaning and collective need. Though from a different tradition, Friedrich Hayek argues that communism and fascism are ultimately linked and that fascism is "simply collectivism freed from all traces of an individualist tradition which might hamper its realization." Hayek, *The Road to Serfdom* (Chicago: University of Chicago Press, 1994), 183. Fascism is, therefore, one form of collectivism, made extreme by the rejection of the importance of the individual. He later quotes Keynes describing a German author of 1915 who believed that "individualism must come to an end absolutely," and as a result "the nation will grow into a 'closed unity'"(201). This radical collectivist thought is, according to Hayek, characteristic of German thought at the time (201).

4   Fukuyama distinguishes between previous authoritarian regimes and the totalitarian regimes of the Soviet Union and Nazi Germany, arguing that while older authoritarian regimes might have sought to control civil society, "totalitarianism sought to destroy civil society in its entirety." Fukuyama, *End of History*, 24. Jose Harris also makes this claim explicit, arguing that collectivism and individualism "advanced in tandem at the expense of more traditional social arrangements such as philanthropy, the family and the local community." See Jose Harris, "Society and the State in Twentieth Century Britain," in *The Cambridge Social History of Britain 1750–1950*, vol. 3, *Social Agencies and Institutions*, ed. F. M. L. Thompson (Cambridge: Cambridge University Press, 2008), 113.

5   According to Hayek, communism opened the door to fascism in Europe by stamping out liberal individualism and the intermediate institutions on which liberal individualism rests. Hayek, *Road to Serfdom*, 33–35.

6   See, e.g., Robert Gellately, *Lenin, Stalin, and Hitler: The Age of Social Catastrophe* (New York: Alfred A. Knopf, 2007).

7   Pangle and Ahrensdorf argue that "from this complex and manifold late-modern reaction to what appeared to be the denuded 'bourgeois' vision of the human vocation sprang the great and diverse idealistic political movements of the past two centuries—not only Wilsonian liberalism . . . but also the varieties of socialism, including communism, and romantic nationalism, distorted finally into fascism." Thomas L. Pangle and Peter J.

Ahrensdorf, *Justice among Nations: On the Moral Basis of Power and Peace* (Lawrence: University Press of Kansas, 1999), 262.

8   The Cold War was the obvious extension of this ideological tension.

9   Marx, e.g., cites precisely these changes in his argument for eventual communist triumph. Karl Marx, *The Marx-Engels Reader*, ed. Robert C. Tucker (New York: Norton, 1978), 345. More recently, Gellately cites the First World War, in conjunction with previous changes wrought by industrialization, as setting the economic, social, and political stage for totalitarianism. Gellately, *Lenin, Stalin, and Hitler*, 4.

10 A precursor was the growth of government power, which gradually made many traditionally autonomous institutions beholden to the government for favors or dependent on the government in other ways: "In many voluntary organisations, however, such autonomy progressively dwindled: they became increasingly the agents and clients of the state, holders of state licences, beneficiaries of state tax concessions, recipients of and competitors for state financial aid. . . . The boundary between public and private spheres became more and more confused than in the late nineteenth century." Harris, "Society and the State," in Thompson, *Cambridge Social History of Britain*, 114.

11 See, e.g., Hannah Arendt's characterization of the Soviet purges: "Mass atomization in Soviet society was achieved by the skillful use of repeated purges which invariably precede actual group liquidation. In order to destroy all social and family ties, the purges are conducted in such a way as to threaten with the same fate the defendant and all his ordinary relations, from mere acquaintances up to his closest friends and relatives." Hannah Arendt, *The Origins of Totalitarianism* (New York: Harcourt, Brace, 1951), 323. Fukuyama echoes this language, arguing that "what was left was a society whose members were reduced to 'atoms,' unconnected to any 'mediating institutions short of an all-powerful government.'" Fukuyama, *End of History*, 24.

12 A key problem for liberalism is that individuals in their abstract state may not be seen as worth preserving. Individual worth requires the assistance of a "civil society" that serves as a buffer between individual and community goals. Arendt argues, "If a human being loses his political status, he should, according to the implications of the inborn and inalienable rights of man, come under exactly the situation for which the declarations of such general rights provided. Actually, the opposite is the case. It seems that a man who is nothing but a man has lost the very qualities which make it possible for other people to treat him as a fellow-man." Arendt, *Origins of Totalitarianism*, 300. Burke makes similar arguments as well. See, e.g., Edmund Burke, *Reflections on the Revolution in France* (Indianapolis: Liberty Fund, 1999), 151. Many of the intermediate institutions that

support the civil society that protects individual rights have been explored at length by political theorists and social scientists. Robert Putnam's work on social capital in southern Italy, which he later expanded into his famous analysis of the lack of civil associations in the United States and the loss of cooperative activity that results, is but one example. See Robert D. Putnam, Robert Leonardi, and Raffaella Nanetti, *Making Democracy Work: Civic Traditions in Modern Italy* (Princeton: Princeton University Press, 1993); Robert D. Putnam, *Bowling Alone: The Collapse and Revival of American Community* (New York: Simon & Schuster, 2000).

13   See Mark A. Largent, *Breeding Contempt: The History of Coerced Sterilization in the United States* (New Brunswick, N.J.: Rutgers University Press, 2008), 3, 66. Individualists like Herbert Spencer, while they decried statist sterilization programs, insisted that helping the poor only served to perpetuate their weak genes in subsequent generations. His thought is somewhat more complex than he is given credit for in that he distinguishes between societal aid and individual aid, arguing that the latter is less likely to find its way into undeserving hands. He is still, nevertheless, persuaded by a flawed understanding of evolution and the causes of poverty. Herbert Spencer, *The Man versus the State: With Six Essays on Government, Society, and Freedom* (Indianapolis: Liberty Fund, 2000), 105. Arendt also discusses the use of Darwinism to support totalitarian mindsets; see Arendt, *Origins of Totalitarianism*, 178, 180.

14   For a balanced discussion of eugenics and how it was supported by both the Right and the Left, see Larry Arnhart, *Darwinian Conservatism: A Disputed Question* (Exeter, UK: Imprint Academic, 2009), 112–29.

15   Edwin Black, *War against the Weak: Eugenics and America's Campaign to Create a Master Race* (New York: Four Walls Eight Windows, 2003), 279–318.

16   Arendt argues that "the most dangerous aspect of these evolutionist doctrines is that they combined the inheritance concept with the insistence on personal achievement and individual character." Arendt, *Origins of Totalitarianism*, 180.

17   Arendt notes that one contributing factor to early anti-Semitism is that the Jewish people had an unusually strong family life, which put them at odds with and allowed them to resist complete assimilation by the dominant culture. A strong internal family life and the resulting strength of cultural traditions made the Jews a target for totalitarian leaders. Arendt, *Origins of Totalitarianism*, 28.

18   Hayek argues that "fascism is the stage reached after communism has proved an illusion." Hayek, *Road to Serfdom*, 33. Though Hayek did not make this claim explicitly, it could be argued that part of the success of Marxism in the early twentieth century can be attributed to the

effects of industrialization on traditional ways of life. The dissatisfaction with industrialization supported communism, which, when it too failed, devolved into fascism. Hayek argues that with the economic benefits of industrialization came also the "discovery of very dark spots in society, spots which men were no longer willing to tolerate" (20). Similarly, Karl Popper argues that Marx was correct in some ways, primarily in his belief that "unrestrained capitalism" could not last much longer. Karl R. Popper, *The Open Society and Its Enemies*, vol. 2 (Princeton: Princeton University Press, 1966), 193. Where Marx was wrong was in his reliance on the historicist belief that historical progress in the direction of communism was inevitable. Extreme individualism was moderated, not eradicated, after capitalism's weaknesses were demonstrated.

19 Arendt argues that it was ultimately the privatized person, concerned only with family and business, that completed the collectivization of humanity by separating individuals from legitimate public life that might serve as a barrier to totalitarian collectivization: "Nothing proved easier to destroy than the privacy and private morality of people who thought of nothing but safeguarding their private lives." Arendt, *Origins of Totalitarianism*, 338. More prosaically, Hayek argues that "individualism has a bad name today, and the term has come to be connected with egotism and selfishness." Hayek, *Road to Serfdom*, 17. He goes on to distinguish the "true" individualism of classical liberalism from "false" individualism, a common theme in his other writings. See, e.g., his essay "Individualism True and False" in F. A. Hayek, *Individualism and Economic Order* (Chicago: University of Chicago Press, 1948).

20 Consider Arendt's argument: "If totalitarianism takes its own claim seriously, it must come to the point where it has 'to finish once and for all with the neutrality of chess,' that is, with the autonomous existence of any activity whatsoever." Arendt, *Origins of Totalitarianism*, 322.

21 Some of Marxism's appeal in the early twentieth century can be traced to the inconsistent thought of some early laissez-faire thinkers. Herbert Spencer vacillated, e.g., between genuine concern for the poor and suspicion of state activity on the one hand and a support for eugenic programs on the other. This inconsistency allows scholars like Weikart to directly connect Darwinian thought with extreme laissez-faire theory. The ambiguity is not resolved, as scholars debate the legacy of early laissez-faire proponents like William Graham Sumner, who some link directly to the worst abuses of social Darwinism, while others argue such a view unnecessarily simplifies the beliefs of a complex thinker. See, e.g., Robert C. Bannister, "William Graham Sumner's Social Darwinism: A Reconsideration," *History of Political Economy* 5, no. 1 (1973). For a more extreme (and I believe flawed) view, see Richard Weikart, *From Darwin to Hitler:*

Evolutionary Ethics, Eugenics, and Racism in Germany (New York: Palgrave Macmillan, 2004); Richard Weikart, "Laissez-Faire Social Darwinism and Individualist Competition in Darwin and Huxley," *European Legacy* 3, no. 1 (1998): 17–30. Weikart's view tends toward an oversimplified view of both Darwin's work and the laissez-faire thinkers he criticizes. The history of laissez-faire individualism in the United States is particularly complex, combining as it does suspicion of government programs for the poor with support for human rights and a corresponding rejection of slavery.

22 For an excellent discussion of the natural foundation of the family and its role as the foundation for human social life, see "Parent and Child" in Larry Arnhart, *Darwinian Natural Right: The Biological Ethics of Human Nature* (Albany: State University of New York Press, 1998), 89–121.

23 Perhaps the most famous example of the ironic interpretation is that of Leo Strauss, laid out most clearly in Allan Bloom's interpretive essay in his translation of Plato. Plato, *The Republic of Plato*, translated with notes and an interpretive essay by Allan Bloom (New York: Basic Books, 1968). Whether ironically or not, Socrates advocates the expansion of the family to the community as a whole, which helps minimize individual interests in favor of unity, eliminating individual wills in favor of a unified community. Plato, *Republic*, para. 426d.

24 Aristotle argues that "the household is the partnership constituted by nature for [the needs of] daily life." Aristotle, *Politics*, para. 1252b10.

25 Locke attempts to understand the position of the individual as separable from the social milieu. Nevertheless, there are restrictions on man's natural freedom, imposed in part by his rational recognition of his need to live with others. John Locke, *Two Treatises of Government*, ed. Peter Laslett (Cambridge: Cambridge University Press, 1988), 269. Locke's new liberal family is characterized by temporary and limited power, and the affections that bond individuals against their rational self-interest are minimized (311).

26 See chapter 4 for a discussion of Montesquieu, Burke, and the moderate classical liberal tradition.

27 See Alexis de Tocqueville, *Democracy in America*, paperback ed. (Chicago: University of Chicago Press, 2002).

28 See the extensive discussion of Marxism and the family in chapter 2.

29 Chapter 3 discusses Rand's attitudes toward the family.

30 Chapter 1 discusses modern liberal distributive justice and its conflicted attitudes toward the family.

31 See chapter 3 on Rand for further discussion of more moderate individualists like Rothbard.

32 See chapter 5 for a discussion of how the family's breakdown has triggered debates about the proper relationship between public and private and the role of family forms like single motherhood in the debate over welfare reform.

33 The recent extremely contentious debate over health insurance and birth control took place in the context of 43 percent of births occurring outside of wedlock. It hardly seems coincidental that as the family erodes in strength and fails to fulfill traditional functions of economic self-sufficiency, education, and moral and emotional development, policy discussions should center, often passionately, on how to solve these problems. See chapter 5 for an extensive discussion of these issues.

Chapter 1

1 "FastStats: Unmarried Childbearing," Centers for Disease Control and Prevention, last updated January 18, 2013, http://www.cdc.gov/nchs/fastats/unmarry.htm.

2 See, e.g., Winston Fletcher, "The Death of Marriage?" *Guardian*, June 26, 2006, http://www.guardian.co.uk/commentisfree/2006/jun/26/thedeathofmarriage; Derek Thompson, "The Death (and Life) of Marriage in America," *Atlantic*, February 7, 2012, http://www.theatlantic.com/business/archive/2012/02/the-death-and-life-of-marriage-in-america/252640/; Matt Richtel, "Marriage Seen through a Contract Lens," *New York Times*, September 28, 2012, http://www.nytimes.com/2012/09/30/fashion/marriage-seen-through-a-contract-lens.html.

3 See, e.g., Australian researcher Meagan Tyler, "Death of Marriage the Path to Equality," November 28, 2011, http://www.abc.net.au/unleashed/3698436.html. She argues that the history of marriage is fundamentally unequal, with particularly damaging effects for women.

4 Scott Yenor has done an excellent job of describing the modern shift to affectionate or companionate marriage; see Scott Yenor, *Family Politics: The Idea of Marriage in Modern Political Thought* (Waco, Tex.: Baylor University Press, 2011).

5 A recent *New York Times* article discusses an apparent trend toward temporary and renewable marriage contracts. See Richtel, "Marriage Seen through a Contract Lens."

6 Susan Moller Okin, *Justice, Gender, and the Family* (New York: Basic Books, 1999).

7 The foundation of much of contemporary liberalism comes from the work of John Rawls, who argues for a society based on a distribution of justice that can only be decided on behind a "veil of ignorance" where individuals cannot know how they will benefit from the rules they agree to ahead of time. This veil, Rawls argues, supports egalitarianism over hierarchy, since all individuals prefer to not be ruled. The family is considered part of the "basic structure" of society, though Rawls argues that the principles of

justice apply only indirectly to the family (i.e., through the protection of the rights of citizens broadly).

Michael Walzer responded by arguing that it is not that justice is not necessary in the family, but that the family is a peculiar sphere that requires its own contextualized justice. His separation of "spheres" of justice from one another supplemented and refined the traditional liberal split between public and private lives, attempting to leave some areas of human life outside the political realm altogether while still preserving the contemporary liberal belief in egalitarianism and distributive justice. Walzer's work was a way of attempting to bridge the gap between traditional liberalism, primarily concerned with protecting a private sphere from community intervention, and contemporary liberalism, concerned as it is with egalitarian outcomes at the community level. Both Rawls and Walzer attempted to preserve the distinction between public and private, placing family life in the private sphere, separate from most community intervention. See John Rawls, *A Theory of Justice* (Cambridge, Mass.: Belknap Press of Harvard University Press, 1971); Deborah Kearns, "A Theory of Justice—And Love; Rawls on the Family," *Politics* 18, no. 2 (1983): 36–42; Michael Walzer, *Spheres of Justice: A Defense of Pluralism and Equality* (New York: Basic Books, 1983).

8   Okin, *Justice, Gender, and the Family*, 160–67.

9   Rawls was persuaded enough by Okin's argument to respond positively to some of her concerns; see John Rawls and Erin Kelly, *Justice as Fairness: A Restatement* (Cambridge, Mass.: Harvard University Press, 2001), 162–68. He argues that protection against abuse, neglect, "and much else, will, as constraints, be a vital part of family law" (165). Though he is silent on what those laws might be, he argues that protecting the equality of women and children "in particular historical conditions is not for political philosophy to decide" (167). Ultimately, however, Rawls' position on the family is more moderate than Okin's, recognizing as it does that the problem of female inequality, e.g., "cannot be settled by a conception of justice alone" (168).

10   Corey Brettschneider, "The Politics of the Personal: A Liberal Approach," *American Political Science Review* 101, no. 1 (2007): 19.

11   Brettschneider, "Politics of the Personal," 27.

12   Brettschneider, "Politics of the Personal," 26.

13   Even more strongly, Brettschneider argues, "The definition of the private sphere must be found through mutual justification." Brettschneider, "Politics of the Personal," 27.

14   "Private life is not a priori distinct from or 'protected' from the political." Brettschneider, "Politics of the Personal," 27.

15   Okin, *Justice, Gender, and the Family*, 177–84.

16 Brettschneider, "Politics of the Personal," 30.

17 Rawls' work is illuminating in this context. He writes in *A Theory of Justice* that monogamous families play a central role in the basic structure, but then argues in *Justice as Fairness* that any such forms (including homosexual unions), compatible with the demands of justice, are acceptable. He never defends the rejection of polygamy or the acceptance of homosexual unions on any theoretical grounds. See Rawls, *Theory of Justice*, 7; Rawls and Kelly, *Justice as Fairness*, 163.

18 Katie Roiphe has written extensively in *Slate* and the *New York Times* defending single motherhood against all detractors. See, e.g., Roiphe, "In Defense of Single Motherhood," *New York Times*, August 11, 2012, http://www .nytimes.com/2012/08/12/opinion/sunday/in-defense-of-single-mother hood.html; idem, "More Single Moms. So What," *Slate*, February 20, 2012, http://www.slate.com/articles/life/roiphe/2012/02/the_new_york _times_condescends_to_single_moms_.html.

19 Roiphe's ideologically based optimism is challenged by one of her own colleagues, who compiled recent research on the outcomes of single motherhood for women and children and found the evidence against single motherhood as a feminist answer to patriarchy overwhelming. See W. Bradford Wilcox, "The Kids Are Not Really Alright," *Slate*, July 20, 2012, http://www.slate.com/articles/double_x/doublex/2012/07/single_mother hood_worse_for_children_.single.html. It is ironic that Roiphe's experience as an Ivy League–educated writer divorced from a Manhattan lawyer differs dramatically from the majority of single mothers, most of whom are lower-middle class or in poverty, did not choose to get pregnant in the first place, and became pregnant before they could finish their education.

20 Roiphe herself admits that her arguments do not reflect any kind of objective reality: "But as far as I am concerned the studies can continue to show whatever they feel like showing. There are things that can't be measured and quantified in studies." Roiphe, "More Single Moms." She argues elsewhere that "we have a wildly outdated but strangely pervasive idea that single motherhood is worse for children, somehow a compromise, a flawed venture, a grave psychological blow to be overcome, our enlightened modern version of shame. It malingers, this idea; it affects us still." Katie Roiphe, "Single Moms Are Crazy!" *Slate*, October 5, 2011, http:// www.slate.com/articles/double_x/doublex/2011/10/shaming_the_single _mom_do_we_all_secretly_think_single_moms_are_.html. Yet this "idea" is not outdated. The evidence from research to date on single parenthood shows decreased social, educational, and economic outcomes for both children and women.

21 A recent article in the *New York Times* traced the current class divide in the United States to differing rates of marriage, attempting to balance an

objective discussion of the economic benefits of marriage with support and tolerance of single mothers and the challenges they face. The article was immediately attacked by Roiphe for "condescending to" single mothers. See Jason Deparle, "Two Classes in America, Divided by 'I Do,'" *New York Times*, July 14, 2012, http://www.nytimes.com/2012/07/15/us/two-classes-in-america-divided-by-i-do.html; Roiphe, "More Single Moms." Other liberal writers are even going so far as to argue that single motherhood is better than other forms of parenting, precisely because of the economic and psychological burdens children have to overcome. See, e.g, Pamela Gwyn Kripke, "It's Better to Be Raised by a Single Mom," *Slate*, January 3, 2013, http://www.slate.com/articles/double_x/doublex/2013/01/single_moms_are_better_kids_raised_by_single_mothers_are_sturdier.html.

22 Deparle, "Two Classes in America."

23 Roiphe, "In Defense of Single Motherhood."

24 See F. A. Hayek, *The Constitution of Liberty* (Chicago: University of Chicago Press, 1960); Steven Pinker, *The Blank Slate: The Modern Denial of Human Nature* (New York: Viking, 2002); Thomas Sowell, *A Conflict of Visions: Ideological Origins of Political Struggles* (New York: Basic Books, 2007).

25 The very word "discrimination," previously used to describe how one makes distinctions between individuals or objects, is now viewed almost exclusively negatively. The suggestion is that any preference of one person over another is somehow unjust or unfair. The ideal human would not discriminate on any basis whatsoever. Saxonhouse has argued persuasively that this particular aspect of contemporary liberalism, and liberal feminism in particular, is dangerous since it does not assist us in determining what traits are worthy of being discriminated against (cruelty and dishonesty) and those that are not (skin color and ethnicity). See Arlene W. Saxonhouse, *Women in the History of Political Thought: Ancient Greece to Machiavelli* (New York: Praeger, 1985), 165–66.

26 See William Donald Hamilton, "The Genetical Evolution of Social Behaviour. I," *Journal of Theoretical Biology* 7, no. 1 (1964): 1–16. For more recent work, see Jennifer Nerissa Davis and Martin Daly, "Evolutionary Theory and the Human Family," *Quarterly Review of Biology* 72, no. 4 (1997).

27 For Hrdy's work on mothers and infants, see Sarah Hrdy, *Mother Nature: A History of Mothers, Infants, and Natural Selection*, 1st ed. (New York: Pantheon Books, 1999).

28 In more complex species, where chemical means of recognizing kin have largely been lost, the mechanism seems to be habituation, thus opening the way for adoption and other forms of culturally recognized kin relationships that do not necessarily follow genetic lineages. See Debra Lieberman,

John Tooby, and Leda Cosmides, "The Architecture of Human Kin Detection," *Nature* 445, no. 7129 (2007): 727–31.

29 See Ashleigh S. Griffin, "Kin Selection," in *Encyclopedia of Ecology*, ed. Sven Erik Jørgensen and Brian D. Fath (Oxford: Academic Press, 2008), 2057–60, http://www.sciencedirect.com/science/article/pii/B978008045 4054000197; see also Kevin R. Foster, Tom Wenseleers, and Francis L. W. Ratnieks, "Kin Selection Is the Key to Altruism," *Trends in Ecology & Evolution* 21, no. 2 (2006): 57–60.

30 See Robert M. Axelrod, *The Evolution of Cooperation* (New York: Basic Books, 1984), 96–98.

31 For an accessible discussion, see Karen Rosenberg and Wenda Trevathan, "Birth, Obstetrics and Human Evolution," *BJOG: An International Journal of Obstetrics & Gynaecology* 109, no. 11 (2002): 1199–1206, doi:10.1046/j.1471-0528.2002.00010.x.

32 Our relationship with our families lasts well beyond even the period of dependence required by complex social learning. This continued relationship may well have adaptive value, since close family relationships can help young adult humans navigate competitive environments by providing additional resources. When offspring are able to have offspring of their own, turning to family like grandparents, aunts, and uncles is an important way of securing more resources and investment in the resulting offspring. Thus, family relationships that last well past independence may assist in the survival and reproduction of close relatives. Some have postulated that female menopause, e.g., may be an adaptation to secure a grandmother's investment in her grandchildren rather than investing in more of her own offspring who, due to the age of her eggs and her failing energy levels, might not be as "high quality" from an evolutionary perspective as her grandchildren. See, e.g., Mhairi A. Gibson and Ruth Mace, "Helpful Grandmothers in Rural Ethiopia: A Study of the Effect of Kin on Child Survival and Growth," *Evolution and Human Behavior* 26, no. 6 (2005): 469–82.

33 David Bjorklund and Anthony D. Pellegrini, *The Origins of Human Nature: Evolutionary Developmental Psychology* (Washington, D.C.: American Psychological Association, 2002), 257.

34 Bjorklund and Pellegrini, *Origins of Human Nature*, 258.

35 Hrdy, *Mother Nature*, 130–31.

36 Hrdy, *Mother Nature*, 130–31.

37 Hrdy, *Mother Nature*, 137.

38 Hrdy, *Mother Nature*, 138.

39 One study found that oxytocin brain receptors existed in much higher numbers in a monogamous species of vole than in a polygynous, though closely related, species. Hrdy, *Mother Nature*, 140. See also Peter Gray,

Fatherhood: Evolution and Human Paternal Behavior (Cambridge, Mass.: Harvard University Press, 2010), 215.

40 Gray, *Fatherhood*, 219.

41 For a discussion of the benefits of lactation, see Hrdy, *Mother Nature*, 121–23.

42 Hrdy, *Mother Nature*, 154.

43 Both Hrdy and de Waal point out this pattern. Hrdy, *Mother Nature*, 155; Frans de Waal, *Chimpanzee Politics: Power and Sex among Apes*, rev. ed. (Baltimore: Johns Hopkins University Press, 1998).

44 Hrdy, *Mother Nature*, 162–64.

45 Gray, *Fatherhood*, 201–2.

46 Gray, *Fatherhood*, 210.

47 Gray, *Fatherhood*, 213.

48 Gray, *Fatherhood*, 220.

49 Gray discusses one study that compared polygynous pastoralists (with little paternal involvement with children) to hunter-gatherers (with high paternal involvement). The polygynous fathers showed no change in testosterone levels compared with nonfathers, while the high-investing fathers of the hunter-gatherers had lower testosterone levels compared to nonfathers. Gray, *Fatherhood*, 37, 216–17.

50 Lee T. Gettler, James J. McKenna, Thomas W. McDade, Sonny S. Agustin, Christopher W. Kuzawa, "Does Cosleeping Contribute to Lower Testosterone Levels in Fathers? Evidence from the Philippines," *PLoS ONE* 7, no. 9 (2012): e41559, published 5 September 2012, http://www.plosone.org/article/info%3Adoi%2F10.1371%2Fjournal.pone.0041559, doi:10.1371/journal.pone.0041559.

51 Gray, *Fatherhood*, 216–19.

52 Hrdy, *Mother Nature*, 251.

53 See Gray, *Fatherhood*, 126–27; Jane Mendle et al., "Associations between Father Absence and Age of First Sexual Intercourse," *Child Development* 80, no. 5 (2009): 1463–80.

54 Gray, *Fatherhood*, 125–27.

55 Hrdy, *Mother Nature*, 536.

56 Hrdy, *Mother Nature*, 414.

57 Hrdy, *Mother Nature*, 416.

58 My grandfather's sister threw him under the porch when he was an infant, much to his parents' consternation. Sibling rivalry is one danger of allo-mothering by siblings.

59 Bjorklund and Pellegrini, *Origins of Human Nature*, 250–54.

60 Bjorklund and Pellegrini, *Origins of Human Nature*, 252.

61 Individuals were much more likely to attend wedding receptions, babysit, and give money to whole siblings than they were to half siblings, even

though culturally and socially no distinctions between half and whole siblings were made and such distinctions were explicitly discouraged. Bjorklund and Pellegrini, *Origins of Human Nature*, 253.

62 Though humans appear to lack the capacity to recognize related individuals through olfactory cues as other species do, the proximity of mothers and their attitudes toward their own children seems to provide a clue to siblings about who is more closely related to whom. Bjorklund and Pellegrini, *Origins of Human Nature*, 254.

63 Hrdy, *Mother Nature*, 394–404.

64 Even in countries like France with high support for government-subsidized day care, such care is not offered free until six months to a year after the child's birth. The assumption seems to be that children cannot be well taken care of communally until after six months of age. See Sarah Henderson and Alana S. Jeydel, *Women and Politics in a Global World* (New York: Oxford University Press, 2010), 154–55.

65 Hrdy, *Mother Nature*, 399.

66 Monkeys separated from their mothers "explored less and played less. . . . More than two years after the original experiment, infants who had been separated from their mothers remained more timid than infants whose mothers had not been removed." Hrdy, *Mother Nature*, 400.

67 Infants smile and imitate facial expressions from a young age and at around six to eight months of age begin to exhibit a fear of strangers. Until around the age of six months, infants are clearly trying to engage with kin. Hrdy, *Mother Nature*, 414. See also Bjorklund and Pellegrini, *Origins of Human Nature*, 280.

68 Hrdy, *Mother Nature*, 398–99.

69 Nursing is, of course, also somewhat stifling, particularly in a society where nursing in public is awkward and where women spend large parts of the day away from their children. The modern working mother is faced with biological, psychological, and emotional burdens that working fathers cannot understand.

70 Hrdy, *Mother Nature*, 535.

71 I discuss family forms in chapter 5.

72 "In traditional societies (and in historical times in Western culture), children without the support of fathers are more likely to die before reaching adulthood than are father-present children." Bjorklund and Pellegrini, *Origins of Human Nature*, 225.

73 Some research demonstrates that "mating strategies are influenced by a history of parental interaction." Bjorklund and Pellegrini, *Origins of Human Nature*, 248.

74 According to some evidence, "the single most important factor contributing to the success of resilient children is competent parenting." Bjorklund

and Pellegrini, *Origins of Human Nature*, 249. The authors point out, however, that raising competent children is well within the abilities of "ordinary parents."

75 Fathers in hunter-gatherer societies have higher levels of paternal involvement than in other societies, which indicates that paternal care has been an important part of human evolution. Gray, *Fatherhood*, 37.

76 Day care has positive effects for the poorest of children, indicating that competent day care can help counter parental absence or lack of education. However, the effects of day care on social and emotional development for the highest-income children were negative, indicating that such children experience lower levels of resources and emotional care in day care than they would have received at home. Day care seems to have a middling effect on child outcomes, increasing poor children's outcomes and decreasing wealthy students' outcomes. See Sarah L. Friedman, "The National Institute of Child Health and Human Development (NICHD) Study of Early Child Care: A Comprehensive Longitudinal Study of Young Children's Lives" (Human Learning and Behavior Branch, National Institute of Child Health and Human Development, Bethesda, Md., 1992).

77 Even in industrial societies with high levels of social welfare, grandparents continue to invest heavily in children and grandchildren. This finding suggests that true egalitarianism is unlikely, barring complete income redistribution. See Raymond Hames, "Grandparental Transfers and Kin Selection," *Behavioral and Brain Sciences* 33, no. 1 (2010): 26–27.

78 Scandinavian countries are often cited as practical examples of this utopian vision. The reality, of course, is that the Scandinavian countries are egalitarian in part because they are extremely homogeneous, ethnically and economically, and it may be easier to see one's neighbors as kin in a homogeneous culture than in a multiethnic and diverse economy like the United States. For a discussion of social capital in heterogeneous communities, see Alberto Alesina, Eliana La Ferrara, and National Bureau of Economic Research, *Participation in Heterogeneous Communities* (Cambridge, Mass.: National Bureau of Economic Research, 1999).

Chapter 2

1   Egalitarian collectivism is characterized by the combination of the beliefs that the group is the primary unit of political and social activity and that equality is the primary value of political and social importance, in part because inequality is seen as dangerous to collective cohesion. This is not to say that collectivists do not have a theoretical interest in human freedom, but the collectivist understanding of human freedom is usually associated with equality of political and economic conditions, and the center

of that freedom is centered primarily in group activity, rather than in individual activity, and group goods (like stability or equality) are assigned higher values than individual goods (like individual freedoms or privacy). Collectivism is rooted in the preference for community desires above individual desires and a preference for public activity (or collective goods) over private activity (or private goods). The preference for public goods over private goods is directly related to the preference for equality of social conditions, since private activity (particularly private market activity and private property) can lead to inequality.

2   In this chapter I use the term "collectivism" rather than "communitarianism" (excepting where authors refer to their theories as communist or socialist explicitly), because collectivism is associated with a more extreme form of privileging of community interests over individual interests than communitarianism is. Part of the rationale for choosing the term "collectivism" over "communitarianism" is that the former makes clear, through its association with collective property, the movement of the family from the private to the public realm. Communitarianism, moreover, has been adopted by more moderate political thinkers like Don Eberly and Robert Putnam and thus does not emphasize the elimination of the private realm (or rather, the incorporation of the private into the public sphere). Communitarianism might be seen as a more moderate version of collectivism, just as liberalism can be seen as the more moderate version of libertarianism. I use the terms "socialism" and "communism" when the authors discussed refer to themselves using these terms. The collectivism I focus on has egalitarianism as a central component, though such a component is by no means part of all collectivist ideologies, e.g., totalitarian nationalism or the later iterations of national socialism.

3   Marx, *Marx-Engels Reader*, 349–50. That the unequal distribution of property stems from this unequal distribution of labor is a related concern. See, e.g., Richard Pipes, "Human Nature and the Fall of Communism," *Bulletin of the American Academy of Arts and Sciences* 49, no. 4 (1996): 38–53.

4   Karl Marx, *On Education, Women, and Children* (New York: McGraw-Hill, 1975), 55. While not natural in the teleological sense, the family is "natural" for Marx in the sense that men and women are naturally drawn together, but not that such pairings are necessary for human happiness or fulfill human nature in any particular way. Contrast Marx with Aristotle, e.g., who believed that relationships between men and women were a necessary part of human flourishing.

5   Marx makes this connection elsewhere as well. In a letter to Ludwig Kugelmann, he humorously writes, "Social progress can be measured accurately

by the social status of the beautiful sex (the ugly ones included)." Marx, *On Education*, 144.

6 "The slavery latent in the family only develops gradually with the increase of population, the growth of wants, and with the extension of external relations, both of war and of barter." Marx, *Marx-Engels Reader*, 151. See also "The nucleus, the first form, of which lies in the family, where wife and children are the slaves of the husband. This latent slavery in the family, though still very crude, is the first property, but even at this early stage it corresponds perfectly to the definition of modern economists who call it the power of disposing of the labour-power of others" (123–24).

7 Marx, *Marx-Engels Reader*, 49.

8 E.g., "it is self-evident that the abolition of the present system of production must bring with it the abolition of the community of women springing from that system, i.e., of prostitution both public and private." Marx, *Marx-Engels Reader*, 350. "From this relationship one can therefore judge man's whole level of development . . . the relation of man to woman is the most natural relation of human being to human being. . . . In this relationship is revealed, too, the extent to which man's need has become a human need; the extent to which, therefore, the other person as a person has become for him a need—the extent to which he in his individual existence is at the same time a social being" (68–70, emphasis in original). See similar discussions of the growth of familial slavery into other forms of life: "The slavery latent in the family only develops gradually with the increase of population, the growth of wants, and with the extension of external relations, both of war and of barter" (115).

9 Friedrich Engels and Eleanor Burke Leacock, *The Origin of the Family, Private Property and the State, in the Light of the Researches of Lewis H. Morgan* (New York: International Publishers, 1972).

10 See Marx's argument that "the bourgeoisie has torn from the family its sentimental veil, and has reduced the family relation to a mere money relation." Marx, *Marx-Engels Reader*, 68, 338. Marx rejects communal love as a mere extension of property, "in which a woman becomes a piece of communal and common property." Marx, *On Education*, 54.

11 Engels and Leacock, *Origin of the Family*, 128.

12 Engels and Leacock, *Origin of the Family*, 129. Engels argues that the family "is the cellular form of civilized society in which the nature of the oppositions and contradictions fully active in that society can be already studied."

13 The husband "is the bourgeois, and the wife represents the proletariat." Engels and Leacock, *Origin of the Family*, 137.

14 E.g., "monogamy arose from the concentration of considerable wealth in the hands of a single individual—a man—and from the need to bequeath

this wealth to the children of that man and no other." Engels and Leacock, *Origin of the Family*, 129.

15 Engels and Leacock, *Origin of the Family*, 129.

16 The first goal of collectivization is to liberate women from "private sphere" work such as child rearing and housework, bringing "the whole female sex back into public industry." Engels and Leacock, *Origin of the Family*, 137–38.

17 Engels wonders whether "prostitution can disappear without dragging monogamy with it into the abyss." Engels and Leacock, *Origin of the Family*, 138.

18 See Engels' scathing critique: "The bourgeois clap-trap about the family and education, about the hallowed co-relation of parent and child, becomes all the more disgusting, the more, by the action of Modern Industry, all family ties among the proletarians are torn asunder, and their children transformed into simple articles of commerce and instruments of labour." Engels and Leacock, *Origin of the Family*, 350. See also Marx, *On Education*, 25, 91.

19 Engels and Leacock, *Origin of the Family*, 139.

20 It is not accidental that theorists who support a simple or noncontradictory vision of human life are usually those who require the radical restructuring of human social relations. Those who believe human life should not contain "contradictions" like conflicting interests, complex desires, or incompatible moral goods are able to do away with messy prudential considerations and advocate the wholesale restructuring of family, friendship, and community. This wholesale restructuring is usually based on an all-or-nothing view of the individual's relationship with the community.

21 It is no accident that Rand picks up on the Marxist belief in simplicity and noncontradiction, though her moral lens is quite different from Marx's. Both, however, believe the instituting of one particular moral good over all others is necessary and, not surprisingly, the family gets in the way of both their chosen ideals.

22 Many "spontaneous order" theorists advocate such an approach, most notably Friedrich Hayek. See chapter 4 for a detailed discussion of moderate political thinkers who support precisely such a harmonic society.

23 See Arnhart, *Darwinian Natural Right*.

24 Engels and Leacock, *Origin of the Family*, 67.

25 He argues, e.g., that the groups that eventually gave rise to humans required "mutual toleration among the adult males, freedom from jealousy." The initial movement toward ownership of women and children by a single male is the first step toward the capitalist precipice. Engels and Leacock, *Origin of the Family*, 100.

26 Engels and Leacock, *Origin of the Family*, 145.

27 Engels exhorts women to "be a mother not only to your child, but to all the children of the workers and peasants," and further argues that "future society, with its communist emotion and understanding, will be as amazed at such egoistic and anti-social acts as we are when we read of the woman in prehistoric society who loved her own child but found the appetite to eat the child of another tribe." Engels and Leacock, *Origin of the Family*, 145.

28 Cf. Federalist No. 10, where Madison discusses precisely this process of creating variation from a diversity of talents. Passing on these diverse talents and their resulting monetary success through inheritance is considered a central desire in a free society. Jacob Ernest Cooke, *The Federalist* (Middletown, Conn.: Wesleyan University Press, 1961), 57.

29 Kollontai argues, "The needs and interests of the individual must be subordinated to the interests and aims of the collective. On the one hand, therefore, the bonds of family and marriage must be weakened, and on the other, men and women need to be educated in solidarity and the subordination of the will of the individual to the will of the collective." Alexandra M. Kollontai, *Selected Writings of Alexandra Kollontai*, trans. Alix Holt (London: Allison & Busby, 1977), 230.

30 Kollontai, *Selected Writings*, 230.

31 Engels and Leacock, *Origin of the Family*, 94, 101.

32 Alexandra Kollontai takes Marx and Engels' theoretical teachings on the family and applies them in the practical world of the Soviet Revolution. An important balancing act of the early Soviet regime involved convincing peasant women that communism provided a way out of poverty while at the same time assuaging fears that the communists meant to eradicate the family by force. Kollontai focuses not on eradicating the family through coercion but on encouraging close emotional ties to the community that will eventually cause the erosion and death of the nuclear family. Kollontai, not surprisingly, focuses on the gradual abolition of the family as ties to the group become ascendant. Marriage, e.g., will eventually be eradicated since "the closer the emotional ties between the members of the community, the less the need to seek a refuge from loneliness in marriage." Kollontai, *Selected Writings*, 227. The family for Kollontai is not a natural object, but is instead a place in which the individual takes refuge when the external community is unwilling or unable to offer space. It is the community and not the family that is the proper home for individuals, according to Kollontai. Compare her to Aristotle, who argues about holding women and children in common: "There are two things above all which make human beings cherish and feel affection, what is one's own and what is dear; and neither of these can be available to those who govern themselves in this way." Aristotle, *Politics*, 59.

33 Engels and Leacock, *Origin of the Family*, 139.

34 Kollontai, *Selected Writings*, 145.

35 Kollontai argues, "In order to give women the possibility of participating in productive labor without violating her nature or breaking with maternity, it is necessary . . . for the collective to assume all the cares of motherhood that have weighed so heavily on women." Kollontai, *Selected Writings*, 143. Moreover, "Soviet power views maternity as a social task. Soviet power, basing itself on this principle, has outlined a number of measures to shift the burden of motherhood from the shoulders of women to those of the state" (143).

36 Marx argues, "But the 'public' education of the State is rather the rational and public existence of the State. Only the State trains its members in that it makes them into political members; in that it transforms individual aims into public aims, raw drive into ethical tendency, natural independence into spiritual freedom; in that the individual enjoys his life in the life of the totality and the totality enjoys itself in the character of the individual." Marx, *On Education*, 17.

37 Marx, *On Education*, 19.

38 Marx, *Marx-Engels Reader*, 437.

39 The rejection of the traditions of the past (in this case the fir-tree) is the tacit rejection of the red grandmother herself. She recognizes her own irrelevance in this new world, a world uncoupled from traditions, ancestry, and inheritance.

   As Kollontai's Soviets of the future tell the red grandmother, the stars "call us to struggle, to achieve things, to move forward. Let the fir-tree burn out. Our festival is in front of us." Kollontai, *Selected Writings*, 236.

40 Kollontai describes her vision of the future fifty years postrevolution, and one of the primary characteristics is that "life is organized so that people do not live in families but in groups, according to their ages." Kollontai, *Selected Writings*, 233.

41 This generational gap is oddly compelling in Kollontai's vignette. The "red grandmother" who tells the children of 1970 about the revolution realizes that "life had forged ahead. The 'great years' were now only history. . . . The social question was settled." Kollontai, *Selected Writings*, 233.

42 E.g., "the worker-mother must learn not to differentiate between yours and mine: she must remember that there are only our children, the children of Russia's communist workers." Kollontai, *Selected Writings*, 259.

43 According to Kollontai, individualists "destroy all the hypocritical restrictions of the obsolete code of sexual behavior," replacing it with the will of the individual, while socialists believe "sexual problems will only be settled when the basic reorganisation of the social and economic structure of society has been tackled." Kollontai, *Selected Writings*, 237.

44 E.g., "with the transfer of educative functions from the family to society, the last tie holding together the modern isolated family will be loosened." Kollontai, *Selected Writings*, 71.

45 Kollontai, *Selected Writings*, 233.

46 I discuss this middle ground between public and private at length in chapter 4.

47 "Legal norms must regulate the relationship between mother and the socially educated child, and between the father and the child. Fatherhood should not be established through marriage or a relationship of a material nature." E.g., "the law of the workers' collective replaces the right of the parents, and the workers' collective keeps a close watch, in the interests of the unified economy and of present and future labour resources." Kollontai, *Selected Writings*, 228.

48 Kollontai, *Selected Writings*, 228.

49 Of course, these early reproductive programs were not merely Marxist in nature. Eugenics programs in Europe were widespread, and the eugenics program in the United States in its laissez-faire heyday resulted in sixty thousand forced sterilizations. See Black, *War against the Weak*; Allen Garland, "Eugenics and Modern Biology: Critiques of Eugenics, 1910–1945," *Annals of Human Genetics* 75, no. 3 (2011), doi:10.1111/j.1469-1809.2011.00649.x.

50 Kollontai, *Selected Writings*, 228–30.

51 In an attempt to convince peasant women particularly that the Soviets had no intention of forcibly collectivizing the family, Kollontai pleads, "Communist society is not intending to take children away from their parents or to tear the baby from the breast of the mother, and neither is it planning to take violent measures to destroy the family. . . . The joys of parenthood will not be taken away from those who are capable of appreciating them." Kollontai, *Selected Writings*, 258.

52 Of course, such equality assumes that the primary cause of inequality between men and women is that of labor, and thus by freeing women from child care, equality would follow soon after. This view ignores the other sources of differential interest in reproduction between men and women such as the effect of pregnancy alone on women's health and desirability.

53 Kollontai refers to the collective as the "society-family" and goes on to argue that in the final stage, "society, that big happy family, will look after everything." Kollontai, *Selected Writings*, 134. Similarly, "working men and women in all countries are fighting for a society and government that will really become a big happy family, where all children will be equal and the family will care equally for all," and "a great universal family will develop" (139).

54 Kollontai's vignette about the Soviets of the 1970s describes the battles the later Soviet generations fight once the social question is "settled." Having

conquered the "social problem," they move onward into the next battle-field, that of nature. The goal of the postrevolutionary generation is "battling against the only enemy, nature." Kollontai, *Selected Writings*, 233.

55 Engels argues, "Nature works dialectically and not metaphysically; that she does not move in the eternal oneness of a perpetually recurring circle, but goes through a real historical evolution." Friedrich Engels, *Socialism: Utopian and Scientific*, trans. Edward Aveling (Moscow: Progress Publishers, 1970), http://www.marxists.org/archive/marx/works/1880/soc-utop/index.htm.

56 Marx's understanding of Darwinism was quite simplistic, as was most people's in that era. Those like Darwin are "few and far between," however, and the majority of naturalists still hold to the view that nature provides us with a standard, not simply for physical laws, but also for the structures and values of the human world. Engels argues, "Modern materialism is essentially dialectic, and no longer requires the assistance of that sort of philosophy which, queen-like, pretended to rule the remaining mob of sciences." Engels, *Socialism: Utopian and Scientific*.

57 That Marx praises Darwin is interesting because he explicitly rejects the central tenet of Darwinism that there exist innate characteristics of animals, including humans, which affect their behavior and structure their social organizations. Marx combines Darwin's theory of natural selection with a simplistic empiricism: "If man derives all knowledge, sensation, etc., from the world of the senses and sense experience, it follows that the empirical world must be so constructed that in it he experiences the truly human and becomes aware of himself as man." Marx argues, "If properly understood interest is the principle of all morality, it follows that the private interests of men coincide with the interest of humanity." Marx, *On Education*, 22.

58 Marxist theory and Darwinian theory are similar in that they are both empirical sciences, attempting to look at how history moves and the ways in which humans adapt to new environments, but the similarity ends there. For Darwin, the empirical nature of his study comes from the weight of the past and the permanent marks of evolution left by eons of adaptation. Marxist empiricism relies on a simplistic cause-and-effect relationship between social conditions and human behavior that denies the existence of innate tendencies or permanent traits. The Marxist dialectic is a rejection of nature because it represents the successive replacement of one empirical system by another over time, rather than an attempt to understand nature through observation. Richard Pipes summarizes the Soviet regime's attitude toward human nature, saying, "Like all socialists, they subscribed to the Lockean notion that man comes into this world

a blank slate." Richard Pipes, *Property and Freedom* (New York: Vintage, 2000), 40.

59 Marx argues, "So far therefore as labour is a creator of use value, is useful labour, it is a necessary condition, independent of all forms of society, for the existence of the human race; it is an eternal nature-imposed necessity, without which there can be no material exchanges between man and Nature, and therefore no life." Karl Marx, *Capital: A Critique of Political Economy*, vol. 1 (Marx/Engels Internet Archive, 1999).

60 See, e.g., Leo Strauss, *Natural Right and History* (Chicago: University of Chicago Press, 1953).

61 Marx's rejection of nature as a standard is clear in his rejection of the French revolutionaries. The French Revolution and its universalistic appeal to human rights were flawed by "representing, not true requirements, but the requirements of Truth; not the interests of the proletariat, but the interests of Human Nature, of Man in general, who belongs to no class, has no reality, who exists only in the misty realm of philosophical fantasy." Karl Marx, *The Communist Manifesto* (Ebrary Electronic Books; London: Electric Book, 2001), 45.

62 Marx criticizes natural law, e.g., arguing, "The selfish misconception that induces you to transform into eternal laws of nature and of reason, the social forms, springing from your present mode of production and form of property—historical relations that rise and disappear in the progress of production—this misconception you share with every ruling class that has preceded you." Marx, *Communist Manifesto*, 32.

63 Studies of early land ownership, e.g., demonstrate that land was always owned or controlled by the immediate family or by an extended kin network: "cultivated land is, as a rule, held privately. Where it is not in family possession, ownership is usually restricted to the broader kinship group." Pipes, *Property and Freedom*, 46.

64 Kollontai argues, "The form of marriage and of the family is thus determined by the economic system of the given epoch, and it changes as the economic base of society changes." Kollontai, *Selected Writings*, 225.

65 Kollontai argues, "It is not surprising then that family ties should loosen and the family begin to fall apart. The circumstances that held the family together no longer exist. The family is ceasing to be necessary either to its members or to the nation as a whole" (emphasis in original). Kollontai, *Selected Writings*, 253.

66 Engels summarizes the Marxist position, arguing, "In short, the animal merely uses its environment, and brings about changes in it simply by his presence; man by his changes makes it serve his ends, masters it. This is the final, essential distinction between man and other animals, and once again

it is labor that brings about this distinction." Engels and Leacock, *Origin of the Family*, 260.

67 One problem with a rejection of nature is that such a move undermines the very arguments that might support the Marxist emphasis on equality. If there is no such thing as a nature and if human nature is infinitely malleable by material and social conditions, there is no ground for preferring one way of life to another. Certainly, there is no real argument to be made for nonoppression, e.g., Marx and Engels recognize this, structuring their rhetoric in a way that eschews normative arguments in favor of empirical arguments based on the inevitability of socialist revolution. But without a stable nature or a historical trajectory rooted in such nature, Marxism must fall back on a kind of deification of history, a kind of materialistic "First Mover" who sets this progressive movement in motion.

68 "If man is by nature social, he will develop his true nature only in society, and the power of his nature must be measured not by the power of separate individuals but by the power of society." Marx, *On Education*, 22.

69 See Pipes' account of property ownership in small children as an extension of this argument. Pipes, *Property and Freedom*.

70 See Hayek, *Constitution of Liberty*.

71 Barbara Evans Clements, *Daughters of Revolution: A History of Women in the USSR* (Arlington Heights, Ill.: Harlan Davidson, 1994).

72 Clements, *Daughters of Revolution*, 80.

73 Though Kollontai herself offered many practical policies to facilitate the movement of Soviet society forward, she trusted in the inevitability of historical progress. As a Kollontai scholar argues, "She gives the impression that with the passage of time all the problems of marriage and the family will mechanically solve themselves." Kollontai, *Selected Writings*, 295–96.

74 The term "familism" became popular in the sociological literature to describe societies whose central focus was the nuclear or extended kin group. While the term is problematic on some levels, it is a useful counterpart to the "collectivism" of the family. See Lionel Tiger and Joseph Shepher, *Women in the Kibbutz* (New York: Harcourt Brace Jovanovich, 1975). "The emphasis on the family as the basic social unit in kibbutz life has been called familism. We use the term in a relative sense; what the kibbutzim practice is far from the true familism of the traditional Chinese, for example. But seen in the light of the early kibbutz ideology about the family, the term is justified today" (225).

75 Kollontai's concerns with the later Soviet regime were rarely expressed; as she spent more and more time abroad on diplomatic work her role in practical policy making correspondingly shrank. She lived to see the Stalin regime give up on almost every hope she had for women's liberation from home and hearth. Kollontai, *Selected Writings*, 297–98.

76   Clements, *Daughters of Revolution*, 76.

77   Early on in the Soviet experience with communism, the family survived, in part because it was politically and economically useful, but also because the Communist Party recognized that eradicating family and the stability it offered would be dangerous to the movement, even as its continued existence threatened the egalitarianism ostensibly at the root of Soviet ideology. Later, as the goals of communism became more and more elusive, the government became more authoritarian. The government then began using the family as a weapon of terror, arresting sons and fathers and encouraging divorce of those arrested. Clements, *Daughters of Revolution*, 78.

78   One of the early failures of communist ideology was the recognition that free sexual pairing, at least in the current transition period, was simply too dangerous for women who would be left with few resources to raise children, particularly since the state was in no financial position to really help them. The movement toward contract marriages was intended to help alleviate this problem by reestablishing the family as the fundamental economic unit. Kollontai, *Selected Writings*, 294.

79   Kollontai, *Selected Writings*, 299.

80   The kibbutzim experience is useful as well because they have been studied extensively for over fifty years, providing social scientists with four or more generations of attitudes toward family structures.

81   Talmon argues, "Kibbutzim curtailed family obligations and attachments and took over most family functions," and "the emphasis on activities outside the family orbit and the masculine-role prototype prevented any intense identification in women with the role of mother, and curbed the desire for children." Yonina Talmon, *Family and Community in the Kibbutz* (Cambridge, Mass.: Harvard University Press, 1972), 7.

82   Melford E. Spiro, "Is the Family Universal?" *American Anthropologist* 56, no. 5 (1954): 839–46.

83   E.g., "the whole system was organized on the basis of a separation between the family and its offspring." Talmon, *Family and Community*, 7. Other attributes of the kibbutzim included sex relations based on "freedom of choice and informality," because "romantic love, by its very nature exclusive, sets lovers apart from their comrades; based as it is on intense emotion, it is in addition not readily amenable to social control, and it can easily get out of hand" (9). Egalitarian parenting was based on the rational agreement of children, and children of the community were referred to as "son" or "daughter" by every individual, not only by their biological parents" (11). One scholar even somewhat retracted his earlier article that had argued that the kibbutzim was proof that the family was not in fact a universal social structure. Spiro, "Is the Family Universal?" Part of the

problem with his first analysis is that he relies on Murdock's somewhat restrictive definition of the family, and the kibbutzim families did not in fact meet that stringent definition. See George Peter Murdock, *Social Structure* (Oxford: Macmillan, 1949).

84 Tiger says about his first long-term study of the kibbutz, "The results startled us. We had had some general notions about the relative intractability of sex roles despite basic social change; we were nonetheless surprised at how the major innovations in kibbutz women's lives have failed to stimulate the expected new social patterns." Tiger and Shepher, *Women in the Kibbutz*, 6.

85 Tiger argues that in the later kibbutzim, "the nuclear family is the most important social unit to both the individual and the social structure," and "we have seen that the most thoroughgoing change the kibbutz has undergone since its early days is in the importance of the family." Tiger and Shepher, *Women in the Kibbutz*, 207, 214.

86 See Talmon, *Family and Community;* Tiger and Shepher, *Women in the Kibbutz.*

87 Tiger and Shepher, *Women in the Kibbutz*, 227. Talmon points to the gradual "circumvention of communal accommodation" as a key symptom of increasing familism. Talmon, *Family and Community*, 86.

88 Tiger and Shepher, *Women in the Kibbutz*, 254.

89 Tiger argues that this trend continued throughout the 1970s. Tiger and Shepher, *Women in the Kibbutz*, 254.

90 Talmon, *Family and Community*, 3.

91 Talmon points out that "public interest and parental emotions here join issue: whereas the former would tend to remove children from the domain of the individual, the latter would tend to separate them from the authority of the community." Talmon, *Family and Community*, 84.

92 Talmon, *Family and Community*, 4.

93 Talmon, *Family and Community*, 73.

94 Talmon argues that the desire to limit the family is found in "two extremes of a continuum—in extreme collectivism at one end and in extreme individualism at the other—whereas the tendency toward family expansion was anchored in moderate collectivism and in familism." Talmon, *Family and Community*, 73.

95 The reintroduction of family forms is well summarized by Talmon, a kibbutz scholar, who notes how the family moderates collective ideals, not the other way around: "The violent antifamilism of the extreme collectivist revolutionary phase gradually abates and disappears. It is superseded by a moderate collectivism that regards the family as a potential though somewhat dangerous ally and employs it for the attainment of collective goals." Talmon, *Family and Community*, 73.

96 Isabel Kershner, "The Kibbutz Sheds Socialism and Gains Popularity," *New York Times*, August 27, 2007, http://www.nytimes.com/2007/08/27/world/middleeast/27kibbutz.html?scp=4&sq=kibbutzim&st=cse. A central contention of the piece is that "the new kibbutz seeks a subtler balance between collective responsibility and individual freedom, with an emphasis on community and values."

97 Many intentional communities, e.g., have limits on the ratio of children to adults. Internet groups like "radical moms," those with radical political beliefs who argue that radical social movements need to take account of and provide a place for the family, demonstrate that despite ideological opposition to the family, it remains a deep-seated human need. See "RADical Moms Resources," n.d., accessed May 26, 2013, http://radicalmoms.wordpress.com. A member of Twin Oaks intentional community explains that they attempt to keep the child to adult ratio at roughly one to five, in part to balance the differential desires of members of the community. Lauren Hall, "Twin Oaks Member Interview" (personal correspondence, June 8, 2011).

98 Tiger and Shepher, *Women in the Kibbutz*, 4.

99 For another discussion of human nature and collectivism, see Arnhart, *Darwinian Conservatism; Arnhart, Darwinian Natural Right.*

100 The economic problem is, of course, an extension of the problem of human nature.

101 As one thinker puts it, "Human goods conflict with one another—and this makes family life much more enduring, important, and indispensable than Marx and Engels had thought." Yenor, *Family Politics*, 156.

102 What this specific kind of equality will look like will be laid out in the chapter on political moderation (chapter 4).

Chapter 3

1 For an overview of this critique, see Jennifer Morse, *Love & Economics: Why the Laissez-Faire Family Doesn't Work* (Dallas: Spence Publishing, 2001).

2 I define radical individualism as the preference for individual-level action above all other kinds of social action, including familial activity. Radical individualism also often includes (and does in the case of Rand) the prioritizing of individual liberty at the expense of all other values without regard to circumstances or enduring human desires. Radical individualism differs from more moderate individualism in its rejection of a distinction between public and private spheres and in its assertion that individual freedom is the highest and perhaps only valuable moral good. Most radical individualism also ascribes to the belief in "moral universalism" or the

idea that "one's life and one's society can be dispassionately and objectively evaluated." See, e.g., Tibor Machan and Douglas Rasmussen, eds., *Liberty for the Twenty-First Century: Contemporary Libertarian Thought* (Lanham, Md.: Rowman & Littlefield, 1995), 265.

3   Most libertarians or individualists do not discuss the family in any length, partly because there is a sort of tacit assumption that the family is important for social cohesion but not terribly important when it comes to individual freedom from coercion. Other reasons may be at play here, some of which are discussed later, but even the libertarians who study the family argue that their study is, by and large, one that requires trying to understand the family's absence in individualist literature rather than analyzing robust arguments for or against it. Steven Horwitz's work on the family is a notable exception. See Steven Horwitz, "The Functions of the Family in the Great Society," *Cambridge Journal of Economics* 29, no. 5 (2005): 669–84, doi:10.1093/cje/bei041; Steven Horwitz, "Two Worlds at Once: Rand, Hayek, and the Ethics of the Micro- and Macro-Cosmos," *Journal of Ayn Rand Studies* 6, no. 2 (2005): 375–403.

4   Rand argues, "Only individual men have the right to decide when or whether they wish to help others; society—as an organized political system—has no rights in the matter at all." Ayn Rand and Nathaniel Branden, *The Virtue of Selfishness: A New Concept of Egoism* (New York: Signet, 1964), 80.

5   She argues, "Can man derive any personal benefit from living in a human society? Yes—if it is a human society. The two great values to be gained from social existence are: knowledge and trade." Rand and Branden, *Virtue of Selfishness*, 32.

6   See, e.g., Galt's theory that "the symbol of all human relations among such men, the moral symbol of respect for human beings, is the trader. . . . A trader is a man who earns what he gets and does not give or take the undeserved." Ayn Rand, *Atlas Shrugged*, centennial ed. (New York: Penguin, 2005), 102 (emphasis in original).

7   The philosopher Akston tells Dagny, "Man is a social being, but not in the way the looters preach." Rand, *Atlas Shrugged*, 747 (emphasis in original). Rand's sociality requires that individuals always be treated as primary. This exclusive focus on the individual is the foundation of the consistency in her work.

8   Rand, *Atlas Shrugged*, 747.

9   Dagny corrects Rearden early in their relationship, arguing, "If you had asked me for more than you meant to me, I would refuse. . . . If ever the pleasure of one has to be bought by the pain of the other, there better be no trade at all. . . . " Rand, *Atlas Shrugged*, 425.

10 Rand apparently held herself to the same standards in her own personal life, breaking off her relationship with Nathanial Branden, not after he cheated on her (they had an open relationship), but because he felt it necessary to lie about it. See Mimi Gladstein, *The New Ayn Rand Companion* (Westport, Conn.: Greenwood Press, 1999), 17.

11 Dagny's brother Jim, e.g., accuses her of inhumanity: "You're lucky—you've never had any feelings. You've never felt anything at all." Rand, *Atlas Shrugged*, 23.

12 When Rearden and the philosopher pirate Ragnar Danneskjöld meet, Rearden accuses Ragnar of being an altruist, giving up his life and time for others. Ragnar replies that far from altruism, he is "investing my time in my own future." He continues, "Because my only love, the only value I care to live for, is that which has never been loved by the world, has never won recognition or friends or defenders: human ability." Rand, *Atlas Shrugged*, 580.

13 Rand, *Atlas Shrugged*, 580.

14 Rand, *Atlas Shrugged*, 199.

15 Chris Matthew Sciabarra, *Ayn Rand: The Russian Radical* (University Park: Pennsylvania State University Press, 1995).

16 Rand parodies the collectivist impulse when she has an anonymous economist remark, "Of what importance is an individual in the titanic collective achievements of our industrial age?" Rand, *Atlas Shrugged*, 27. Similarly, Boyle, a leading "looter," rails against the "anti-social individual," arguing, "After all, private property is a trusteeship held for the benefit of society as a whole" (46).

17 Dr. Pritchett, a prominent "looter," describes his support of the bill: "But I believe I made it clear that I am in favor of it, because I am in favor of a free economy. A free economy cannot exist without competition. Therefore, men must be forced to compete. Therefore, we must control men in order to force them to be free." Rand, *Atlas Shrugged*, 132.

18 Rand, *Atlas Shrugged*, 132.

19 Rearden slowly learns to fight against what collectivists describe as "the noblest ideal—that man live for the sake of his brothers, that the strong work for the weak, that he who has ability serve him who hasn't." Rand, *Atlas Shrugged*, 223.

20 E.g., Rand describes the slow destruction of Starnesville, after the collectivization of the factory, through the eyes of one of the workers: "We're all one big family, they told us, we're all in this together." Rand, *Atlas Shrugged*, 662.

21 One worker describes how familial love is twisted by collectivist ideology, sighing, "Love of our brothers? That's when we learned to hate our

brothers for the first time in our lives. We began to hate them for every meal they swallowed." Rand, *Atlas Shrugged*, 665.

22 Rand, *Atlas Shrugged*, 147.

23 The engineer, before being forced to send a trainload of people to their deaths, reflects on what the looter mentality has wrought: "He saw, in astonished horror, that the choice which he now had to make was between the lives of his children and the lives of the passengers on the Comet. A conflict of this kind had never been possible before. It was by protecting the safety of the passengers that he had earned the security of his children; he had served one by serving the other; there had been no clash of interests, no call for victims." Rand, *Atlas Shrugged*, 598.

24 Rand, *Atlas Shrugged*, 60.

25 Rand directly links families with chance, arguing, "The world of chance— of families, meals, schools, people, of aimless people dragging the load of some unknown guilt—was not theirs, could not change him, could not matter." Rand, *Atlas Shrugged*, 98.

26 Rand, *Atlas Shrugged*, 91.

27 Cherryl, perhaps one of the most tragic characters in the work, explains why she left her family: "I thought if I didn't get out, it would get me— I'd rot all the way through, like the rest of them." Rand, *Atlas Shrugged*, 261. Unfortunately, she flees from her family of looters into the arms of Jim Taggart, a man who does not want to be loved for any reason other than blind affection. Cherryl's demise is a cautionary tale about the effects of the looting philosophy on those with opposing principles who are not strong enough to fight it.

28 Jim argues that his marriage creates certain duties for Dagny: "Don't you think that a person such as your brother's bride does deserve some interest?" Rand, *Atlas Shrugged*, 400. Dagny, of course, replies in the negative.

29 Rand, *Atlas Shrugged*, 93.

30 Rand, *Atlas Shrugged*, 537.

31 Akston describes his own struggle during the hardships born by the three heroes: "It was the kind of emotion that makes men capable of killing— when I thought that the purpose of the world's trend was to destroy these children, that these three sons of mine were marked for immolation." Rand, *Atlas Shrugged*, 788.

32 Rand, *Atlas Shrugged*, 780.

33 Rand, *Atlas Shrugged*, 785.

34 The attitude of the valley toward family life demonstrates the difficulty of Rand's approach in practice and how the family will, at least eventually, become the thorn in the side of the Objectivist ideal. Rand's assertion that life be constructed of independent convictions is not compatible with parenthood and family life generally. What happens when one of the

Objectivist children decides he or she prefers equality to liberty? Would mothers and fathers, in turn, support the banishment of children who reject the Objectivist way of life? One can only assume that Rand's answer is that children raised properly (by the right parents, of course) would not reject the values of the society and that if an individual did reject his parents' trader values, the parents themselves would be willing and able to reject their child as objective observers. The difficulty with which Rearden casts off his admittedly worthless family should demonstrate the difficulty of eradicating unchosen ties, even in an ideal world. That Rand has the valley mother speak to Dagny when her children are young, before they become fully independent individuals, indicates that there are some practical difficulties with the Objectivist family that Rand herself does not know how to confront.

35 Other scholars, such as Friedrich Hayek and Larry Arnhart, have pointed out that true collectivism is only possible in the family. See Arnhart, *Darwinian Conservatism*.

36 See Horwitz, "Two Worlds at Once." Horwitz argues against Rand's moral universalism and in favor of a Hayekian moral contextualism in which the moral rules of the market differ from those of the family.

37 "Once, you believed it was 'only a compromise': you conceded it was evil to live for yourself but moral to live for the sake of your children. Then you conceded that it was selfish to live for your children, but moral to live for your community." Rand, *Atlas Shrugged*, 1055. Peter Singer, a philosopher focusing on distributive justice, argues for precisely this kind of moral movement away from the individual and the family and toward cosmopolitanism. See, e.g., Peter Singer, *The Expanding Circle: Ethics and Sociobiology*, 1st ed. (New York: Farrar, Straus & Giroux, 1981). Thus, the claim that Rand misunderstands the goal of theorists of distributive justice is at least somewhat belied by the explicit arguments of these theorists.

38 E.g., Sciabarra argues, "Devotion to the Family was a con game in Rand's view, in which the weaker and irresponsible family members are dependent on those who are stronger. Frequently, the relations within the family mirror those of master and slave. Just as the stronger members are exploited, they are also obeyed." Sciabarra, *Ayn Rand*, 350.

39 One inhabitant describes the valley: "Here, we trade achievements, not failures—values, not needs. We're free of one another, yet we all grow together." Rand, *Atlas Shrugged*, 772.

40 As Rearden opines early in the work, "I can't stand people who need me." Rand, *Atlas Shrugged*, 276.

41 Rand, *Atlas Shrugged*, 276.

42 Rand, *Atlas Shrugged*, 1019.

43 Rand, *Atlas Shrugged*, 307.

44 Rand, *Atlas Shrugged*, 314.

45 Jim confronts his new wife: "So you think that love is a matter of mathematics, of exchange, of weighing and measuring, like a pound of butter
on a grocery counter? I don't want to be loved for anything. I want to
be loved for myself—not for anything I do or have or say or think. For
myself—not for my body or mind or words or works or actions." Cherryl,
understandably bewildered, replies, "But then . . . what is *yourself?*" Rand,
Atlas Shrugged, 883 (emphasis in original).

46 Rearden rejects this kind of thoughtless unconditional attachment, reflect-
ing in despair, "They professed to love him for some unknown reason and
they ignored all the things for which he could wish to be loved." Rand,
Atlas Shrugged, 37.

47 Galt tells Dagny that "some of us have wives and children, but there is a
mutual trade involved in that, and a mutual payment," and the rules of
the valley are clear that individuals can only enter on the basis of their own
judgment. Rand, *Atlas Shrugged*, 760.

48 Rand does not adequately separate legitimate emotional attachments from
illegitimate ones, which means that she cannot tell us when a family is
a trader family and when it is a looter family. Rand solves this problem
by providing only families on the extremes. Rearden's parasitic family is
contrasted with the trader wives and husbands of the valley, but of course
families themselves rarely come in these shapes and sizes.

49 For an example of this Randian view, see Richard B. McKenzie and Gordon Tullock, *The New World of Economics* (Homewood, Ill.: Richard D.
Irwin, 1985). They view family as a contract, discuss the benefits and costs
of marriage (76), and argue that "the benefits of marriage and the family
are derived mainly from the ability of the family to produce goods and
services wanted" (79). They do, however, argue that the family "may, and
very likely will, also agree to make many decisions by democratic or collective action" (77). Overall, the focus of their discussion is on the family
as a kind of trading relationship, based on the rational interests of the
constituent individuals (81, 83). Part of Rand's criticism is the implied
slippery slope between living for one's family and then living for the collective: "Once, you believed it was 'only a compromise': you conceded it
was evil to live for yourself but moral to live for the sake of your children.
Then you conceded that it was selfish to live for your children, but moral
to live for your community." Rand, *Atlas Shrugged*, 1055.

50 Rand's rejection of the farce of unconditional love, where such love means
to be loved for no reason at all, does not mean that the opposite is necessarily true. Rand is not wrong about the existence of "looter" families.
Rearden's family is the extreme of exploitation and parasitism, and one
cannot but help be sympathetic when he describes the initial trap in which

he finds himself: "I thought it was my duty to grant an unearned love to a wife I despised, an unearned respect to a mother who hated me, an unearned support to a brother who plotted for my destruction." Rand, *Atlas Shrugged*, 858.

51 Rearden's rejection of his mother's request for nepotistic employment of his useless brother is recognized by the reader as both rational and just. Rearden's brother is not only parasitic, but he even attempts to sabotage Rearden's business. No just person would argue that Rearden owes his adult brother anything under the circumstances.

52 It is perhaps no surprise that as the capitalism idealized by Rand's trader mentality spread, the desire to quantify the worth of familial caretaking grew, and such caretaking inevitably moved outside the household into the public sphere, where such relationships do have a price and thus do represent trade. The lack of multigenerational homes and the increasing incidence of group homes, institutions, and day-care centers all demonstrate that while we have freed people from the burden of caring for dependent relatives, we have shifted that burden onto the community as a whole. Rand is not forced to deal with the problem of how to pay for the existence of true dependents in society because she has created a society with no legitimate dependents.

53 Rand criticizes the tendency to require generations to sacrifice for each other: "Only such a [collectivized] brain can contemplate as 'moral' or 'desirable' the sacrifice of generations of living men for the alleged benefits which public science or public industry or public concerts will bring to the unborn. . . . Two generations of Russians have lived, toiled and died in misery, waiting for the abundance promised by their rulers, who pleaded for patience and commanded austerity." Rand and Branden, *Virtue of Self-ishness*, 84.

54 Dagny's relationship to Nat Taggart, regardless of how hard she tries to make it one of choice, is still one of blood, and Francisco's birth and education in an industrial family must have played some role in the kind of man he became. In fact, much is made of how Francisco, in his early incarnation as playboy, has betrayed the values of his family. No one knows at the time, of course, that his goal is to create a world consistent with precisely those familial values.

55 One Rand scholar attempts to defend Rand's view of the family: "What Rand objected to was the practice of those who sought to substitute their lineage for an authentic self-esteem. Self-efficacy and self-worth cannot be derived from others—past or present." Sciabarra, *Ayn Rand*, 344. But again, most people would object to that kind of extreme.

56 Rand, *Atlas Shrugged*, 181 (emphasis added).

57 See, e.g., Rearden's conversation with harvester operator Ward: "So I'll say that what I need the steel for is to save my own business. Because it's mine." Rand, *Atlas Shrugged*, 211. Dagny reflects on the importance of property rights as well: "Ownership—she thought, glancing back at him—weren't there those who knew nothing of its nature and doubted its reality?" (240). In both cases, ownership and the extension of self into an object is what supports the desire for innovation and improvement.

58 Rand, *Atlas Shrugged*, 1080.

59 Rand, *Atlas Shrugged*, 208.

60 Hayek explicitly argues that different rules apply in the "microcosmos" of family and friends than apply in the "macrocosmos" of markets. The primary reason I consider his individualism more moderate than Rand's is that he recognizes the importance of context in ethical decision making and does not attempt to apply one principle consistently across human affairs. See F. A. Hayek, *The Fatal Conceit: The Errors of Socialism*, University of Chicago Press ed. (Chicago: University of Chicago Press, 1989).

61 Rand, *Atlas Shrugged*, 138.

62 Rand, *Atlas Shrugged*, 948.

63 When Dagny and Rearden take a cross-country tour, both comment on the wilderness they pass through, noting the lack of billboards. Both clearly feel that the achievements of civilization trump those of nature and that man's natural role is to triumph over that nature.

64 A new branch of "deep" libertarianism, however, pushes for the inclusion of social power as a potentially dangerous limitation on human freedom. Somewhat ironically, these libertarians follow John Stuart Mill, one of the founders of modern liberalism. At some point, radical libertarianism meets up with radical collectivism in the creation of anarchic consensus-based societies. See Kerry Howley's work at *Reason* magazine and her blog (http://kerryhowley.com/) as an example.

65 I follow Hayek here in his distinction between "true individualism" and "false individualism." See Hayek, *Constitution of Liberty*.

66 See Stephen Cullen, *Children in Society: A Libertarian Critique* (London: Freedom Press, 1991).

67 Rothbard, e.g., follows Rand's individualist epistemology, arguing, "The individualist holds that only individuals exist, think, freely choose, and act." Murray Newton Rothbard, *For a New Liberty: The Libertarian Manifesto* (Auburn, Ala.: Ludwig von Mises Institute, 2006), 37.

68 The individualist concern with the family's collective nature is ultimately shortsighted, however. Failing to deal with the family as a peculiar institution with its own set of rules actually weakens individualist arguments against government coercion. Murray Rothbard, e.g., defines freedom as "a condition in which a person's ownership rights in his own body and his

legitimate material property are NOT invaded, are not aggressed against."
He argues, " 'Crime' is an act of aggression against a man's property right,
either in his own person or his materially owned objects." Rothbard, *For
a New Liberty*, 41 (emphasis in original). This of course begs the question
of whether crimes against one's children harm parents. Kidnapping, as
mentioned above, is one example where it would be difficult to argue that
a crime has not been committed against the parents as well as against the
child. His definition cannot take into account crimes against individuals
such as kidnapping, which is a crime against both the child and his parents. Similarly, in a chapter on education, Rothbard decries governmental
coercion in the realm of education but is silent on who is responsible for
providing it. It is the family of an individual, and not the individual in
question, who decides the kind of education that individual will get. Rothbard's discussion of freedom requires something other than one's body and
one's legitimate property, unless we grant that families are, in fact, a kind
of property of an individual because they are an extension of that individual's body (in both a literal and figurative sense). The right to educate
one's children is neither a right founded in a simplistic understanding of
body or property but instead implies a kind of ownership of parent over
child that recognizes the right of that parent to make fundamental decisions on the child's behalf.

69 One of Rand's characters describes the slow slide into despotism: "Once,
you believed it was 'only a compromise': you conceded it was evil to live
for yourself but moral to live for the sake of your children. Then you conceded that it was selfish to live for your children, but moral to live for your
community," and so on until the individual is eradicated in the name of
the good of all humankind. Rand, *Atlas Shrugged*, 1055.

70 Rand, *Atlas Shrugged*, 206–7.

71 One of the very few libertarian scholars studying the family, Steven Horwitz, argues that Rand's philosophy is ultimately less successful than that
of classical liberals like Friedrich Hayek, because Rand does not recognize
that the moral rules of the trader may not work well in the collective of the
family and vice versa. See Horwitz, "Two Worlds at Once."

72 A nice contrast is the social individualism espoused by Friedrich Hayek.
Rand recognizes intergenerational continuity in the market but not in the
family and social worlds. Hayek recognizes the importance of intergenerational continuity because he understands the limitations on individual
reason and the importance of habit and custom, which are the purview of
the family. Rand's businessman, with his long-sighted wisdom, recognizes
the importance of planning ahead, but the future success of his enterprise relies also on the existence of other rational individuals in the future
who will carry on his plans. Rand's work is conflicted; she recognizes the

need for generational continuity in business endeavors but rejects the very institutions, like the family, that are likely to pass on and preserve these individualistic values over time. This conflict is based on Rand's insistence that individuals must be self-made and thus not the vessels into which the values of a particular family (and perhaps through the family the greater society) are poured. For Rand, the goal of the family is, as one thinker puts it, to "facilitate, and then get out of the way of, the child's traverse toward individuality and independence." Horwitz argues that for Rand, "what mattered most was the development of those mental skills and habits that would encourage individuality and rationality." On the other hand, for "Hayek, the key was the intergenerational transmission of the discipline of rule following." Horwitz, "Two Worlds at Once," 394.

73 Horwitz argues that the family is an important commitment mechanism that helps reinforce the bonds people have to their communities. While Rand sees these bonds as dangerous, more moderate individualists like Hayek see them as beneficial to the commitments required in a voluntary society: "Freedom from external coercion is necessary to generate and sustain that commitment, but it is not sufficient, which is why the family can and should play such a central and positive role for Hayek." Horwitz, "Two Worlds at Once," 395.

74 Machan and Rasmussen, *Liberty for the Twenty-First Century*, 259.

Chapter 4

1 That era, incidentally, is perhaps the main era in which the conflict between individualism and collectivism becomes clear, and the thought of the eighteenth century lays the groundwork for the more severe conflicts between individualism and collectivism that culminate in the twentieth century.

2 I use Tocqueville's phrase here, since it is indicative of the rejection of extreme or overly simplistic political ideals in favor of more nuanced and more moderate ideals that can be combined and harmonized with other political goods. See Tocqueville, *Democracy in America*.

3 Scott Yenor's recent work is perhaps the most comprehensive treatment of the family in political thought since Elshtain's (1982) work. See Yenor, *Family Politics*; Jean Elshtain, *The Family in Political Thought* (Amherst: University of Massachusetts Press, 1982). Neither, however, deals with either Montesquieu or Burke's work at length.

4 See Francis P. Canavan, "Edmund Burke's Conception of the Role of Reason in Politics," *Journal of Politics* 21, no. 1 (1959): 60.

5 See, e.g., Elshtain, *Family in Political Thought*.

6 He lists the procreative desire as the third law, arguing, "The charm that the two sexes inspire in each other by their difference would increase this

pleasure, and the natural entreaty they always make to one another would be a third law [of nature]." Charles de Secondat, baron de La Brède et de Montesquieu, *The Spirit of the Laws* (New York: Cambridge University Press, 1989), 7. Montesquieu rejects the early modern theory of a state of nature based on individuals who are unconnected by political or social bonds. Instead, we are born into families. The family is the first of the social groups to which men belong. It is only after men enter society that the state of war begins. Losing their fear of one another that characterized their behavior presociety, humans "seek to turn to their favor the principal advantages of this society," which results in a state of war (7). This is one of the many important respects in which Montesquieu differs from Locke and Hobbes. Out of this state of war, laws are created to control it, including international law, political laws, and civil laws. The family remains central since "political power necessarily includes the union of many families" (8).

7   Montesquieu's apparent relativism is in fact a recognition that nature works through general natural laws that are applied in particular situations: "It is better to say that the government most in conformity with nature is the one whose particular arrangement best relates to the disposition of the people for whom it is established," and "laws should be so appropriate to the people for whom they are made that it is very unlikely that the laws of one nation can suit another." Montesquieu, *Spirit of the Laws*, 8. A more extensive discussion of the relationships between the different levels of law is below.

8   Montesquieu references, e.g., the Cretan practice of homosexuality as a means of birth control described by Aristotle. He believes this practice violates the natural law of modesty. Montesquieu, *Spirit of the Laws*, 438.

9   Montesquieu, *Spirit of the Laws*, 200–201.

10 Montesquieu, *Spirit of the Laws*, 497.

11 Montesquieu refers to attachment to kin as "that which is best in the world by its nature." Montesquieu, *Spirit of the Laws*, 271.

12 Montesquieu recognizes that such conflicts cannot always be avoided. His long section on inheritance and demographic concerns demonstrate that what happens in the family does not always stay in the family. Yet he is clear that in cases where a violation of mores is purely internal to the family (i.e., sexual activity, adultery, or the decision to enter into or exit a marriage), the state should have as little to do with the decision as possible.

13 Burke's treatment of family and politics differs from Montesquieu's partially because he is attacking a particular evil that he fears will spread to England. The natural rights of the French revolutionaries have been used, Burke believes, to overturn the customary rights that are the protection of both individual and society. Burke, *Reflections on the Revolution*, 151.

14 Of the two ways of understanding nature, Burke clearly rejects a mathematical or physical understanding of nature (à la Hobbes) and focuses instead on an organic or biological understanding of nature that focuses not on mathematical certainty but on slow organic growth.

15 Burke, *Reflections on the Revolution*, 121.

16 He argues, "By a constitutional policy, working after the pattern of nature, we receive, we hold, we transmit our government and our privileges, in the same manner in which we enjoy and transmit our property and our lives." Burke, *Reflections on the Revolution*, 122.

17 Inheritance is discussed more fully in the section on intergenerational relationships below.

18 Burke is particularly critical of the "metaphysicians" of the French Revolution, who ground their theory of rights in an abstract state of nature that never existed. Burke counsels them, "All your sophisters cannot produce anything better adapted to preserve a rational and manly freedom than the course that we have pursued, who have chosen our nature rather than our speculations, our breasts rather than our inventions, for the great conservatories and magazines of our rights and privileges." Burke, *Reflections on the Revolution*, 123.

19 Burke, *Reflections on the Revolution*, 292.

20 Burke argues that the "second nature" of custom slowly alters and shifts the "first nature," creating new combinations requiring new laws. Burke, *Reflections on the Revolution*, 292.

21 For Strauss' criticism of Burke, see Strauss, *Natural Right and History*; for a rejoinder, see Steven J. Lenzner, "Strauss's Three Burkes: The Problem of Edmund Burke in Natural Right and History," *Political Theory* 19, no. 3 (1991): 364–90.

22 Burke, *Reflections on the Revolution*, 122, 192.

23 Burke believes that the affections we have for our country make the use of coercive force less necessary, thus securing the voluntary obedience to the laws. These affections are not spontaneous, but arise from our affections for our families and then extend outward to the country as a whole: "In this choice of inheritance we have given to our frame of polity the image of a relation in blood; binding up the constitution of our country with our dearest domestic ties; adopting our fundamental laws into the bosom of our family affections; keeping inseparable, and cherishing with the warmth of all their combined and mutually reflected charities, our state, our hearths, our sepulchres, and our altars." Burke, *Reflections on the Revolution*, 122.

24 Both collectivists and individualists tend to support the sovereignty of the present generation as a way to facilitate social change and individual freedom. Marx is clearest in his disdain for the past: "The tradition of all

the dead generations weighs like a nightmare on the brain of the living."
Marx, *Marx-Engels Reader*, 437.

25 Burke's argument is not merely that we learn from the past but that the
values of past generations should play a role in determining the course for
the future: "Where the great interests of mankind are concerned through
a long succession of generations, that succession ought to be admitted
into some share in the councils which are so deeply to affect them." Burke,
Reflections on the Revolution, 276.

26 Burke, *Reflections on the Revolution*, 193.

27 Burke describes this peculiar kind of contract as an extension of the natural intergenerational bonds tying all humans to each other: "Each contract
of each particular state is but a clause in the great primaeval contract of
eternal society, linking the lower with the higher natures, connecting the
visible and invisible world, according to a fixed compact sanctioned by
the inviolable oath which holds all physical and all moral natures, each in
their appointed place." Burke, *Reflections on the Revolution*, 193.

28 Burke probably has in mind aristocracy and the commons in this context, but the mixing of higher and lower natures within individuals would
hardly be antithetical to his thought.

29 Describing the English against the French, Burke argues that the English
make decisions on the basis of sentimental attachment to homeland and
hearth. These sentiments are "the faithful guardians, the active monitors
of our duty, the true supporters of all liberal and manly morals." Burke,
Reflections on the Revolution, 181.

30 Burke's most famous formulation of the extension of familial attachments
to patriotic objects argues that "to be attached to the subdivision, to love
the little platoon we belong to in society, is the first principle (the germ
as it were) of public affections. It is the first link in the series by which we
proceed towards a love to our country and to mankind." Burke, *Reflections
on the Revolution*, 136–37.

31 E.g., he argues that "to make us love our country, our country ought to be
lovely." Burke, *Reflections on the Revolution*, 68.

32 This sentimental conservatism does not, however, preclude social progress,
though it does preclude radical social change. Much like the growth of a
tree, where particular branches are either growing or decaying at any given
point in time without danger to the tree as a whole, the collective is kept
alive through gradual reform, decay, and progression, but such changes
happen slowly over time in a way that allows the entire system to adapt.
Such a system is only possible when the society is bound together by affection for the past, the traditions and values of the people, and a people
whose sentiments support the passing on of those traditions and values
to the future. He argues, "By the disposition of a stupenduous wisdom,

moulding together the great mysterious incorporation of the human race, the whole, at one time, is never old or middle-aged, or young, but in a condition of unchangeable constancy, moves on through the varied tenour of perpetual decay, fall, renovation, and progression." Burke, *Reflections on the Revolution*, 122. See Burke's comment that "a spirit of innovation is generally the result of a selfish temper and confined views" (121).

33 The analogy between family and state, by extending our familial affections to our homeland as a whole, secures the voluntary obedience to the laws necessary for a free people. These affections are extended from the family to the state precisely because we inherit our rights and duties as citizens from and through our families.

34 Burke, *Reflections on the Revolution*, 171.

35 Montesquieu, *Spirit of the Laws*, 7.

36 "It is a rule drawn from nature that the more one decreases the number of marriages that can be made, the more one corrupts those that are made." Montesquieu, *Spirit of the Laws*, 450.

37 Montesquieu, *Spirit of the Laws*, 448.

38 He argues, "Where celibacy was preeminent, marriage could no longer be honored." Montesquieu, *Spirit of the Laws*, 449.

39 Montesquieu, *Spirit of the Laws*, 505.

40 Montesquieu, *Spirit of the Laws*, 505.

41 But, because it deals only directly with interactions between citizens and other citizens and not between citizen and ruler (except in cases of royal succession), marriage is not a political but is instead a civil affair.

42 In the regulation of marriage to prevent incest, e.g., "it is a very delicate thing to set clearly the point at which the laws of nature cease and where the civil laws begin." Montesquieu, *Spirit of the Laws*, 506.

43 E.g., sons owe their mother unlimited respect and wives owe their husbands unlimited respect, thus making an incestuous relationship between mother and son unnatural in that it overturns the natural balance of power between the members of the union. Montesquieu's discussion of domestic relations is heavily influenced by his political theory; much of what he sees as problematic in domestic relations from polygamy to incest stems from the imbalances of power that result from these unnatural forms.

44 He argues, "Do not clear the way for this crime, let it be proscribed by an exact police, as are all the violations of mores, and one will immediately see nature either defend her rights or take them back." Montesquieu, *Spirit of the Laws*, 194.

45 In general, he argues that violations of the mores should be punished primarily with fines and social censure, not with imprisonment or physical punishment. Montesquieu, *Spirit of the Laws*, 190, 191.

46 Burke argues that human nature is a mix of both nature and custom: "The state of civil society, which necessarily generates this aristocracy, is a state of nature; and much more truly so than a savage and incoherent way of life. For man is by nature reasonable; and he is never perfectly in his natural state, but when is placed where reason may be best cultivated, and most predominates. Art is man's nature. We are as much, at least, in a state of nature in formed manhood, as in immature and helpless infancy." Edmund Burke, *Further Reflections on the Revolution in France* (Indianapolis: Liberty Fund, 1992), 91.

47 Burke argues, "All your sophisters cannot produce anything better adapted to preserve a rational and manly freedom than the course that we have pursued, who have chosen our nature rather than our speculation, our breasts rather than our inventions, for the great conservatories and magazines of our rights and privileges." Burke, *Reflections on the Revolution*, 123. Burke does acknowledge the importance of our country being objectively worthy of our love: "To make us love our country, our country ought to be lovely" (172). For David Womersley's excellent discussion of Burke's criticism of British treatment of the American colonists, in particular, the way the English policies alienated American affections, see Eduardo Velásquez, *Love and Friendship: Rethinking Politics and Affection in Modern Times* (Lanham, Md.: Rowman & Littlefield, 2003), 270–71.

48 He argues, "We procure reverence to our civil institutions on the principle upon which nature teaches us to revere individual men; on account of their age; and on account of those from whom they are descended." Burke, *Reflections on the Revolution*, 123.

49 Burke condemns the French revolutionaries for losing sight of "natural morality" in their quest after abstract rights. See his prediction that "justifying perfidy and murder for public benefit, public benefit would soon become the pretext, and perfidy and murder the end; until rapacity, malice, revenge, and fear more dreadful than revenge, could satiate their insatiable appetites. Such must be the consequences of losing in the splendour of these triumphs of the rights of men, all natural sense of wrong and right." Burke, *Reflections on the Revolution*, 176.

50 For a more extensive discussion, see Lauren Hall, "Rights and the Heart: Emotions and Rights Claims in the Political Theory of Edmund Burke," *Review of Politics* 73 (2011): 1–23.

51 E.g., see Burke's discussion of the "real rights of men." Burke, *Reflections on the Revolution*, 150.

52 E.g., Burke argues that the abstract rights of the Lockean theorists have no practical or legal limits, making them dangerous for the societies they are supposed to protect: "Government is not made in virtue of natural rights, which may and do exist in total independence of it; and exist in much

greater clearness, and in a much greater degree of abstract perfection: but their abstract perfection is their practical defect. By having a right to every thing they want every thing." Burke, *Reflections on the Revolution*, 151.

53 Burke continues his argument for a mixed human nature, arguing that man is "a creature of prejudice, a creature of opinions, a creature of habits, and of sentiments growing out of them. These form our second nature, as inhabitants of the country and members of the society in which Providence has placed us." Edmund Burke, *The Works of the Right Honourable Edmund Burke: With a Portrait, and Life of the Author* (London: T. M'Lean, Haymarket, 1823), 12:164.

54 He argues, "The worst of these politics of revolution is this; they temper and harden the breast, in order to prepare it for the desperate strokes which are sometimes used in extreme occasions. But as these occasions may never arrive, the mind receives a gratuitous taint; and the moral sentiments suffer not a little, when no political purpose is served by the depravation." Burke, *Reflections on the Revolution*, 157.

55 Pappin makes a similar point when he argues, "Burke emphasizes our duties and obligations to society against the dominance of will." Joseph Pappin III, "A Symposium on Edmund Burke—Edmund Burke's Progeny: Recent Scholarship on Burke's Political Philosophy," *Political Science Reviewer* 35 (2006): 119. Burke explicitly links the emotions with man's nature, arguing, "This sort of people are so taken up with their theories about the rights of man, that they have totally forgot his nature. Without opening one new avenue to the understanding, they have succeeded in stopping up those that lead to the heart." Burke, *Reflections on the Revolution*, 157.

56 At one point Burke quotes Juvenal: "Never was there a jar or discord between genuine sentiment and sound policy. Never, no, never, did Nature say one thing, and Wisdom another. Nor are sentiments of elevation in themselves turgid and unnatural." Edmund Burke, *Select Works of Edmund Burke: A New Imprint of the Payne Edition* (Indianapolis: Liberty Fund, 1999), 3:217.

57 Burke uses an analogy between rights and light, and between the vicissitudes of political life and objects that refract light, changing its form. Abstract rights are fine in the abstract, but political life acts like waves, changing the character of those rights. His conclusion is that "the nature of man is intricate; the objects of society are of the greatest possible complexity; and therefore no simple disposition or direction of power can be suitable either to man's nature, or to the quality of his affairs." Burke, *Reflections on the Revolution*, 153.

58 He argues that unlike the French, with their commitment to abstract individual rights, "in England we have not yet been completely embowelled of

our natural entrails: we still feel within us, and we still cherish and culti-
vate, those inbred sentiments which are the faithful guardians, the active
monitors of our duty, the true supporters of all liberal and manly morals.
. . . We have real hearts of flesh and blood beating in our bosom." Burke,
Reflections on the Revolution, 181.

59 He famously argued, "To be attached to the subdivision, to love the little
platoon we belong to in society, is the first principle (the germ as it were)
of public affections. It is the first link in the series by which we proceed
towards a love to our country and to mankind." Burke, *Reflections on the
Revolution*, 136–37.

60 Burke, *Reflections on the Revolution*, 122.

61 Burke, *Reflections on the Revolution*, 122.

62 The link between property and family is clear: "The power of perpetuating
our property in our families is one of the most valuable and interesting
circumstances belonging to it, and that which tends the most to the per-
petuation of society itself. It makes our weakness subservient to our virtue;
it grafts benevolence even upon avarice." Burke, *Reflections on the Revolution*, 142.

63 Burke, *Reflections on the Revolution*, 171.

64 Both Marx and Rand recognize the existence of conflicts, but both also
believe that these conflicts can be overcome or eradicated if the proper
social system is achieved. Montesquieu and Burke believe that politics will
always be about balancing conflicts and differences, and thus the utopian
fantasies of the individualists and the collectivists are, in fact, utopian.
They occur nowhere.

65 Moderate governments require that "one must combine powers, regulate
them, temper them, make them act; one must give power a ballast, so
to speak, to put it in a position to resist another; this is a masterpiece of
legislation that chance rarely produces and prudence is rarely allowed to
produce." Montesquieu, *Spirit of the Laws*, 63.

66 Other elements that require balance include nature and custom and political rule (particularly obvious when discussing family forms), the needs of
individuals and the needs of the community (obvious in his discussions of
the different kinds of regime principles and the laws appropriate to each),
and the private and public spheres broadly (as can be seen in his discussion
of modesty and family life). See, e.g., Montesquieu's argument that "it is
a fallacy to say that the good of the individual should yield to the public
good; this occurs only when it is a question of the empire of the city, that
is, of the liberty of the citizen; it does not occur when it is a question of
the ownership of goods because it is always in the public good for each one
to preserve invariably the property given him by the civil laws." Montesquieu, *Spirit of the Laws*, 510.

67 See Montesquieu's initial discussion of natural laws. Procreation and intimate bonding come just after self-preservation and nourishment and before other social groupings.

68 "But when you disturb this harmony; when you break up this beautiful order, this array of truth and nature, as well as of habit and prejudice; when you separate the common sort of men from their proper chieftains so as to form them into an adverse army, I no longer know that venerable object called the people in such a disbanded race of deserters and vagabonds." Burke, *Further Reflections*, 169.

69 "We compensate, we reconcile, we balance. We are enabled to unite into a consistent whole the various anomalies and contending principles that are found in the minds and affairs of men." Burke, *Reflections on the Revolution*, 276. He further chastises the French for choosing simplicity over harmony: "In your old states you possessed that variety of parts corresponding with the various descriptions of which your community was happily composed; you had all that combination, and all that opposition of interests, you had that action and counteraction which, in the natural and in the political world, from the reciprocal struggle of discordant powers, draws out the harmony of the universe" (124).

70 Burke, *Reflections on the Revolution*, 126.

Chapter 5

1 Thinkers differ on the primary reasons for the family's loss of self-sufficiency over time. Some ascribe the primary cause to industrialization, which changed the family in various important ways, separating extended families and loosening kin ties. See André Burguière, *A History of the Family* (Cambridge, Mass.: Belknap Press of Harvard University Press, 1996), 377–415. Other thinkers trace the major changes in family structure that created a loss of self-sufficiency to the increased availability of contraception and the separation of marriage from procreation during the sexual revolution of the 1960s. See Robert P. George and Jean Bethke Elshtain, *The Meaning of Marriage: Family, State, Market, and Morals* (Dallas: Spence, 2006), 246.

2 These costs include everything from economic inefficiency to concerns about justice. See, e.g., critiques of economic centralization by Hayek. For Hayek's most famous formulation of the importance of local-level knowledge, see F. A. Hayek, "The Use of Knowledge in Society," *American Economic Review* 35, no. 4 (1945): 519–30. See also Ben Lockwood and Centre for Economic Policy Research (Great Britain), *Distributive Politics and the Costs of Centralization* (London: Centre for Economic Policy Research, 1998). For specific arguments against centralization of family

duties on the basis of justice and on the basis of emotional and psychological well-being, see Walzer, *Spheres of Justice*; Allan C. Carlson, *Family Questions: Reflections on the American Social Crisis* (New Brunswick, N.J.: Transaction Publishers, 1988), 13.

3   The national school lunch program, school counselors, and, in some areas, community-based schools provide extensive community services. Increasingly, these services are centered in public schools already strapped for money and resources. See Governor Cuomo's 2013 State of the State address. Press release available online at http://www.governor.ny.gov/press/01092013-cuomo-agenda-2013.

4   Arlene Saxonhouse discusses the collectivization of the family through her exploration of Aristophanes' *Ecclesiazusae*, arguing that as the family is collectivized, the unique characteristics of individuals are ignored in favor of conformity. The result is an inability to discriminate between good and bad, between the beautiful and the ugly. The result is that no individual preferences matter and that all individual worth is decided by the collective. See "Political Woman: Ancient Comedies and Modern Dilemmas," in Pamela Jensen, *Finding a New Feminism: Rethinking the Woman Question for Liberal Democracy* (Lanham, Md.: Rowman & Littlefield, 1996).

5   This social individualism could be considered a central component of what has been called "social capital." Putnam describes social capital as "connections among individuals—social networks and the norms of reciprocity and trustworthiness that arise from them." See Putnam, *Bowling Alone*, 19. Crucially, in one of the earliest descriptions of social capital, it is described as benefiting both individual and community: "The community as a whole will benefit by the cooperation of all its parts, while the individual will find in his associations the advantages of the help, the sympathy, and the fellowship of his neighbors" (19). Tocqueville anticipated this point when he discussed the unique way in which the Americans were able to balance both individualism and collective action through "self-interest well understood," where "particular interest happens to meet the general interest." Not coincidentally, the family is central to his analysis. See Tocqueville, *Democracy in America*, 500–503.

6   For the "Moynihan Report," see United States Department of Labor, Office of Policy Planning and Research, *The Negro Family: The Case for National Action* (Washington, D.C.: For sale by the Supt. of Docs., U.S. Govt. Print. Off., 1965). For current rates of single parenthood, see "FastStats: Unmarried Childbearing," Centers for Disease Control and Prevention, last updated January 18, 2013, http://www.cdc.gov/nchs/fastats/unmarry.htm.

7   "FastStats: Unmarried Childbearing," Centers for Disease Control and Prevention, last updated January 18, 2013, http://www.cdc.gov/nchs/fastats/unmarry.htm.

8   Single mothers (particularly those who have never been married) have lower than average education levels. See Department of Health and Human Services, *Report to Congress on Out-of-Wedlock Childbearing* (Hyattsville, Md.: U.S. Department of Health and Human Services, September 1995), xvi, www.cdc.gov/nchs/data/misc/wedlock.pdf.

9   Sweden notably narrows the gap. See Karen Christopher, Paula England, Timothy M. Smeeding, and Katherin Ross Phillips, "The Gender Gap in Poverty in Modern Nations: Single Motherhood, the Market, and the State," *Sociological Perspectives* 45, no. 3 (2002): 219–42.

10 Reynolds Farley and John Haaga, *The American People: Census 2000* (New York: Russell Sage Foundation, 2005), 212.

11 George and Elshtain, *Meaning of Marriage*, 251.

12 Department of Health and Human Services, *Out-of-Wedlock Childbearing*, 63.

13 Merril Sobie, "The Family Court—A Short History," *1 Jud. Notice* 6 (2011), accessed May 27, 2013, available at http://digitalcommons.pace.edu/cgi/viewcontent.cgi?article=1856&context=lawfaculty.

14 Jill Duerr Berrick, "When Children Cannot Remain Home: Foster Family Care and Kinship Care," *Protecting Children from Abuse and Neglect* 8, no. 1 (1998): 37.

15 William J. Doherty, National Marriage Coalition, and Fatherhood Foundation, *Twenty-One Reasons Why Marriage Matters* (Wollongong, N.S.W.: Fatherhood Foundation in cooperation with the National Marriage Coalition, 2004), 6. See also Gudrun Neises and Christian Grüneberg, "Socioeconomic Situation and Health Outcomes of Single Parents," *Journal of Public Health* 13, no. 5 (2005): 270–78.

16 Institute for American Values, "The Taxpayer Costs of Divorce and Unwed Childbearing," accessed April 23, 2013, http://www.americanvalues.org/html/coff_mediaadvisory.htm. Another analysis finds similar results; see George and Elshtain, *Meaning of Marriage*, 252.

17 David T. Lykken, "Parental Licensure," *American Psychologist* 56, no. 11 (2001): 885–94.

18 Diana Romero, Wendy Chavkin, and Paul Wise, "The Impact of Welfare Reform Policies on Child Protective Services: A National Study," *Journal of Social Sciences* 56, no. 4 (2000), 799.

19 Family scholars are often torn between public interventions in the family for the sake of the family (which often backfire or have unintended consequences) and a focus on private solutions, which take time and may not be sufficient to deal with the complexity of the problem. Because

innocent parties in the form of children are involved, however, the state's ability to withdraw these benefits is inherently limited. The result is a self-reinforcing cycle of familial disintegration and political centralization. As the family disintegrates, state intervention in the family becomes routine, which further erodes traditional family functions. The solution to this snowball effect, other than spontaneous cultural change, is unclear. See Carlson, *Family Questions*; George and Elshtain, *Meaning of Marriage*. For an excellent example of unintended side effects, see Allan C. Carlson, *The Swedish Experiment in Family Politics: The Myrdals and the Interwar Population Crisis* (New Brunswick, N.J.: Transaction Publishers, 1990).

20 Gray, *Fatherhood*, 130.

21 See Robert J. Quinlan, "Father Absence, Parental Care, and Female Reproductive Development," *Evolution and Human Behavior* 24, no. 6 (2003): 376–90. See also Mendle et al., "Associations between Father Absence."

22 Cynthia C. Harper and Sara S. McLanahan, "Father Absence and Youth Incarceration," *Journal of Research on Adolescence* 14, no. 3 (2004): 369–97.

23 Kathryn Harker Tillman, "Family Structure Pathways and Academic Disadvantage among Adolescents in Stepfamilies," *Sociological Inquiry* 77, no. 3 (2007): 383–424.

24 For a discussion of educational and psychological outcomes on children in single-parent families, see Department of Health and Human Services, *Out-of-Wedlock Childbearing*.

25 See, e.g., Melissa M. Ghera et al., "The Effects of Foster Care Intervention on Socially Deprived Institutionalized Children's Attention and Positive Affect: Results from the BEIP Study," *Journal of Child Psychology and Psychiatry* 50, no. 3 (2009): 246–53. For an American case study, see Sandra J. Altshuler and John Poertner, "The Child Health and Illness Profile—Adolescent Edition: Assessing Well-Being in Group Homes or Institutions," *Child Welfare* 81, no. 3 (2002): 495–513. Both studies demonstrate that children separated from family life show persistent emotional deficits into adulthood.

26 See Francis Fukuyama, *The Great Disruption: Human Nature and the Reconstitution of Social Order* (New York: Free Press, 1999), 36–37.

27 I follow Chantal Delsol's excellent analysis here. See Delsol, *Icarus Fallen: The Search for Meaning in an Uncertain World*, 2nd ed. (Wilmington, Del.: ISI Books, 2010).

28 Some family scholars object to using the sociological terminology of functionalism precisely because it allows one to separate the various "functions" the family serves away from the family itself, leaving families as merely "emotional or affective institutions." The concern is that the functionalist approach "ignores the nuances and textures of those human relations that make up the heart of the family's existence." David Blankenhorn,

Steven Bayme, and Jean Bethke Elshtain, eds., *Rebuilding the Nest: A New Commitment to the American Family* (Milwaukee, Wis.: Family Service America, 1990), 259.

29 One criticism of polygamous families in the United States and Canada is that such family forms often rely on public assistance, with the nonlegal wives considered as single mothers for purposes of state aid. See Jon Krakauer, *Under the Banner of Heaven: A Story of Violent Faith*, 1st ed. (New York: Doubleday, 2003), 12–13. In other societies, it is clear that polygamy is limited by the resources controllable by the male of the family. Because polygamous unions tend to be more traditional, fewer women contribute to family income, though this may be changing.

30 Some researchers on polygamy have gone so far as to say that polygamy makes equal gender relations impossible. See Miriam Koktvedgaard Zeitzen, *Polygamy: A Cross-Cultural Analysis* (Oxford: Berg, 2008), 125.

31 Riley Bove and Claudia Valeggia, "Polygyny and Women's Health in Sub-Saharan Africa," *Social Science & Medicine* 68, no. 1 (2009): 21–29. See also Dena Hassouneh-Phillips, "Polygamy and Wife Abuse: A Qualitative Study of Muslim Women in America," *Health Care for Women International* 22, no. 8 (2001): 735–48.

32 Joseph Henrich, *Affidavit*, no. S-097767 (Vancouver, B.C.: Supreme Court of British Columbia, Ministry of Attorney General, 2010), 36–37, accessed May 27, 2013, http://www.vancouversun.com/pdf/affidavit.pdf.

33 Henrich, *Affidavit*, 36–38.

34 Krakauer, *Under the Banner*, 14–17. See also Joseph Henrich, Robert Boyd, and Peter J. Richerson, "The Puzzle of Monogamous Marriage," *Philosophical Transactions of the Royal Society of London, Series B, Biological Sciences* 367, no. 1589 (2012): 661.

35 Henrich, *Affidavit*.

36 Henrich, *Affidavit*, 36–37.

37 Warren Jeffs, one of the most infamous of the Fundamentalist Mormon polygamists, was arrested and convicted not for plural marriage, but for child abuse, since many of his wives were under the age of consent and he also claimed the right to have sex with virgins in the group prior to their marriage to other men. See Krakauer, *Under the Banner*.

38 Krakauer, *Under the Banner*, 13–17.

39 Montesquieu's comment in *The Spirit of the Laws* that the polygamous family seems extensive but amounts to nothing reveals that the problem of maintaining affection for children and siblings in an extended polygamous union is not a new phenomenon. (63)

40 Henrich, *Affidavit*, 20.

41 Bjorklund and Pellegrini, *Origins of Human Nature*, 253.

42 See, e.g., Putnam, Leonardi, and Nanetti, *Making Democracy Work*, 99–111.

43 Paul Rubin discusses the patriarchal and hierarchical nature of polygamous societies, arguing that free societies may be incompatible with polygamous domestic structures. See Rubin, *Darwinian Politics: The Evolutionary Origin of Freedom* (New Brunswick, N.J.: Rutgers University Press, 2002).

44 Daphne Bramham, "Polygamy, Impunity and Human Rights," *Inroads: A Journal of Opinion*, no. 23 (2008).

45 Nicholas S. Hopkins, *The New Arab Family* (Cairo: American University in Cairo Press, 2003).

46 Michele Tertilt, "Polygyny, Human Rights, and Development," *Journal of the European Economic Association* 4, nos. 2–3 (2006): 523–30. See also David P. Barash and Judith Eve Lipton, *The Myth of Monogamy: Fidelity and Infidelity in Animals and People* (New York: W. H. Freeman, 2001), 113–38.

47 Carle Zimmerman uses the phrase "atomistic family," though his usage describes a broader trend in family life than mere nonreproduction. His concern was the shift toward a free and individualistic family. Because his use is broader than my own, I use "atomic" family rather than "atomistic" to avoid confusing our two slightly different concepts. Carle Clark Zimmerman, *Family and Civilization* (New York: Harper & Bros., 1947).

48 For an extended discussion on this point, see George and Elshtain, *Meaning of Marriage*.

49 One might say of a friend from high school with whom one has since lost touch, "We were friends many years ago," but one does not say about a great aunt whom one has little contact with, "She used to be my aunt." Biological relationships, however distant, remain despite time and distance.

50 This is, of course, not always the case, and very often families agree with one another politically since family members share common experiences and education.

51 In the case of legal trouble, a nonatomic individual is more likely to have the support of family for legal bills, jailhouse visits, and media attention to prevent abuses. An atomic individual must rely on the energy of friends and acquaintances, whose interest may die away with time, particularly when difficulties persist. These individuals too may bow to collective pressure precisely because the bond of friendship is a public bond more than a private one, because friendships, unlike families, are predicated on shared interests that are often (though not always) public in nature. Additionally, friendships are not given the same kind of public respect that familial relationships are, and so friends, e.g., are not accorded the protections of familial privilege, legally or socially. This is not to say that friendships always falter or that families always support their members. But because

of the permanence of family bonds, family relationships create duties to individuals that other kinds of relationships do not create.

52 One analysis finds a link between increasingly "atomistic" eras and dictatorships and gross violations of human rights in the name of collective ideals. See Zimmerman, *Family and Civilization*, 245. For a theoretical argument, see Arendt, *Origins of Totalitarianism*, 300. Recent empirical research demonstrates the importance of close social relationships for everything from health to foster care outcomes. Social relationships have important benefits for health outcomes. James S. House, Karl R. Landis, and Debra Umberson, "Social Relationships and Health," *Science* 241, no. 4865 (1988): 540–45. A recent study found that removing children into foster care resulted in lower outcomes than leaving children with potentially abusive or neglectful parents. This suggests that even in dysfunctional families, individuals may be treated more as individuals. See Joseph J. Doyle, "Child Protection and Child Outcomes: Measuring the Effects of Foster Care," *American Economic Review* 97, no. 5 (2007): 1583–1610.

53 Putnam argues that close relationships with families and neighbors benefit child welfare and development, child and adult health, economic growth, and political performance. Just as individuals are shaped by the relationships they have with others, the community is shaped by those individuals as well: "People who have active and trusting connections to others—whether family members, friends, or fellow bowlers—develop or maintain character traits that are good for the rest of society. Joiners become more tolerant, less cynical, and more empathetic to the misfortunes of others." Putnam, *Bowling Alone*, 288, 290.

54 See Kollontai's treatment of the "red grandmother," e.g., who recognizes her own irrelevance in the face of a unigenerational collectivism. Kollontai, *Selected Writings of Alexandra Kollontai*, 235.

55 Gloria Gutman and Charmaine Spencer, *Aging, Ageism and Abuse: Moving from Awareness to Action* (Boston: Elsevier, 2010), vi. See also Randall Summers and Allan Hoffman, *Elder Abuse: A Public Health Perspective* (Washington, D.C.: American Public Health Association, 2006).

56 Less than 6 percent of the elderly in Sweden, e.g., live without close contact to kin. While the social welfare state provides important resources, emotional and psychological support still comes primarily from kin connections. See Burguière, *History of the Family*, 498.

57 Traditional religious conservatives occupy the only political position that actively supports the growth of the family, though they are generally not in favor of political interventions. Populist collectivists and traditional classical liberal individualists also tend to support the family, though in both cases support for the family represents the moderation of their particular principles, rather than an extension of these principles. For Elshtain's

conclusion, see Blankenhorn, Bayme, and Elshtain, *Rebuilding the Nest*, 254–55. She argues for a centrist policy that avoids the extremes of either social or economic conservatives or liberal progressives.

58 Many individual families, whatever their form, may support political moderation, and because families are made of unique individuals with different strengths and weaknesses, no family form is determinate. However, in terms of probabilities and likelihoods, some family forms will be more likely to maintain these moderate characteristics than others. The monogamous family discussed here can be nuclear or extended, though our highly mobile society often prevents extended family members from living near each other. For practical reasons, the most common kind of ideal family will be a monogamous pair and their children.

59 Zeitzen, *Polygamy*, 16.

60 Single motherhood and polygamy are reproductive strategies that benefit males at the expense of females. Males have a greater reproductive potential over their life spans than females do, and males can fulfill that potential optimally by mating with multiple women. Women, on the other hand, are limited in their reproductive potential because, prior to menopause, they bear the costs of gestating, birthing, and nursing offspring. Thus, women are more vulnerable to reproductive exploitation than males are because they are left with the burden of raising children. Monogamy, by forcing males to invest in the offspring of one female, equalizes the investments of the sexes. See Henrich, *Affidavit*, 4–6.

61 Research finds that monogamous families have greater equality of investment between the sexes and that monogamy increases male investment in children. See Henrich, Boyd, and Richerson, "Puzzle of Monogamous Marriage," 665.

62 George and Elshtain cite the conclusion of family researchers to support the contention that the most stable family form is a family headed by two parents, ideally a father and a mother. This system is ideal because it balances the interests of men and women: "Such a design, in theory, would not only ensure that children had access to the time and money of two adults, it also would provide a system of checks and balances that promoted quality parenting. The fact that both parents have a biological connection to the child would increase the likelihood that the parents would identify with the child and be willing to sacrifice for that child, and it would reduce the likelihood that either parent would abuse the child." George and Elshtain, *Meaning of Marriage*, 251–52.

63 Current research on changing social norms demonstrates that increasing support for gay rights and gay marriage is likely partly the result of close relationships with openly gay individuals who provide an intimate "wedge" into long-held beliefs. See "New Surveys on Experiences of Lesbians,

Gays and Bisexuals and the Public's Views Related to Sexual Orientation," Kaiser Family Foundation, accessed February 9, 2013, http://www .kff.org/kaiserpolls/3193-index.cfm.

64 Single-parent households may be more likely to have some degree of connection to grandparents, depending on the culture and geographic circumstances. In some urban environments, e.g., grandmothers may take the place of absent fathers, encouraging a degree of intergenerationality not seen in other systems. While this intergenerational contact may be beneficial in some lights, it cannot make up for the lack of close bonds between father and child and the lack of resources across the generations. Thus, while some single-parent households may have an extensive network of intergenerational relationships, this intergenerationality is likely to be outweighed by other considerations, particularly the lack of male involvement and the reduction in resources characteristic of these families.

65 Bjorklund and Pellegrini, *Origins of Human Nature.*

66 See, e.g., the conference publication "Changing Population Age Structures: Demographic and Economic Consequences and Implications," from the United Nations' Conference of European Statisticians, United Nations, Economic Commission for Europe, and United Nations Population Fund (Geneva, 1992).

67 See discussion above on the impacts of polygamy for female outcomes.

68 E.g., the rise in female genital mutilation as African families move to Europe and the United States. See, e.g., Maligaye Bikoo et al., "Female Genital Mutilation: A Growing Challenge for Midwives in the UK," *British Journal of Midwifery* 14, no. 7 (2006): 403–5.

69 Physical abuse is just one example. Literature and pop culture alike are filled with examples of the varied ways in which families can exert coercive pressure on their members.

70 See, e.g., the recent controversial article that criticizes inequalities in how the public and private spheres are structured and the effects on elite women. Anne-Marie Slaughter, "Why Women Still Can't Have It All," *Atlantic*, July/August 2012, http://www.theatlantic.com/magazine/ archive/2012/07/why-women-still-can-8217-t-have-it-all/9020/.

71 See Jennifer Lawless, *It Takes a Candidate: Why Women Don't Run for Office* (Cambridge: Cambridge University Press, 2005). Another excellent discussion looks at how biological differences including pregnancy and lactation are magnified by cultural and social norms to produce gendered division of labor. See Wendy Wood and Alice H. Eagly, "Biosocial Construction of Sex Differences and Similarities in Behavior," *Advances in Experimental Social Psychology* 46 (2012): 55–123.

72 Henderson and Jeydel, *Women and Politics*, 139–41.

73 Susan Moller Okin's spirited rejection of the injustice of the family argues for numerous policy reforms to create just families and communities. See Okin, *Justice, Gender, and the Family.*

74 The experience of the kibbutzim suggests that social programs intended to move women into political and economic parity with men against their desires to care for children will be short lived.

75 Elshtain too denies the false choice between absolutism and relativism, though her solution centers on combining pro-family policies with a reinvigorated moral movement. See Blankenhorn, Bayme, and Elshtain, *Rebuilding the Nest,* 155.

76 The empirical evidence is clear across the board that different family forms are associated with differing levels of economic, political, social, emotional, and health outcomes for individuals. It is simply not possible to treat family forms as though they all equally provide for the well-being of children or the adult individuals involved. For excellent overviews of the outcomes associated with various family forms, see the discussion above; see also George and Elshtain, *Meaning of Marriage*; Henrich, Boyd, and Richerson, "Puzzle of Monogamous Marriage." For an evolutionary developmental view, see Bjorklund and Pellegrini, *Origins of Human Nature.*

77 What is meant by "support" here could range from mere social sanction to state-level marriage laws to amendment of the federal constitution. In a federal system where marriage laws have traditionally been decided at the state or local level, these lower levels of government seem the most logical places to deal with whether and how to publicly recognize such unions.

78 As more people become acquainted with same-sex partnerships, opposition is likely to die down even further. E.g., the reaction of young conservatives to the banning of GOProud from the Conservative Political Action Committee (CPAC) was largely negative. Younger conservatives tend to believe that political and economic policy stances are more important than sexual orientation. See Stephen Richer, "CPAC Bans Gay Group. But Not for Sake of Young Attendees," *Forbes*, February 10, 2012, online edition, http://www.forbes.com/sites/stephenricher/2012/02/10/cpac-bans-gay-group-but-not-for-the-sake-of-young-attendants/.

Conclusion

1 Fukuyama, following Hegel, famously termed this the "end of history," though he has indicated that history could be "restarted" again. See Fukuyama, *End of History.*

2 See, e.g., the essays by Arlene Saxonhouse and Mary Nichols in Jensen, *Finding a New Feminism.* Both authors argue that liberal democracy and its focus on equal rights ignores both individual distinction and community

cohesion. The result is groups of undifferentiated individuals who are unworthy of love.

3   Tocqueville, *Democracy in America*.

4   For Fukuyama's extended analysis, see Fukuyama, *End of History*.

5   See Robert Kagan, "The End of the End of History," *New Republic*, April 23, 2008, http://www.newrepublic.com/article/environment-energy/the -end-the-end-history. Huntington's earlier discussion also made the argument that cultures are pulling away from each other rather than converging. See Samuel P. Huntington, *The Clash of Civilizations and the Remaking of World Order* (New York: Simon & Schuster, 1996).

6   Elshtain discusses the problem of political polarization and its effects on the family, criticizing the false choice between moral absolutism and moral relativism. Blankenhorn, Bayme, and Elshtain, *Rebuilding the Nest*, 255. More recent political commentary argues either that we are indeed polarized or that we are not as polarized as people think. Whatever the actual level of polarization, the last decade has been a particularly bruising one for American politics. See Clive Crook, "Why Does Polarization Pay?" *Atlantic*, November 23, 2011, http://www.theatlantic .com/politics/archive/2011/11/why-does-polarization-pay/249059/; Andrew Gelman, "Why America Isn't as Polarized as You Think," *Atlantic*, July 8, 2011, http://www.theatlantic.com/politics/archive/2011/07/why -america-isnt-as-polarized-as-you-think/240653/.

7   See George and Elshtain, *Meaning of Marriage*, 53–73, 242–54.

8   Chantal Delsol argues, "There will be no post-totalitarian future without a clear and well-argued rejection of everything that built the anti-worlds of the twentieth century. The future will not take shape without the loss of illusions, which are laid to rest only by a clear-minded examination of experience." Delsol, *Unlearned Lessons*, 30.

9   The problem with perfection is not idealism per se. All human progress is grounded in the efforts of individuals to improve their lives and their communities. It is not idealism that is dangerous, but what happens when idealism is combined with moral absolutism. What makes perfection as a goal so dangerous is that in the course of pursuing a particular vision of "perfection," other values and goods become lost or are targeted for extinction. Elshtain discusses this problem in a section titled "Neatness isn't everything": "For the discordance embodied in this uneasy coexistence of familial and democratic authority sustains the struggles over identity, purpose, and meaning that form the very stuff of democratic life. To resolve this untidiness, we could simply declare a set of unitary authoritative norms. Or we could simply eliminate all norms as arbitrary and oppressive. But to do either is to jeopardize the social goods that democratic and familial authority—paradoxical in relation to one another—promise to

citizens and their children." Blankenhorn, Bayme, and Elshtain, *Rebuilding the Nest*, 131.

10 Burke's words are perhaps the best formulation of this process: "We compensate, we reconcile, we balance. We are enabled to unite into a consistent whole the various anomalies and contending principles that are found in the minds and affairs of men. From hence arises, not an excellence in simplicity, but one far superior, an excellence in composition." Burke, *Further Reflections*, 276.

11 Burke argues, "The nature of man is intricate; the objects of society are of the greatest possible complexity: and therefore no simple disposition or direction of power can be suitable either to man's nature or to the quality of his affairs. When I hear the simplicity of contrivance aimed at and boasted of in any new political constitutions, I am at no loss to decide that the artificers are grossly ignorant of their trade or totally negligent of their duty." Burke, *Further Reflections*, 153.

12 Peter Lawler's discussion of Heidegger and Wendell Berry's critiques of technology is useful here. See Peter Augustine Lawler, *Stuck with Virtue: The American Individual and Our Biotechnological Future* (Wilmington, Del.: ISI Books, 2005), 45–71.

13 It is the loss of reproduction that many see as a signal of the decline and perhaps eventual fall of society. When people no longer see reproduction as worthwhile, when they see nothing worth passing on, a society is doomed.

14 Yet there may be some stability even amid such flux. The desire to reproduce, so fundamental to human life, is unlikely to change. The major biotechnologies under discussion are primarily reproductive in nature, suggesting that the core of human life will remain unchanged, at least in the near term. Most people are likely to use these technologies to rid their genetic legacies of diseases and secure long and healthy lives for their descendants. New biotechnologies may be used in the service of the family rather than radically changing it. As long as the fundamental desire to reproduce, to love, and to be loved continues, the family will remain, though its form may change.

15 Putnam's discussion is only one example of the recent resurgence of interest in intermediate institutions or social capital broadly. See Putnam, *Bowling Alone*.

BIBLIOGRAPHY

Alesina, Alberto, Eliana La Ferrara, and National Bureau of Economic Research. *Participation in Heterogeneous Communities*. Cambridge, Mass.: National Bureau of Economic Research, 1999.

Allen, Garland. "Eugenics and Modern Biology: Critiques of Eugenics, 1910–1945." *Annals of Human Genetics* 75, no. 3 (2011). doi: 10.1111/j.1469-1809.2011.00649.x.

Altshuler, Sandra J., and John Poertner. "The Child Health and Illness Profile—Adolescent Edition: Assessing Well-Being in Group Homes or Institutions." *Child Welfare* 81, no. 3 (2002): 495–513.

Arendt, Hannah. *The Origins of Totalitarianism*. New York: Harcourt, Brace, 1951.

Aristotle. *The Politics*. Translated by Carnes Lord. Chicago: University of Chicago Press, 1984.

Arnhart, Larry. *Darwinian Conservatism: A Disputed Question*. Exeter, UK: Imprint Academic, 2009.

———. *Darwinian Natural Right: The Biological Ethics of Human Nature*. Albany: State University of New York Press, 1998.

Axelrod, Robert M. *The Evolution of Cooperation.* New York: Basic Books, 1984.

Bannister, Robert C. "William Graham Sumner's Social Darwinism: A Reconsideration." *History of Political Economy* 5, no. 1 (1973).

Barash, David P., and Judith Eve Lipton. *The Myth of Monogamy: Fidelity and Infidelity in Animals and People.* New York: W. H. Freeman, 2001.

Berrick, Jill Duerr. "When Children Cannot Remain Home: Foster Family Care and Kinship Care." *Protecting Children from Abuse and Neglect* 8, no. 1 (1998): 72–87.

Bikoo, Maligaye, Melissa Davies, Yana Richens, and Sarah Creighton. "Female Genital Mutilation: A Growing Challenge for Midwives in the UK." *British Journal of Midwifery* 14, no. 7 (2006): 403–5.

Bjorklund, David, and Anthony D. Pellegrini. *The Origins of Human Nature: Evolutionary Developmental Psychology.* Washington, D.C.: American Psychological Association, 2002.

Black, Edwin. *War against the Weak: Eugenics and America's Campaign to Create a Master Race.* New York: Four Walls Eight Windows, 2003.

Blankenhorn, David, Steven Bayme, and Jean Bethke Elshtain, eds. *Rebuilding the Nest: A New Commitment to the American Family.* Milwaukee, Wis.: Family Service America, 1990.

Bove, Riley, and Claudia Valeggia. "Polygyny and Women's Health in Sub-Saharan Africa." *Social Science & Medicine* 68, no. 1 (2009): 21–29. doi: 10.1016/j.socscimed.2008.09.045.

Bramham, Daphne. "Polygamy, Impunity and Human Rights." *Inroads: A Journal of Opinion,* no. 23 (2008).

Brettschneider, Corey. "The Politics of the Personal: A Liberal Approach." *American Political Science Review* 101, no. 1 (2007): 19–31. doi:10.1017/S0003055407070104.

Burguière, André. *A History of the Family.* Cambridge, Mass.: Belknap Press of Harvard University Press, 1996.

Burke, Edmund. *Further Reflections on the Revolution in France.* Indianapolis: Liberty Fund, 1992.

———. *Reflections on the Revolution in France.* Indianapolis: Liberty Fund, 1999.

———. *Select Works of Edmund Burke: A New Imprint of the Payne Edition.* Indianapolis: Liberty Fund, 1999.

———. *The Works of the Right Honourable Edmund Burke: With a Portrait, and Life of the Author.* London: T. M'Lean, Haymarket, 1823.

Canavan, Francis P. "Edmund Burke's Conception of the Role of Reason in Politics." *Journal of Politics* 21, no. 1 (1959): 60.

Carlson, Allan C. *Family Questions: Reflections on the American Social Crisis.* New Brunswick, N.J.: Transaction Publishers, 1988.

―――. *The Swedish Experiment in Family Politics: The Myrdals and the Interwar Population Crisis.* New Brunswick, N.J.: Transaction Publishers, 1990.

"Changing Population Age Structures: Demographic and Economic Consequences and Implications." Conference publication from the United Nations' Conference of European Statisticians, United Nations, Economic Commission for Europe, and United Nations Population Fund. Geneva, 1992.

Christopher, Karen, Paula England, Timothy M. Smeeding, and Katherin Ross Phillips. "The Gender Gap in Poverty in Modern Nations: Single Motherhood, the Market, and the State." *Sociological Perspectives* 45, no. 3 (2002): 219–42.

Clements, Barbara Evans. *Daughters of Revolution: A History of Women in the USSR.* Arlington Heights, Ill.: Harlan Davidson, 1994.

Cooke, Jacob Ernest. *The Federalist.* Middletown, Conn.: Wesleyan University Press, 1961.

Courtwright, David. *Violent Land: Single Men and Social Disorder from the Frontier to the Inner City.* Cambridge, Mass.: Harvard University Press, 1996.

Crook, Clive. "Why Does Polarization Pay?" *Atlantic,* November 23, 2011. http://www.theatlantic.com/politics/archive/2011/11/why-does-polarization-pay/249059/.

Cullen, Stephen. *Children in Society: A Libertarian Critique.* London: Freedom Press, 1991.

Davis, Jennifer Nerissa, and Martin Daly. "Evolutionary Theory and the Human Family." *The Quarterly Review of Biology* 72, no. 4 (1997).

De Waal, Frans. *Chimpanzee Politics: Power and Sex among Apes.* Rev. ed. Baltimore: Johns Hopkins University Press, 1998.

Delsol, Chantal. *Icarus Fallen: The Search for Meaning in an Uncertain World.* 2nd ed. Wilmington, Del.: ISI Books, 2010.

―――. *The Unlearned Lessons of the Twentieth Century: An Essay on Late Modernity.* 1st ed. Wilmington, Del.: ISI Books, 2006.

Deparle, Jason. "Two Classes in America, Divided by 'I Do.'" *New York Times,* July 14, 2012. http://www.nytimes.com/2012/07/15/us/two-classes-in-america-divided-by-i-do.html.

Department of Health and Human Services. *Report to Congress on Out-of-Wedlock Childbearing.* Hyattsville, Md.: U.S. Department of Health and Human Services, September 1995. www.cdc.gov/nchs/data/misc/wedlock.pdf.

Doherty, William J., National Marriage Coalition, and Fatherhood Foundation. *Twenty-One Reasons Why Marriage Matters.* Wollongong, N.S.W.: Fatherhood Foundation in co-operation with the National Marriage Coalition, 2004.

Doyle, Joseph J. "Child Protection and Child Outcomes: Measuring the Effects of Foster Care." *American Economic Review* 97, no. 5 (2007): 1583–1610.

Elshtain, Jean. *The Family in Political Thought.* Amherst: University of Massachusetts Press, 1982.

Engels, Friedrich. *Socialism: Utopian and Scientific.* Translated by Edward Aveling. Moscow: Progress Publishers, 1970. http://www.marxists.org/archive/marx/works/1880/soc-utop/index.htm.

Engels, Friedrich, and Eleanor Burke Leacock. *The Origin of the Family, Private Property and the State, in the Light of the Researches of Lewis H. Morgan.* New York: International Publishers, 1972.

Farley, Reynolds, and John Haaga. *The American People: Census 2000.* New York: Russell Sage Foundation, 2005.

Fletcher, Winston. "The Death of Marriage?" *Guardian*, June 26, 2006. http://www.guardian.co.uk/commentisfree/2006/jun/26/thedeathofmarriage.

Foster, Kevin R., Tom Wenseleers, and Francis L. W. Ratnieks. "Kin Selection Is the Key to Altruism." *Trends in Ecology & Evolution* 21, no. 2 (2006): 57–60. doi:10.1016/j.tree.2005.11.020.

Friedman, Sarah L. "The National Institute of Child Health and Human Development (NICHD) Study of Early Child Care: A Comprehensive Longitudinal Study of Young Children's Lives." Human Learning and Behavior Branch, National Institute of Child Health and Human Development, Bethesda, Md., 1992.

Fukuyama, Francis. *The End of History and the Last Man.* New York: Free Press, 1992.

———. *The Great Disruption: Human Nature and the Reconstitution of Social Order.* New York: Free Press, 1999.

Gellately, Robert. *Lenin, Stalin, and Hitler: The Age of Social Catastrophe.* New York: Alfred A. Knopf, 2007.

Gelman, Andrew. "Why America Isn't as Polarized as You Think." *Atlantic*, July 8, 2011. http://www.theatlantic.com/politics/archive/2011/07/why-america-isnt-as-polarized-as-you-think/240653/.

George, Robert P., and Jean Bethke Elshtain. *The Meaning of Marriage: Family, State, Market, and Morals.* Dallas: Spence, 2006.

Gettler, Lee T., James J. McKenna, Thomas W. McDade, Sonny S. Agustin, and Christopher W. Kuzawa. "Does Cosleeping Contribute to

Lower Testosterone Levels in Fathers? Evidence from the Philippines." *PLoS ONE* 7, no. 9 (2012): e41559, published 5 September 2012, http://www.plosone.org/article/info%3Adoi%2F10.1371%2Fjournal .pone.0041559, doi: 10.1371/journal.pone.0041559.

Ghera, Melissa M., Peter J. Marshall, Nathan A. Fox, Charles H. Zeanah, Charles A. Nelson, Anna T. Smyke, and Donald Guthrie. "The Effects of Foster Care Intervention on Socially Deprived Institutionalized Children's Attention and Positive Affect: Results from the BEIP Study." *Journal of Child Psychology and Psychiatry* 50, no. 3 (2009): 246–53.

Gibson, Mhairi A., and Ruth Mace. "Helpful Grandmothers in Rural Ethiopia: A Study of the Effect of Kin on Child Survival and Growth." *Evolution and Human Behavior* 26, no. 6 (2005): 469–82. doi:10.1016/j .evolhumbehav.2005.03.004.

Gladstein, Mimi. *The New Ayn Rand Companion*. Westport, Conn.: Greenwood Press, 1999.

Gray, Peter. *Fatherhood: Evolution and Human Paternal Behavior*. Cambridge, Mass.: Harvard University Press, 2010.

Griffin, Ashleigh S. "Kin Selection." In *Encyclopedia of Ecology*, ed. Sven Erik Jørgensen and Brian D. Fath, 2057–60. Oxford: Academic Press, 2008. http://www.sciencedirect.com/science/article/pii/B9780 080454054000197.

Gutman, Gloria, and Charmaine Spencer. *Aging, Ageism and Abuse: Moving from Awareness to Action*. Boston: Elsevier, 2010.

Hall, Lauren. "Rights and the Heart: Emotions and Rights Claims in the Political Theory of Edmund Burke." *Review of Politics* 73 (2011): 1–23.

Hames, Raymond. "Grandparental Transfers and Kin Selection." *Behavioral and Brain Sciences* 33, no. 1 (2010): 26–27.

Hamilton, William Donald. "The Genetical Evolution of Social Behaviour. I." *Journal of Theoretical Biology* 7, no. 1 (1964): 1–16.

Harper, Cynthia C., and Sara S. McLanahan. "Father Absence and Youth Incarceration." *Journal of Research on Adolescence* 14, no. 3 (2004): 369–97.

Harris, Jose. "Society and the State in Twentieth Century Britain." In *The Cambridge Social History of Britain 1750–1950*, edited by F. M. L. Thompson. Vol. 3, *Social Agencies and Institutions*. Cambridge: Cambridge University Press, 2008.

Hassouneh-Phillips, Dena. "Polygamy and Wife Abuse: A Qualitative Study of Muslim Women in America." *Health Care for Women International* 22, no. 8 (2001): 735–48.

Hayek, F. A. [Friedrich A. von Hayek]. *The Constitution of Liberty*. Chicago: University of Chicago Press, 1960.

———. *The Fatal Conceit: The Errors of Socialism*. University of Chicago Press ed. Chicago: University of Chicago Press, 1989.

———. *Individualism and Economic Order*. Chicago: University of Chicago Press, 1948.

———. *The Road to Serfdom*. Chicago: University of Chicago Press, 1994.

———. "The Use of Knowledge in Society." *American Economic Review* 35, no. 4 (1945): 519–30.

Henderson, Sarah, and Alana S. Jeydel. *Women and Politics in a Global World*. New York: Oxford University Press, 2010.

Henrich, Joseph. *Affidavit*, no. S-097767 (Vancouver, B.C.: Supreme Court of British Columbia, Ministry of Attorney General, 2010), 36–37, accessed May 27, 2013, http://www.vancouversun.com/pdf/affidavit.pdf.

Henrich, Joseph, Robert Boyd, and Peter J. Richerson. "The Puzzle of Monogamous Marriage." *Philosophical Transactions of the Royal Society of London. Series B, Biological Sciences* 367, no. 1589 (2012): 657–69.

Hopkins, Nicholas S. *The New Arab Family*. Cairo: American University in Cairo Press, 2003.

Horwitz, Steven. "The Functions of the Family in the Great Society." *Cambridge Journal of Economics* 29, no. 5 (2005): 669–84. doi:10.1093/cje/bei041.

———. "Two Worlds at Once: Rand, Hayek, and the Ethics of the Micro- and Macro-Cosmos." *Journal of Ayn Rand Studies* 6, no. 2. (2005): 375–403.

House, James S., Karl R. Landis, and Debra Umberson. "Social Relationships and Health." *Science* 241, no. 4865 (1988): 540–45.

Hrdy, Sarah. *Mother Nature: A History of Mothers, Infants, and Natural Selection*. 1st ed. New York: Pantheon Books, 1999.

Hudson, Valerie. *Bare Branches: The Security Implications of Asia's Surplus Male Population*. Cambridge, Mass.: MIT Press, 2004.

Huntington, Samuel P. *The Clash of Civilizations and the Remaking of World Order*. New York: Simon & Schuster, 1996.

Jefferson, Thomas. *Writings: Autobiography; A Summary View of the Rights of British America; Notes on the State of Virginia; Public Papers; Addresses, Messages, and Replies; Miscellany; Letters*. Edited by Merrill D. Peterson. New York: Literary Classics of the United States, 1984.

Jensen, Pamela, ed. *Finding a New Feminism: Rethinking the Woman Question for Liberal Democracy*. Lanham, Md.: Rowman & Littlefield, 1996.

Kagan, Robert. "The End of the End of History." *New Republic*, April 23, 2008. http://www.newrepublic.com/article/environment-energy/the -end-the-end-history.

Kearns, Deborah. "A Theory of Justice—And Love; Rawls on the Family." *Politics* 18, no. 2 (1983): 36–42. doi:10.1080/00323268308401886.

Kershner, Isabel. "The Kibbutz Sheds Socialism and Gains Popularity." *New York Times*, August 27, 2007. http://www.nytimes.com/2007/08/27/world/middleeast/27kibbutz.html?scp=4&sq=kibbutzim&st=cse.

Kollontai, Alexandra M. *Selected Writings of Alexandra Kollontai*. Translated by Alix Holt. London: Allison & Busby, 1977.

Krakauer, Jon. *Under the Banner of Heaven: A Story of Violent Faith*. 1st ed. New York: Doubleday, 2003.

Kripke, Pamela Gwyn. "It's Better to Be Raised by a Single Mom." *Slate*, January 3, 2013. http://www.slate.com/articles/double_x/doublex/2013/01/single_moms_are_better_kids_raised_by_single_mothers _are_sturdier.html.

Largent, Mark A. *Breeding Contempt: The History of Coerced Sterilization in the United States*. New Brunswick, N.J.: Rutgers University Press, 2008.

Lawler, Peter Augustine. *Stuck with Virtue: The American Individual and Our Biotechnological Future*. Wilmington, Del.: ISI Books, 2005.

Lawless, Jennifer. *It Takes a Candidate: Why Women Don't Run for Office*. Cambridge: Cambridge University Press, 2005.

Lenzner, Steven J. "Strauss's Three Burkes: The Problem of Edmund Burke in Natural Right and History." *Political Theory* 19, no. 3 (1991): 364–90.

Lewin, Tamar. "Three New Studies Assess Effects of Child Care." *New York Times*, November 1, 2005. http://www.nytimes.com/2005/11/01/national/01child.html.

Lieberman, Debra, John Tooby, and Leda Cosmides. "The Architecture of Human Kin Detection." *Nature* 445, no. 7129 (2007): 727–31. doi:10.1038/nature05510.

Locke, John. *Two Treatises of Government*. Edited by Peter Laslett. Cambridge: Cambridge University Press, 1988.

Lockwood, Ben, and Centre for Economic Policy Research (Great Britain). *Distributive Politics and the Costs of Centralization*. London: Centre for Economic Policy Research, 1998.

Lykken, David T. "Parental Licensure." *American Psychologist* 56, no. 11 (2001): 885–94.

Machan, Tibor, and Douglas Rasmussen, eds. *Liberty for the Twenty-First Century: Contemporary Libertarian Thought*. Lanham, Md.: Rowman & Littlefield, 1995.

Marx, Karl. *Capital: A Critique of Political Economy.* Vol. 1. Marx/Engels Internet Archive, 1999.

———. *The Communist Manifesto.* Ebrary Electronic Books. London: Electric Book, 2001.

———. *The Marx-Engels Reader.* Edited by Robert C. Tucker. New York: Norton, 1978.

———. *On Education, Women, and Children.* New York: McGraw-Hill, 1975.

McKenzie, Richard B., and Gordon Tullock. *The New World of Economics.* Homewood, Ill.: Richard D. Irwin, 1985.

Mendle, Jane, K. Paige Harden, Eric Turkheimer, Carol A. Van Hulle, Brian M. D'Onofrio, Jeanne Brooks-Gunn, Joseph L. Rodgers, Robert E. Emery, and Benjamin B. Lahey. "Associations between Father Absence and Age of First Sexual Intercourse." *Child Development* 80, no. 5 (2009): 1463–80.

Montesquieu, Charles de Secondat, Baron de. *Persian Letters.* Indianapolis: Bobbs-Merrill, 1964.

———. *The Spirit of the Laws.* New York: Cambridge University Press, 1989.

Morse, Jennifer. *Love & Economics: Why the Laissez-Faire Family Doesn't Work.* Dallas: Spence Publishing, 2001.

Murdock, George Peter. *Social Structure.* Oxford: Macmillan, 1949.

Neises, Gudrun, and Christian Grüneberg. "Socioeconomic Situation and Health Outcomes of Single Parents." *Journal of Public Health* 13, no. 5 (2005): 270–78.

Okin, Susan Moller. *Justice, Gender, and the Family.* New York: Basic Books, 1999.

Pangle, Thomas L., and Peter J. Ahrensdorf. *Justice among Nations: On the Moral Basis of Power and Peace.* Lawrence: University Press of Kansas, 1999.

Pappin, Joseph, III. "A Symposium on Edmund Burke—Edmund Burke's Progeny: Recent Scholarship on Burke's Political Philosophy." *Political Science Reviewer* 35 (2006): 10.

Pinker, Steven. *The Blank Slate: The Modern Denial of Human Nature.* New York: Viking, 2002.

Pipes, Richard. "Human Nature and the Fall of Communism." *Bulletin of the American Academy of Arts and Sciences* 49, no. 4 (1996): 38–53.

———. *Property and Freedom.* New York: Vintage, 2000.

Plato. *The Republic of Plato.* Translated with notes and an interpretive essay by Allan Bloom. New York: Basic Books, 1968.

Popper, Karl R. *The Open Society and Its Enemies*. Princeton, N.J.: Princeton University Press, 1966.

President's Council on Bioethics (U.S.) and Leon Kass. *Beyond Therapy: Biotechnology and the Pursuit of Happiness*. Washington, D.C.: President's Council on Bioethics, 2003.

Putnam, Robert D. *Bowling Alone: The Collapse and Revival of American Community*. New York: Simon & Schuster, 2000.

Putnam, Robert D., Robert Leonardi, and Raffaella Nanetti. *Making Democracy Work: Civic Traditions in Modern Italy*. Princeton, N.J.: Princeton University Press, 1993.

Quinlan, Robert J. "Father Absence, Parental Care, and Female Reproductive Development." *Evolution and Human Behavior* 24, no. 6 (2003): 376–90.

Rand, Ayn. *Atlas Shrugged*. Centennial ed. New York: Penguin, 2005.

Rand, Ayn, and Nathaniel Branden. *The Virtue of Selfishness: A New Concept of Egoism*. New York: Signet, 1964.

Rawls, John. *A Theory of Justice*. Cambridge, Mass.: Belknap Press of Harvard University Press, 1971.

Rawls, John, and Erin Kelly. *Justice as Fairness: A Restatement*. Cambridge, Mass.: Harvard University Press, 2001.

Richer, Stephen. "CPAC Bans Gay Group. But Not for Sake of Young Attendees." *Forbes*, February 10, 2012, online edition. http://www .forbes.com/sites/stephenricher/2012/02/10/cpac-bans-gay-group-but -not-for-the-sake-of-young-attendants/.

Richtel, Matt. "Marriage Seen through a Contract Lens." *New York Times*, September 28, 2012. http://www.nytimes.com/2012/09/30/fashion/ marriage-seen-through-a-contract-lens.html.

Roiphe, Katie. "In Defense of Single Motherhood." *New York Times*, August 11, 2012. http://www.nytimes.com/2012/08/12/opinion/sunday/in -defense-of-single-motherhood.html.

———. "More Single Moms. So What." *Slate*, February 20, 2012. http:// www.slate.com/articles/life/roiphe/2012/02/the_new_york_times _condescends_to_single_moms_.html.

———. "Single Moms Are Crazy!" *Slate*, October 5, 2011. http://www .slate.com/articles/double_x/doublex/2011/10/shaming_the_single _mom_do_we_all_secretly_think_single_moms_are_.html.

Romero, Diana, Wendy Chavkin, and Paul Wise. "The Impact of Welfare Reform Policies on Child Protective Services: A National Study." *Journal of Social Sciences* 56, no. 4 (2000), 799.

Rosenberg, Karen, and Wenda Trevathan. "Birth, Obstetrics and Human Evolution." *BJOG: An International Journal of Obstetrics & Gynaecology* 109, no. 11 (2002): 1199–1206. doi:10.1046/j.1471-0528.2002.00010.x.

Rothbard, Murray Newton. *For a New Liberty: The Libertarian Manifesto.* Auburn, Al.: Ludwig von Mises Institute, 2006.

Rubin, Paul H. *Darwinian Politics: The Evolutionary Origin of Freedom.* New Brunswick, N.J.: Rutgers University Press, 2002.

Saxonhouse, Arlene W. *Women in the History of Political Thought: Ancient Greece to Machiavelli.* New York: Praeger, 1985.

Sciabarra, Chris Matthew. *Ayn Rand: The Russian Radical.* University Park: Pennsylvania State University Press, 1995.

Singer, Peter. *The Expanding Circle: Ethics and Sociobiology.* 1st ed. New York: Farrar, Straus & Giroux, 1981.

Slaughter, Anne-Marie. "Why Women Still Can't Have It All." *Atlantic,* July/August 2012. http://www.theatlantic.com/magazine/archive/2012/07/why-women-still-can-8217-t-have-it-all/9020/.

Sobie, Merril. "The Family Court—A Short History." *1 Jud. Notice* 6 (2011). Accessed May 27, 2013. Available at http://digitalcommons.pace.edu/cgi/viewcontent.cgi?article=1856&context=lawfaculty.

Sowell, Thomas. *A Conflict of Visions: Ideological Origins of Political Struggles.* New York: Basic Books, 2007.

Spencer, Herbert. *The Man versus the State: With Six Essays on Government, Society, and Freedom.* Indianapolis: Liberty Fund, 2000.

Spiro, Melford E. "Is the Family Universal?" *American Anthropologist* 56, no. 5 (1954): 839–46.

Strauss, Leo. *Natural Right and History.* Chicago: University of Chicago Press, 1953.

Summers, Randall, and Allan Hoffman. *Elder Abuse: A Public Health Perspective.* Washington, D.C.: American Public Health Association, 2006.

Talmon, Yonina. *Family and Community in the Kibbutz.* Cambridge, Mass.: Harvard University Press, 1972.

Tertilt, Michele. "Polygyny, Human Rights, and Development." *Journal of the European Economic Association* 4, no. 2–3 (2006): 523–30.

Thompson, Derek. "The Death (and Life) of Marriage in America." *Atlantic,* February 7, 2012. http://www.theatlantic.com/business/archive/2012/02/the-death-and-life-of-marriage-in-america/252640/.

Tiger, Lionel, and Joseph Shepher. *Women in the Kibbutz.* New York: Harcourt Brace Jovanovich, 1975.

Tillman, Kathryn Harker. "Family Structure Pathways and Academic Disadvantage among Adolescents in Stepfamilies." *Sociological Inquiry* 77, no. 3 (2007): 383–424.

Tocqueville, Alexis de. *Democracy in America.* Paperback ed. Chicago: University of Chicago Press, 2002.

Tyler, Meagan. "Death of Marriage the Path to Equality." November 28, 2011. http://www.abc.net.au/unleashed/3698436.html.

United States Department of Labor, Office of Policy Planning and Research. *The Negro Family: The Case for National Action.* Washington, D.C.: For sale by the Supt. of Docs., U.S. Govt. Print. Off., 1965.

Velásquez, Eduardo. *Love and Friendship: Rethinking Politics and Affection in Modern Times.* Lanham, Md.: Rowman & Littlefield, 2003.

Walzer, Michael. *Spheres of Justice: A Defense of Pluralism and Equality.* New York: Basic Books, 1983.

Weikart, Richard. *From Darwin to Hitler: Evolutionary Ethics, Eugenics, and Racism in Germany.* New York: Palgrave Macmillan, 2004.

———. "Laissez-Faire Social Darwinism and Individualist Competition in Darwin and Huxley." *European Legacy* 3, no. 1 (1998): 17–30.

Wilcox, W. Bradford. "The Kids Are Not Really Alright." *Slate,* July 20, 2012. http://www.slate.com/articles/double_x/doublex/2012/07/single _motherhood_worse_for_children_.single.html.

Wood, Wendy, and Alice H. Eagly. "Biosocial Construction of Sex Differences and Similarities in Behavior." *Advances in Experimental Social Psychology* 46 (2012): 55–123.

Yenor, Scott. *Family Politics: The Idea of Marriage in Modern Political Thought.* Waco, Tex.: Baylor University Press, 2011.

Zeitzen, Miriam Koktvedgaard. *Polygamy: A Cross-Cultural Analysis.* Oxford: Berg, 2008.

Zimmerman, Carle Clark. *Family and Civilization.* New York: Harper & Bros., 1947.

INDEX

abortion, 11, 36, 86
adultery, 16; Montesquieu on, 67–68, 74, 152n13
Ahrensdorf, Peter J., 118n7
altruism, 43, 54–55, 102
Arendt, Hannah, 119n11; on anti-Semitism, 120n17; on human rights, 119n12; on individualism, 121nn19–20
Aristophanes, 160n4
Aristotle, 33, 82; on birth control, 152n8; on cities, 117n1; on family, 5, 122n24, 131n4; on polygamy, 134n32
Arnhart, Larry, 122n22, 146n35

Berry, Wendell, 170n12
biotechnology, 113–14, 170n14
birth control, 99, 159n1; Aristotle on, 152n8; in China, 95; eugenics and,

3, 120nn13–16, 121n21, 136n49; health insurance for, 86, 123n33; in USSR, 32–33
Bjorklund, David, 129nn61–62, 129nn72–74
Bloom, Allan, 122n23
Branden, Nathanial, 144n10
Brettschneider, Corey, 124nn13–14
Burguière, André, 159n1
Burke, Edmund, 5, 65–70, 81–83, 85, 87; on civil society, 82–83, 156n46; on French Revolution, 71, 152n13, 153n18, 156n49; on harmony, 82–83, 170n10; and Hobbes, 153n14; on human nature, 67–69, 72, 170n11; on human rights, 79–81, 119n12, 157nn57–58; on intergenerational relationships, 70–72, 77–78, 80, 96, 102; and Locke, 156n52; and Marxism,

183